GUTEN TAG, Y'ALL

GUTEN TAG, Y'ALL

GLOBALIZATION AND THE SOUTH CAROLINA PIEDMONT, 1950–2000

Marko Maunula

THE UNIVERSITY OF GEORGIA PRESS

Athens and London

Set in Electra LH by Integrated Book Technology
Printed digitally in the United States of America

Library of Congress Cataloging-in-Publication Data
Maunula, Marko, 1966–
Guten tag, y'all : globalization and the South Carolina
Piedmont, 1950–2000 / by Marko Maunula.
        p. cm. — (Politics and culture in the
twentieth-century South)
Includes bibliographical references and index.
ISBN-13: 978-0-8203-2901-7 (cloth : alk. paper)
ISBN-10: 0-8203-2901-0 (cloth : alk. paper)
1. Spartanburg (S.C.)—History—20th century.
2. Spartanburg (S.C.)—Economic conditions.
3. Spartanburg (S.C.)—Social conditions.
4. Business enterprises—South Carolina—Spartanburg.
5. Southern States—Economic conditions.
6. Southern States—Social conditions.
7. Social history—1945–   8. Globalization.   I. Title.
   F279.S7M38 2009
   303.48'20975729—dc22   2008049638

British Library Cataloging-in-Publication Data available

CONTENTS

ACKNOWLEDGMENTS

Writing a book is a very undemocratic process. A labor of many people goes into it, yet only one person gets the credit.

This book benefits from the help of scores of individuals, covering three continents and a number of years. First, I would like to thank the late Gary Fink and my friend and mentor John M. Matthews at Georgia State University. At the University of Georgia, my master's committee of William W. Stueck, William F. Holmes, and James C. Cobb further helped in turning my raw ideas into a workable project.

At the University of North Carolina, Peter A. Coclanis was simply the best dissertation advisor one can imagine. His combination of cheery helpfulness and relentless gentle pressure pushed me steadily forward, and his encyclopedic knowledge of historiography helped me to regain my footing whenever my research or analysis began to slip. The entire history department of the University of North Carolina at Chapel Hill deserves generous credit. With its seminar rooms and discussions in the graduate student lounge, Hamilton Hall was a fantastic incubator of ideas and arguments.

My colleagues at Clayton State University have been very helpful. My department heads, Gene Hatfield and Randy Rosenburg, showed great support and flexibility when accommodating my research needs. Professors Adam Tate and Chris Ward have provided their cheerful companionship and astute counsel.

Enormous thanks go to the Dwight D. Eisenhower Presidential Library, the Lyndon B. Johnson Presidential Library, and the Gerald R. Ford Presidential Library for their generous financial support and excellent staffs. Librarians at the Southern Labor Archives at Georgia State University, the Southern Historical Collections at the University of North Carolina, the Perkins Library at Duke University, the Woodruff Library at Emory University, the Sandor Teszler Library at Wofford College, the Spartanburg Main Library in Spartanburg, and the South Caroliniana Library at the University of South Carolina all deserve my sincere gratitude.

Thanks to Bryant Simon for his invitation to participate in this series. Thank you to everybody at the University of Georgia Press, especially Derek Krissoff for his insightful editorial help and Jon Davies for his skillful management. Thanks to Polly Kummel for her thorough and thoughtful copyediting.

My friends have offered their unwavering support throughout the years. Their companionship has cheered me up when necessary, and their probing questions have made the work much better. Thank you Dave, Matthew, Leah, Ethan, Blaine, Joel, Josh, Matt, Adam, Mike, Trey, Jari, Tree, Leona, James, George, Bill, Lauri, Jan, Margaretha, and, especially, Johanna. You have made my life brighter and my work better.

My family deserves enormous gratitude for their emotional and material support. Throughout the years they encouraged and helped me in my academic pursuits. Sisko and Ilmari Maunula, Mirva and Harri Kuni, Henrik and Matias. I particularly want to single out Gail Maunula and Nate and Betty Bowers. Thank you so much for your help.

This book is dedicated to my sons: Matthew, Langston, and Caleb Maunula. Never stop asking questions—even if I don't always answer.

To the Souths—
Both the New and the Latest

The first, vague idea for this book emerged in July 1991 on my first trip to the United States. While working in my native Finland as a young journalist, I had decided to spend my summer vacation touring the American South. The idea behind the trip was unabashedly romantic, shaped by my long-standing fascination with southern history and culture. I visited such storied places as Memphis and Nashville, Columbia and Atlanta, as well as many smaller towns, determined to find a region that would correspond with the idea of the South that I had soaked up as a teenager by reading Tennessee Williams, William Faulkner, Flannery O'Connor, and Richard Wright and by listening to Delta blues, Memphis soul, and old rock 'n' roll.

I did find the romantic gothic South I was looking for. Simultaneously, however, I discovered another, equally fascinating version of the region. While driving through the South Carolina Piedmont with my traveling companion, I saw a thoroughly industrialized and even cosmopolitan slice of the South. Through the windshield of our rental car I spotted factories bearing familiar names—Hoechst, Michelin, Sulzer—dotting the roadsides of Interstate 85. After taking an exit ramp and venturing into the Greenville-Spartanburg area, I heard people speaking German with an unmistakable Swiss dialect at a local convenience store. A French flag was flying atop the porch of one house in a nearby neighborhood.

I cannot remember what I thought about this surprising pocket of cosmopolitanism in the foothills of the Blue Ridge Mountains. Perhaps I was lamenting the unorthodox presence of these multinationals in the South and the corrupting, homogenizing power of European corporate capitalism. Or perhaps I was a bit pleased, taken by some exaggerated notions of a European-southern bond so visible in this region. Despite these obvious outward signs of the South's transformation, even the South Carolina Piedmont still felt very southern. It radiated the same sense of place and culture I had recognized in other small and midsize towns I had visited earlier in my trip.

Later, afforded an opportunity to further my studies in Atlanta, I determined to inspect more closely the Piedmont I had discovered the previous summer. During my ensuing studies at the universities of Georgia and North Carolina at Chapel Hill, I learned about boosters, industrial recruitment, textiles, unions, chambers of commerce, and globalization's impact on the South. Towns named Greenville, Spartanburg, Rock Hill, and Anderson became quite familiar to me, alongside regionally prominent family names such as Tukey, Black, Foerster, and Milliken.

I chose to focus my studies on post–World War II Spartanburg County. With its impressive manufacturing centers and seemingly never-ending construction, the Greenville-Spartanburg axis forms the buckle of the Southern Piedmont's Interstate 85 Boom Belt.[1] With notable success, the area has answered the challenges of the new economy while staying true to its socioeconomic traditions. South Carolinians in general and Spartans in particular do not believe in revolutions or quick fixes of any sort. Spartanburg has been, and is, an industrial town, where money is made by putting things together or turning raw materials into processed goods. Relying on the economic strategy that has dominated the community since the early post–Civil War era, the town adds value with the physical labor of men and women dressed in overalls.

For more than three decades many academics and journalists have widely celebrated Spartanburg as the model community of globalization. Numerous widely published articles have told the story of the textile town that modernized its economy with forward-looking openness to new industries and a willingness to take on new challenges and revamp its entire economic structure. Most notably, Milton Friedman and Rosabeth Moss Kantner, two deservedly reputable scholars and unapologetic business romanticists, have nominated Spartanburg as the proud symbol of the economic opportunities offered by globalization, neoliberal economic freedoms, and hard work.[2]

The merits of their theories notwithstanding, a closer look at Spartanburg reveals more continuity than change, strict control rather than economic freedom. My thesis, in short, is that the transformation in Spartanburg has been a classic revolution from above. Although the external representations of the community's economy have often changed, its fundamental character and power structures have largely remained intact. The changes might appear on the surface to be radical departures, but the community leadership's decision to recruit foreign corporations actually helped the preexisting elites maintain control of the community. Foreign corporations and their Spartanburg-based executives have been incorporated effectively and surprisingly easily into local economic and social power structures.

While the concept of revolution from above, as used here, is useful and accurate in pointing out the dramatic and substantial economic changes that took place in Spartanburg during the post–World War II era, the term simultaneously acknowledges the strength of the institutions and individuals that controlled Spartanburg both before and after the economic transformation. The origins of large-scale industrialization in Spartanburg were created by new men and new money, C. Vann Woodward's intellectual descendants of Whigs and David Carlton's postbellum middle-class boosters.[3] By the time of the Great Depression, these men had gained impressive economic control of Spartanburg. However, these practical boosters and industrial entrepreneurs did not allow quixotic notions to destroy their economic and political dominance. They proved very capable of adapting their economic modus operandi and cultural values to correspond with changing times.[4]

One can question whether globalization itself is a new or radical concept in South Carolina, especially considering that the state was born of transatlantic economic dreams and motives. South Carolina's economic survival and character have always depended on global markets—and occasionally even on international recruitment. The state and its communities have a long tradition of seeking economic salvation from abroad. Waves of promoting immigration have periodically swept the Palmetto State, for example, its Reconstruction-era campaign to attract skilled and industrious laborers from northern Europe, especially Germany.[5]

Until the last few decades South Carolina's international recruitment efforts targeted individuals, while more recent recruitment has concentrated on corporations. During both time periods the recruitment has largely focused on northern Europe. Then and now international recruitment also served political motives, including a desire to preserve the status quo. During Reconstruction South Carolina's white elite envisioned the white European immigration as a potential political weapon against an emerging African American and carpet-bagger majority.[6] During the post–World War II era incoming foreign corporations offered economic benefits without posing substantial challenges to the community's economic and political power structures.

Initially, many South Carolinians recognized the cultural concerns surrounding a large-scale influx of foreign stock. Although xenophobic fears about the native culture's survival would express themselves with initial strength, they would be shot down by more pressing economic and political concerns. Then and now, as many South Carolinians discovered, it was better "to lose the relics of antiquity than to make no bequests to posterity," as one proponent of immigration, addressing the Charleston Board of Trade in April 1869, concluded.[7] During the post–World War II years even those fears proved largely unfounded, as the immigrant corporations proved to be very willing to comply with local customs, often more so than northern companies, with their more fluent understanding of U.S. culture and aggressive desire to assert their beliefs and practices.

This book is about control and continuity in one southern community. Spartanburg is definitely an unusual community, but like much of the rest of the South Carolina Piedmont it is, in many ways, many Souths in one. It holds on to the idea of the Old South while simultaneously celebrating and living the New South creed. Its position between Appalachia and the coastal plain, close to Interstate 85, alongside the state's historical and current trade routes, has ensured its exposure to commerce, ideas, and people from multiple corners of the South and the nation. Spartanburg has successfully soaked it all in, adopting and shaping the ideas and attitudes that have made their way through the community over centuries.

Spartanburg has often harnessed new social and economic forces to serve its existing culture and institutions. The town is widely noted for its staunch individualism and commitment to capitalist rhetoric, yet it is a highly organized, hierarchical community whose leadership has often fought unionization and open, competitive capitalism with almost equal determination. A cynical observer can easily say that the willingness and ability to live with contradictions form essential aspects of the southern experience. This seems to be especially true of Spartanburg, which has a conflictual relationship with globalization and free-market capitalism. The community and its citizens demonstrate an impressive ability to equate justice with economic self-interest, with fairness often serving merely as a semantic tool to justify blatant pursuit of personal benefit.

The work at hand focuses heavily on international industrial recruitment, but its scope is wider than that. This book analyzes the mechanisms and influences of globalization, both of which suggest more continuity than change. Spartanburg's social and economic characteristics lie on a foundation that is more than a century old. The community's new branches reflect hopes and strategies that are as old as the entire community and as young as its latest incarnation. The economic changes in Spartanburg are obviously real and meaningful, and they often have benefited most of its residents. However, the changes are mostly economic, with little corresponding effects on social hierarchies or political power.

The discussion shifts between Washington and Spartanburg, and many events that shape Spartanburg and this book occur in the placeless world of the modern global economy. The size and scope of foreign direct investment in Spartanburg depended upon the economic situation elsewhere, whether in the Southeast, the United States, or global investment markets. However, I have attempted to connect the global economic developments to Spartanburg, leaving the community only when absolutely necessary, and even then, focusing on showing the influence of global developments on Spartanburg's grass roots.

The book also touches on various other fields. It is mostly economic and social history, but it also flirts with labor history, diplomatic history, and classic political economy. I am attempting to use various methodologies to paint a panoramic picture of Spartanburg under intense economic and social change. Occasionally, and admittedly, width has replaced breadth. I am consciously trying to create a larger view of Spartanburg and its connections with the world. I hope that it helps communicate the complexities of this town's evolving relationship with the world and its role in the world economy.

The role of labor in the creation of Spartanburg is crucial. Its sizable, nonunionized, and relatively skilled pool of labor was one of Spartanburg's key selling points. During the era under study the politics and culture of labor in the South Carolina Piedmont was changing. The old militancy, mill village culture, labor activism, and tensions between the mill people and town people were disappearing, replaced by the post–World War II era sense of cold war consensus, economic optimism, and a new sense of belonging, enforced by esoteric notions of community and very real status brought by homeownership.

In the last decades of the twentieth century and the first decade of the twenty-first, southern labor history has experienced impressive maturation in both size and scope. Influenced by the new labor history movement that emerged in the 1960s, the pioneering efforts of Gary Fink, Merl E. Reed, and other founders of modern southern labor history revolutionized the field by telling the stories of the workers themselves.[8] Earlier narratives, such as Broadus Mitchell's classic study from the 1920s, *The Rise of the Cotton Mills in the South*, had centralized the industrialists and boosters, treating workers as a slightly detached side story within the larger narrative of southern industrialization. Marjorie Potwin had shown more attention to workers in her 1927

Cotton Mill People of the Piedmont, but, as a social worker at Saxon Mills in Spartanburg, her account is guilty of not-so-subtle condescension.

Collections edited by Fink and Reed helped to invigorate southern labor history, and the field continued to grow and form new branches. During the 1970s and 1980s scholarship on the mill village culture, workers' conceptions of race and gender, and the nature of the relationships between mill workers and their occasional enemies—mill bosses and middle-class townspeople— started to emerge.[9] In Chapel Hill, Jacqueline Hall and her students and col- laborators began groundbreaking work in studying southern labor culture. Their articles and books, especially *Like a Family: The Making of a Southern Cotton Mill World*, radically expanded our knowledge and understanding of cotton mill people and their values, culture, and ideas. The importance of *Like a Family* has lost very little of its luster, as the book's emphasis on culture and identity in understanding the mill village culture has shaped almost an entire generation of southern labor historians.

During the late 1990s and early 2000s, the image of southern labor con- tinued to become more diverse—and, undoubtedly, more complete—as more detached analyses have started to supplement the victimization and occasional romantic treatment of the workers. While expanding our understanding of concepts of race, class, and gender in the worlds of southern mill workers, books such as Bryant Simon, *A Fabric of Defeat: The Politics of South Carolina Millhands, 1910–1948* and Michelle Brattain, *The Politics of Whiteness: Race, Workers, and Culture in the Modern South* have also stripped some of the myth of innocent victimhood that had occasionally shaped the discussion of southern labor. Simon and Brattain showed the complexities and occasional moral shortcomings of southern workers, including their susceptibility to politics of racism. In good and bad alike, southern workers were not docile victims but active agents, shaping the world that they had both inherited and created—and not always for the better.

Timothy J. Minchin's *What Do We Need a Union For? The TWUA in the South, 1945–1955* also corrected the often simplistic view that unioniza- tion failed because of ruthless antiunion activities by the bosses. Minchin acknowledges, both here and in his more recent synthesis, *Fighting against the Odds: A History of Southern Labor since World War II*, the brutal effec- tiveness of the southern antiunion machine. However, Minchin shows how southern textile mill bosses were also learning softer and less confrontational labor management techniques. The old tools of spying, oppression, and even direct violence were supplemented by new methods, such as improved wages and working conditions.

My approach continues in the vein of recent labor history. My analysis questions whether the old, dualistic, and juxtaposing perspective of studying labor-employer relations in Spartanburg explains the workers' repeated rejection of the unions. The antiunion efforts of Spartanburg's boosters, authorities, and mill owners were often morally questionable and even illegal. Additionally, union agents themselves occasionally proved to be incompetent, no match for the local antiunion machine. However, the oppression and periodic incompetence do not entirely explain the failure to unionize. Both explanations, when used alone, could easily reduce the workers to objects, passive targets of successful or failed strategies by their manipulators in the boardrooms of both corporations and the unions.

Spartanburg's workforce was not a victim, nor was it a bamboozled and a docile lot. In Spartanburg occasional dreams of unionization continued to exist during the second half of the twentieth century, but a new, communal, and consensus-driven approach gradually started to emerge. In Spartanburg this new mind-set emphasized stability and identified workers' success with the success of their town. After the disappointments of the failed union drives of the 1950s large segments of Spartanburg's workers learned to appreciate a peaceful labor climate and steady economic growth. For thousands of Spartanburg's workers, the decision to abandon unionization was a calculated and rational one, not a cowering choice of the defeated.

Dismantling mill villages and selling the homes to mill workers helped to transform the highly mobile mill people into townspeople. The organic, active, and isolated mill village culture gave way to a growing commitment to a place. Their new status as property owners tied their fortunes to that of the town. The workers had a growing stake in the success of the community, and former tensions between the mill village and the town began to ease. Mill workers increasingly identified with the town. They benefited from the town's growth, as reflected in increasing property values and improving employment opportunities.

This book is also about migration to the Sunbelt—the economic and demographic shift of money, jobs, political power, and people from the Rustbelt to the Sunbelt, a high-growth region stretching from Virginia to California. The enormous scale of this migration attracted the attention of journalists and scores of scholars, representing a wide range of social scientists. The literature in the field started to fully develop during the 1970s. Kirkpatrick Sale's *Power Shift: The Rise of the Southern Rim and Its Challenge to the Eastern Establishment*, first published in 1975, was an ominous warning to the Northeast of the South's—and southern conservatism's—new role in the nation. Bernard L. Weinstein and Robert E. Firestine, two economists, probed the size and scope of the Sunbelt migration in *Regional Growth and Decline in the United States*. Another edited collection, by E. Blaine Liner and Lawrence K. Lynch, *The Economics of Southern Growth*, also studies the pocketbook reasons behind the South's growth. Taken together these two books argue that the South's growth was not so much a function of tax breaks, federal spending, or even promotional efforts as growing markets, good weather, and low taxes. In his groundbreaking *The Selling of the South: The Southern Crusade for Industrial Development, 1936–1980*, the historian James C. Cobb also questions the wisdom of using enormous tax breaks and other perks to lure industry. Bruce J. Schulman's *From Cotton Belt to Sunbelt* focuses on the continued and substantial presence of federal money in the making of the Sunbelt South, especially in the fields of defense and aerospace.

The influx of new men and money to the South has also produced many scholarly studies—and occasional speculations—about the future of the South itself. An impressive volume edited by H. Brandt Ayers and Thomas H. Naylor, *You Can't Eat Magnolias*, was one of the early, substantial works to deal with the South's role and identity in the changing nation. John Egerton's pessimistic work, *The Americanization of Dixie: The Southernization of America*, predicts the disappearance of the distinctive South, as interaction across the Mason-Dixon Line begins to homogenize South and North. In taking an economic look at the region's changes, no book has surpassed Gavin Wright's *Old South, New South: Revolutions in Southern Economy since the Civil War*. Wright observes the gradual erosion of separate southern labor markets, a major force in bringing the South economically into the American mainstream.

Since the late 1980s new and interesting trends have emerged in the study of the South's relationship with the world. With the growing focus on globalization, the study of the South has, naturally, switched much of its attention from contrasting the South against the North to studying the South in global context. From the University of Georgia's 2000 conference on the South and globalization to the University of North Carolina's annual spring meetings on various aspects of the South's globalization, the field has moved beyond the early questions about the character and survival of southern culture. New scholarship on the South has begun to emphasize the region's active involvement and interaction with the world rather than its isolated, contrarian character as the conscientious objector to the modern West. As a result, the arguments about the South's survival and the determined strength of the region's culture have started to strengthen as well. The new scholarship has reminded us of the South's historical connections with the rest of the world.[10] The work is still in progress and the debate continues, but the emerging scholarship has already opened interesting paths to viewing the South in a new, global light.[11]

Chapter 1 introduces Spartanburg and describes the culture, economy, and politics immediately after World War II that enabled local textile companies and community leaders to fend off the threat of unionization. That period turned out to be crucial in shaping Spartanburg for the remainder of the twentieth century. While the focus of this chapter is broad and some of its assertions admittedly somewhat generalized, this big picture approach sets the stage for the history and analysis in subsequent chapters.

Chapter 2 focuses on the conflicting economic news of the mid-1950s in Spartanburg. While the town had just experienced the most prosperous decade in its history, international competition, in the form of Japanese textile imports, was threatening to take this prosperity away. The reaction of community leaders, which would become a habit, was to simultaneously fight against and prepare for the change. This chapter also discusses the motives and workings of the economic aspects of U.S. foreign policy, and their effect upon Spartanburg. Finally, the chapter addresses the arrival of new people, namely, the textile magnate Roger Milliken and Richard E. (Dick) Tukey, CEO of the Spartanburg Chamber of Commerce, both of whom would play crucial roles in shaping the town for rest of the twentieth century.

The origins of international recruitment in Spartanburg and, later, South Carolina emerge in the third chapter. The chapter describes the motives and methods of wooing foreign corporations, paying careful attention to the pioneering and enduring efforts of Spartanburg's improved recruitment machine and Tukey, its unquestioned leader and visionary. Spartanburg's boosters turned the entire town into a commodity, selling it as a complete community for business and good living. The townspeople were both invited and coerced to contribute to the sales campaigns, enforcing the sense of community as a commodity among sellers and buyers alike.

In chapter 4 I again delve into the international fiscal developments and U.S. foreign policy, as I discuss and analyze the macroeconomic factors affecting international investment flows, paying specific attention to their effects upon Spartanburg. American balance-of-payments problems and President Richard Nixon's termination of the Bretton Woods agreement triggered a rapid and substantial interest among foreign corporations to invest in the United States. In Spartanburg global developments provided an enormous boost for local recruitment efforts, as the proverbial flood of foreign corporations to town began. Their arrival on such a large scale triggered both social and economic reactions in the town. The challenge for Spartanburg's leaders was to maximize the economic benefits while keeping the cultural and social effects of the expansion tightly in check. They succeeded.

The decline in textile employment fully began to hit Spartanburg during the 1970s. While the community had been intensely worried about textile employment since the mid-1950s, it took fifteen years for the town's worries to become reality. Chapter 5 discusses this decline and Spartanburg's reactions to it—its perplexing efforts at both protectionism and internationalization of its economy. The chapter also discusses the tightening competition in international recruitment and its effect on Spartanburg.

I conclude my study in chapter 6. The successful recruitment of the BMW car factory in 1992 marked the culmination of Spartanburg's economic transition. In four decades foreign corporations had established themselves as natural members of the town's industrial landscape, and the culture and contributions of the foreign corporations differed little, if at all, from those of U.S. or South Carolina corporations. All contributed to the economic well-being and enforcement of the character of the community.

In a matter of a few decades the early fears and romanticism of a foreign presence in Spartanburg turned into local satisfaction at the economic contributions of the international firms and the casual, nonreflective acceptance of foreigners and foreign companies by local residents. Foreigners and foreign corporations began as a late twentieth-century version of the carpetbagger, arriving with their ideas and factories; after a few decades of cultural give-and-take, they had melted into the local business culture and taken on its traditions.

CHAPTER ONE

A New Game in South Carolina

The cartoon dominating the editorial page of the *Spartanburg Herald* on June 27, 1945, was especially savvy, reeling readers in with a sports theme starring their home town. The cartoonist had converted the Carolina Piedmont into a massive baseball diamond, a symbolic playing field for the postwar economic forces in the region. The artist had designated Columbia as first base, Charlotte as second, and Asheville as third. Greenville formed home plate. The outfield covered most of the Carolina coast and Piedmont, stretching from the seaports of Charleston and Wilmington toward the greater Winston-Salem tobacco, furniture, and textile manufacturing area. In the middle of this field of economic dreams stood a dominating pitcher, none other than Spartanburg himself. The lanky, confident hurler was in the middle of his windup, getting ready to deliver the pitch that would push the entire Southern Piedmont into frenzied action.

The cartoon's message was clear. In the emerging post–World War II order, Spartanburg had an opportunity to control the game, to direct the pace and character of the entire region's economic development. The cartoon and its headline, "Let's Get in the Game and Pitch!" sought to make Spartans aware of their community's potential. The war in Europe was over. News from the Pacific theater, while still prominent in Spartanburg's media and consciousness, had the unmistakable undertone that Allied victory was inevitable. The war was won, the peace was at hand. Now it was time to convert the wartime drive and determination to serve the region's commercial impulses. The townspeople's attention was turning from world affairs to practical tasks closer to home, and Spartanburg's leading newspaper was eager to do its share in directing these energies.

For the *Herald* choosing the proper tool for harnessing the postwar energies and development was obvious. The task called for ministrations of the Greater Spartanburg Chamber of Commerce. Like many papers in the region the *Herald* was born out of the booster impulse, never deviating far from the spirit of the community as an enterprise.[1] The paper's ties to the chamber were of blood, money, and tradition; top newspaper officials, especially the publisher,

Bill Buchheit, often served in the chamber and other business-minded civic organizations in Spartanburg. As the community was preparing for the transformation from war to peace, the *Herald* saw and promoted the chamber as the natural force to oversee the process.

The editorial board sought to maintain the wartime civic and communal spirit by expanding the chamber's membership base. The message was clear. It was time to put aside the labor strife and class conflict of the Depression era. Both labor and management needed revamping. The paper sought to preserve and nourish the unity of the war years, calling for all segments and members of the community to gather behind the economic home team. "The Chamber of Commerce wants YOUR ideas and YOUR help," the editorial page announced: "Let's ALL get in the game and PITCH for Spartanburg and the Piedmont."[2]

The chamber of commerce membership drive was but one, albeit important, part of Spartanburg's postwar strategy for success. Throughout the spring and summer of 1945 the community had searched for ways to keep the wartime economic momentum going and prepare the region for changes that the peace would foster both at home and abroad. The chamber had, naturally, assumed responsibility for most of the planning. By May its Postwar Planning Committee had set up a junior chamber and completed an "11-point roadmap" for Spartanburg's future. The *Herald* again communicated these efforts to the public through glowing editorials and cartoons reflecting the style and spirit of something resembling socialist realism.[3] In a state—and nation—fluctuating between wild economic optimism and fears of a returning depression, the chamber and newspaper radiated unwavering faith in the future of Spartanburg.

The plans of the chamber called for improved zoning and urban beautification to please potential industrial immigrants, directing local capital to investments in office space and production facilities for small businesses, and thorough improvements in local transportation infrastructure. On the agricultural side the chamber emphasized how the pastures in the region were suitable for aspiring peach farmers and dairy producers. Working to reinforce the confidence of farmers and townspeople alike, the chamber and its supporters declared what a sure thing the growth was. The challenges of the postwar economy were centered more around serving and controlling rather than seeking expansion. For many leaders of Spartanburg the main economic question of the day was how to direct, foster, and exploit the growth for the maximum benefit of the community—as defined by the boosters of the town.[4]

The fundamental dilemma facing Spartanburg and South Carolina was change. The town and state were in flux, and the future social and political direction of the community was far from determined. Continued threats of unionization, disappearance of the mill villages, the substantial political transformation taking place in the state, the budding civil rights movement, and other ominous forces were threatening the established elites and cultural norms that had guided life in the community for decades. The enthusiasm and excitement about the postwar promise were complicated by local worries and concerns associated with change. The cycle of creative destruction forebode substantial changes for Spartanburg's social, economic, and political structures. The old anchors of the local economy and culture, from cotton farming to the role of mill villages in the life of the community, faced growing challenges from outside as well as from within. Although optimism prevailed, Spartanburg vacillated between preservation and reformation, hopeful visions and questions of concern regarding its future development.

The local economic situation would, naturally, play the biggest role in settling Spartanburg's labor question. The ingredients for Spartanburg's economic takeoff were present. Since the 1930s Spartanburg had enjoyed the fruits of the New Deal and the federal government's World War II spending. As for so many communities around the South and the nation, the Great Depression in Spartanburg had meant an economically devastated countryside and declining wages. Unlike most communities, however, Spartanburg in the 1930s was actually able to increase the number of its industrial facilities, helping the community to survive the challenges of the decade with somewhat less economic devastation than that faced by many of the northeastern textile towns—or even Southern Piedmont communities—with similar economic monocultures.[5]

During the 1930s and 1940s the economic crisis pushed many New England textile mills to relocate to the South. The low wages of the region enabled these companies to chew the last few dollars out of their aging machinery, which would have been obsolete and unprofitable in the mills of Massachusetts or Rhode Island.[6] Even in the midst of the worst economic crisis in American history, the number of manufacturing establishments in Spartanburg County increased from 99 in 1929 to 104 in 1939.[7] Additionally, Camp Croft, the U.S. Army's massive training facility, opened in February 1941, bringing service jobs and a sense of rigorous activity to Spartanburg.[8] Its peak complement of twenty-five thousand personnel, including hundreds of local support jobs, injected the town with an invigorating mixture of patriotic military spirit and much-needed federal dollars.

By the mid-1940s the relatively positive state of Spartanburg's industry was countered by a massive influx of rural refugees. The county population had grown rapidly throughout the Great Depression and World War II. The Agricultural Adjustment Act (AAA) of 1933 saved hundreds of South Carolina Piedmont farmers from bankruptcy by raising cotton prices through cuts in production. However, the cuts also pushed thousands of sharecroppers, tenant farmers, and small landholders out of agriculture and into the urban centers to seek meager employment in the mill towns of the region.[9] Piedmont farmers of the Depression era, black and white alike, ventured away from their homelands. While the African American migration often led families away from the farms and the South, their white counterparts often moved their lives to the nearby towns, such as Anderson, Greenville, and Spartanburg.[10]

Between 1930 and 1940 the population of Spartanburg County grew from 116,323 to 127,733. During the period, however, the number of Spartans who earned their livelihood from agriculture dropped from 17,530 to 10,175. That the county's total employed workforce grew by only 3,000, reaching 50,140 by 1940, reflects the despondency of its Depression-era economy.[11] Until World War II invigorated Spartanburg's economy through its textile mills, local farmers were pushed out of the rural areas by the collapse of the agricultural system; functioning labor markets did not lure them to the urban centers. The result was a reluctant migration and newcomers with a lukewarm attachment to their new homes. The rapid increase in marginally skilled laborers further reinforced the low wage structure, and the surplus of workers continued to affect the county's development throughout the war and early postwar years.[12]

By 1945, with Spartanburg County's textile industry humming at practically full speed, the increased population had become a valuable asset. Although the war had ended, the town's mills continued to operate near full capacity, struggling to satisfy the demands of rapidly growing consumer markets at home and abroad. The industry was reaping record profits, as wartime orders were first supplemented and then replaced by rapidly escalating demand from the civilian markets.[13] As the town and its surroundings sought new ways to secure their newfound prosperity and industrial progress, the large population became a magnet, offering both a motivation to invest and a suitable pool of labor for corporations considering relocation. The labor was present and motivated, and the indicators of further economic development suggested substantial potential for growth.

The first order of business for the economic leadership in Spartanburg was maintaining and strengthening the industrial peace that had gradually emerged during the war years. Long familiar with the town's strong, independent, and potentially militant labor force, Spartanburg's economic leaders understood the need for a thoroughly revamped strategy and attitude toward workers. A successful battle against the unions alone would not secure a permanent victory. In order to achieve a long-lasting, meaningful industrial peace, the chamber needed to build ties between the mill and town to incorporate the county's working classes more thoroughly into the town.

Since the advent of large-scale industrialization in the late nineteenth century, people from the textile mill villages, "lintheads," had formed the white pariah class of the New South Piedmont, an isolated and ostracized community of poor whites that provided most of the muscle behind the industrialization. The changing political landscape of the New Deal, the unity of the World War II years, and the warning examples of the labor strife of the 1930s helped to foster a new attitude and policy toward the mill people. As the economic and cultural changes of the era soon proved to be durable, Spartanburg's leaders learned to base their control on managing rather than resisting the changes. An important front in this campaign for control would focus on getting the workers to share the boosters' vision of the city, to see their roles and interests as intertwined with those of the traditional enemy of the community and the workers, namely, the local middle class.

Since its settlement in 1785 Spartanburg was built from diverse pieces of the human mosaic. Scots-Irish from the nearby Blue Ridge Mountains, Germans, African Americans, affluent summer visitors from the coast, and migrating Yankee industrialists had met here, creating a community that in many ways epitomized the New South.[14] The social structures of Spartanburg celebrated order and deference, combining its Old South ideals with the dynamic and aggressive New South commercial instincts. The economic leaders of the town were willing to seek new avenues of wealth, but they were equally committed to the ideas of continuity and control. Now, securing success on both fronts demanded consensus and teamwork, a need to incorporate the workers fully into the larger community, and to eradicate the remaining demarcation lines between the mill villages and the town itself. Spartanburg's leaders began to react to the forces of change as managerial challenges, seeking new ways to adjust their techniques of community control in order to maintain continuity with as few disrupting changes as possible.

The challenges of recruiting the working class to support the business-progressive vision of the boosters were sizable. The South Carolina Piedmont had been one of the most violent fronts of the 1930s labor unrest, including the 1934 massacre at Honea Path, Anderson County, where a confrontation between striking textile workers and the police-backed mill owners had led to the deaths of seven strikers. Throughout the decades since, Spartanburg's textile workers had joined their colleagues throughout the Piedmont, resisting the bosses and fighting for the union with dogged determination. Culturally and physically isolated, often ridiculed mill workers had turned inward, creating their own culture and social structures inside the mill villages and developing a well-justified suspicion toward the people outside their communities.[15]

To make workers receptive to their message, boosters would have to narrow the physical, economic, and cultural gaps between the mill people and the rest of Spartanburg. As the war was winding down, the divide between the mill and town remained wide and high. Thousands of mill workers dreamed of unions, hoping for rapid and extensive unionization to secure the advances they had made during the fat years of the war economy. The occasional, partial acceptance of a paternalistic system was offset by the workers' habitual dislike of new owners and managers, impersonality of modern factory production, and full knowledge of the ownership's resources and commitment to fight any nascent signs of unionization. The mill villages entertained both militant and accommodating sentiments, worried about securing their jobs, and wanted to improve their lot. These were proud, strong, and fiercely independent people, not easily led to either follow the union or blindly obey their bosses. They waited to see what the union and the bosses had to offer. Whatever decision the mill villages made would be based on a calculated, individualistic rationale, with careful evaluation of positives and negatives.

Unionization, perhaps the biggest fear of the town's boosters and mill owners, reemerged almost immediately after the war. The Textile Workers' Union of America (TWUA), reinvigorated by its success in the North and the federal support for unionization during the administrations of Franklin Delano Roosevelt and Harry S. Truman, embarked on a determined push to unionize the southern textile mills. The effort formed an important front in the CIO-led Operation Dixie, a larger campaign to bring unionization in the South closer to the levels of the industrial Northeast and Midwest. Union bosses saw, with good reason, that success in the South was crucial to their larger struggles of cementing the wartime advances of the nation's labor movement.[16] As any observer could easily conclude, the South's success in recruiting northern textile manufacturers was in large part based on its scarcity of unions, and the same recruiting success was largely responsible for the decline of unionized mills in New England and rest of the Northeast. In order to ensure their future nationally, the unions could not afford to lose in the South, the cornerstone of the antiunion movement.

In South Carolina unionization efforts focused on the Greenville-Spartanburg axis, the spiritual and geographic center of the entire southern textile industry.[17] The unions and local textile bosses had learned the lessons of 1934. Management, assisted by the improved economic situation and cognizant of the changes in federal attitudes toward labor, knew that a return to their more combative stance was undesirable and probably even impossible. In postwar America fighting the unions required softer, smarter, and more accommodating strategies. For their part the unions had learned that organizing southern labor posed a different set of challenges than in the North. The battles of 1934 had shown that the southern textile mill workers were not any less brave or potentially militant than their northern brethren. However, the cultures of northern factory towns differed substantially from the seemingly paradoxical combination of fierce individualism and strong sense of community that prevailed in southern mill villages. The Appalachian and agrarian roots of the southern mill villagers remained strong. The battle about unionization was fought at the fronts of wallet and *weltanschauung*.

The first order of business for the unions was to show that unionization was compatible with regional traditions, including the roles of religion and of the highly personal relationship between workers and bosses. But this was compounded by the need to also help locals forget the bitter failures of the previous decade and introduce modern ideas of industrial relationships. Combining sensitivity to southern working-class traditions and prejudices with the union's modern and moral convictions in matters such as race made the task almost impossible.

From the start, TWUA's union recruiters acknowledged the unique nature of southern labor and labor-management relationships. When the union organizers entered the South Carolina Piedmont, their first step was to convince workers to change their relationship with their bosses, from the quasi paternalism of the past to a formal, contractually defined triangle involving a worker, the union, and the company. The task was formidable for a variety of reasons, including some important cultural ones. Southern textile mill workers rarely greeted with joy any suggestions of thorough reorganization of their social and economic relationships. The workers appreciated stability and safety, especially after the disruptions of the war years. To sell the benefits of unionization to the South, labor organizers had to convince the region's workers of the unreliability and unpredictability of the paternalistic labor system. In the end, the fundamental question for most workers was to determine which institution, mill owners or the union, could offer them more money and security.

Union organizers tried to convince Spartanburg's workers that the world they wanted to preserve was already gone, thanks to the substantial consolidation of the textile industry. Agents worked hard to educate southern textile mill workers about the impersonality of the new corporate system. "In the old days . . . your boss knew you, knew your problems, and you could talk to him face-to-face when things weren't going right," reminded a union drive flyer that circulated around the South. "But you can't talk face-to-face to with a big corporation—it hasn't even got a face."[18] Appealing to the local knowledge of ownership changes and increased concentration of textile industries during the Great Depression, union representatives tried to point out how the new industrial world belonged to faceless corporations and impersonal forces operating from some remote offices on Wall Street. The change was inevitable, nostalgia was pointless. In this new world, a nonunionized worker would not be an individual but a lonely and powerless peon, unable to rely on his fellow workers or his boss.

The challenge for the unions was to represent change without threatening traditions and to offer security in an age of transition. In this struggle unions hoped to demonstrate their compatibility with local values and traditions, including religion. Southern union meetings usually started with a prayer. Organizers hoped to create networks of pastors and preachers sympathetic to labor's cause, so that they would convince mill villagers, who were often exposed to the fiery theology of biblical antiunionism, of the Christianity of unionization.[19] On a secular level local agents organized fish fries, concerts, and other entertainment to get new members and cement a sense of community and brotherhood within the union.[20] TWUA's recruiters hoped to educate South Carolina textile workers about the impersonal economic forces controlling new industrial production and present the union as a nonoppressive fraternity that would offer its members not only political and economic leverage but also a sense of security and a buffer against the increasingly impersonal, contemporary capitalistic corporate model of production.

This new capitalism—unsettling as it occasionally might be to employees— seemed to treat the South Carolina Piedmont workers well. The economic benefits to the area's textile workers were real and tangible, as domestic and international demand kept the Piedmont mills humming. Between 1941 and 1951 the wages of southern textile workers rose faster than those of any other industrial group in the nation: their real average weekly earnings increased from $13.83 ($206 in 2007 dollars) in October 1939 to $29.32 ($252) in October 1950.[21] TWUA could not take direct credit for the material improvement in the lives of these working men and women, as southern mill owners cleverly resisted unionization by offering their nonunionized workers the same wage that workers received in the organized mills nearby.[22] In those rare cases where workers resorted to strikes, such as the failed twenty-two-month Gaffney strike of 1948–50, the usually discouraging results convinced many workers of the folly of unionization.[23]

Operation Dixie failed to ignite a massive wave of unionization, but the reasons behind the failure were often surprising for many union activists. Frustrated union officials had anticipated and prepared for rigorous opposition from employers, and they did not disappoint. However, union activists were soon to discover that in many parts of the South, such as in Spartanburg, not all workers were naturally enthusiastic about unionization. The reluctance of Spartanburg's laborers to abandon their traditional concept of industrial relations or their hesitance to risk their increasingly better-paid jobs in order to unionize drove the recruiters to periodic bouts of frustration and despair.

In short order, union organizers felt forced to focus their efforts increasingly on proselytizing workers about the benefits of unionization rather than actually organizing elections and working to establish new locals. As early as the fall of 1946 some activists began to view the entire CIO campaign in the South as a miserable failure. Expressing the sentiments of thousands, a December 11, 1946, letter from the labor activist Jesse B. Smith, who was organizing in Greenville, South Carolina, to the CIO Organizing Committee, declared the campaign in the South Carolina Piedmont all but lost: "As the workers at Brandon Mills will phrase it, . . . the whole CIO campaign is a flop, and many of them express their regret that they had ever confided in the CIO."[24]

The aspirations of the unions went unfulfilled. By the early 1950s it was clear that substantial, regionwide unionization was a nonstarter, and local boosters considered the stability of Spartanburg's labor markets secured. Union activities continued in the region, but they largely failed to form a serious challenge to the local textile bosses' control of the community. Workers often refused to believe the messages of TWUA and other unions about the impersonality of industrial relations, more often putting their faith in the bosses than in their union brothers. When the International Ladies Garment Workers' Union worked to get bargaining rights for 165 workers at JaLog Industries in Spartanburg, the ILGWU had difficulty getting the workers' signatures for their union cards, despite the company's positive attitude and cooperation with the union drive. Some workers went to management, expressing their desire to remain "neutral" from unionization. "Even though a union is given to them on a silver platter, they are still reluctant to accept it," commented a frustrated regional director of the AFL-CIO.[25]

After years of hard and occasionally desperate work, the drive ended in an enormous disappointment for the TWUA and the CIO, cementing the reputation and character of the South, and especially the South Carolina Piedmont, as decidedly antiunion. The dreams of unionization did not die completely but struggled and withered under the pressure of previous failures, managerial resistance, and a subtle but noticeable transformation in the workers' attitude toward their jobs and their community. Periodic waves of interest in the unions emerged, and organized labor could occasionally celebrate small victories, but the larger war was practically lost.[26]

The enormous challenges of organizing the industrial South, with its mill village demography and owners' oligarchic rule, proved to be too big a challenge even for a well-organized labor union operating with a substantial war chest. The legal and extralegal challenges that the mill owners, antiunion middle class, and local authorities operating under their command threw in the path of the union organizers created constant challenges and hardships.[27] The fairness of the local unionization votes were often disputable, as union organizers and their supporters on the shop floor faced constant harassment and thinly veiled threats of economic and legal consequences for their activism.

External pressure is an important factor but not an end-all argument in addressing the failure of large-scale unionization in South Carolina and Spartanburg. Despite the existence of antiunion activities, in Spartanburg, as in most textile communities throughout the South, a more thorough understanding of labor's attitudes toward organization—and occasional complicity in the defeat of the union drives—is necessary to get the full picture of what happened and why. Ultimately, it was the workers who rejected the TWUA. While many mill owners and communities worked tirelessly and often unethically to defeat the union, their opposition was not as violent as the Depression-era efforts to crush labor activism. The South Carolina Piedmont of the postwar years did not experience large-scale organized violence or systematic class warfare. This time the town's conservative leaders and mill bosses were smarter and better equipped to fight the union recruiters, with carrots as well as sticks in their arsenal.

The sticks did not disappear. If anything, a few new ones emerged alongside the familiar weapons. After the war the methods of factory owners and public officials for fighting the unions became increasingly more creative. In Spartanburg municipal government emerged as a reliable partner of local textile bosses in curbing labor activism. In January 1954 the city passed a "License Tax Ordinance" that required people to pay a tax for passing out flyers on city streets. The ordinance gave the town and mill bosses one more tool for fighting the unions, as the measure was used to fine union organizers, who customarily targeted factory workers as they were leaving their shifts.[28] In 1962 a union lawyer wryly commented about the City of Spartanburg's efforts to "kill two birds with one stone" with its new antipicketing ordinance. The ordinance, which targeted both union picketing and the NAACP's picketing against segregated facilities, required picketers to register their intentions with the city, with harassing and intimidating rules requiring the names and addresses of picketers and their stated purpose for picketing. The city reserved the right to punish violators with fines and jail sentences as long as thirty days.[29]

During a spring 1960 organizing drive in Spartanburg's Powell Knitting Mill Company, the union organizer Robert Dixon Beame reported on the efforts of mill owners to get him arrested on trumped-up charges of threats and verbal abuse toward workers who were allegedly not keen on unionizing. Discussing the event, a union official familiar with the Carolinas informed higher-ups about the situation: "I am surprised that the police officers didn't issue warrants for brother Beame as they are rather over zealous [*sic*] in performance of their duties where union representatives are concerned."[30] Workers interested in unions also received letters from their owners advising how a union was not in their best interests. Factory supervisors and mill owners, sitting in cars parked conspicuously outside union halls, recorded the names and faces of their workers as they entered the meetings.[31] The intimidating stare, suggestive letter, burdensome and ominous bureaucratic pressure all contributed to union organizers' lack of success. Union agents and workers received a range of thinly veiled threats, and there was no mistaking their message. The town, the company, and the good people of Spartanburg did not want the unions, and if workers knew what was best for them, they would stay away from these worrisome organizations.

These efforts were nothing new—although they were considerably more civil than in the past. Union organizers working in Spartanburg had faced police officers and other public servants who were exceptionally zealous in protecting local workers from the harassment of outside agitators.[32] The workers rarely felt encouraged to join or free to make up their minds, but they were not violently prevented from unionizing either. While their parents had mustered the conviction and courage to march against bayonets during the great southern textile strikes of the 1930s, postwar workers in Spartanburg and the

South in general did not face the same level of threats, nor did they feel the same urge for unionization.

While antiunion activism, some organizers' poor organizational skills, and other external factors contributed to the failure of thorough unionization in Spartanburg, other factors in the reluctance of workers to organize was their suspicious nature and their abhorrence of change, as reflected in managerial reform, the sale of mill villages, and defining labor relations through written, strict contracts. Throughout the South the excitement about the growing prosperity was mitigated by concern about change. As instinctive cultural conservatives, southern textile mill workers often preferred the devil they knew, especially when the devil was finally beginning to pay them a true living wage.[33] Some mill communities tacitly accepted modified paternalism, the contested and much-maligned southern institution, because it was a familiar system for organizing life and labor in mills and mill villages. Regardless of whether paternalism was forced externally or incorporated into the workers' psyche through some peculiar variation of the Stockholm syndrome, working people in Spartanburg did not let the pharaoh go easily. This was not a union of love but of habit and convenience.

Additionally, despite all the good efforts of the union, for many of the men and women working on the factory floors, unions sometimes represented an impersonalized force that threatened the informal, traditional way of communicating between workers and bosses. In some ways unions were like the book-smart managers who entered supervisory positions through college rather than the spindle hall. Traditional managerial methods of personal interaction and custom-based rules were increasingly challenged by formal, written, and impersonal workplace relationships. The same spirit of reform and rapid modernization of southern civil services that fueled GI revolts around the region found its way to the factory floors and management offices of the region's mills.[34]

The change was contested and controversial. Ever since the 1920s scholars and other observers had noted the Southern Piedmont's highly individualistic, improvised, and personalized way of solving conflicts and other issues affecting its industrial relationships.[35] Mostly small, but even some larger regional, textile corporations operated without a formal labor policy, relying instead on a flexible system of give-and-take and patriarchal benevolence, based on tradition and constant negotiation between the parties. "We don't have any written body of policy for the plant," one Georgia-based textile manager emphasized. "We don't want it written. As soon as you write policy down, you freeze it." Increased structure and professionalization of the supervisory tasks, worker testing, and improved bookkeeping and personnel management faced occasional resistance from the workers as well as their bosses.[36]

Major decisions about unionization and adjusting to changes in managerial culture were not the only factors altering the world of the mill workers. The mobile culture of the textile workers, and the dividing lines between the mill and the town, were gradually eroding. Through the disappearance of the mill villages, workers' identities and sense of community were gradually shifting from the village to the town. The townspeople witnessed how the people oft-maligned as "lintheads" were gradually becoming full citizens and fellow Spartans. The process was substantial and no doubt encouraged by the booster interests, who were now willing to invite these new townspeople, with their evolving status as members of the community, to join Spartanburg's bullpen.

The rapid sale of mill villages contributed to the changing identity of South Carolina's, and Spartanburg's, textile workers. Since the early years of the Great Depression, growing numbers of southern textile mill companies had attempted to unload their mill villages as part of the industry's efforts to survive and reorganize itself. As textile mills changed hands, the new management was not often interested in acquiring the villages that surrounded its new possession. Scarcity of capital, ready availability of labor, and management's desire to focus the company's resources on running the mill provided the impetus for the sale of mill villages throughout the South. The sales boom started in the early 1930s and picked up steam until World War II put a temporary halt to sales. With such a large labor market management did not need to offer housing as an incentive to get skilled hands.[37] Additionally, as the transition from the archaic family labor system to modern, one- or two-worker households neared its completion, textile companies saw little need to provide housing for families when only one or two of their members worked in the mill.[38]

The breakdown of the old housing system signaled a thorough reorganization of life and labor in the South Carolina Piedmont's textile towns. The mill village, a demographic icon in the Southern Piedmont since the early postbellum era, had been born of the mill owners' material necessity, patriarchal aspirations, and spiritual desires. It grew out of the mill owners' need to attract itinerant mill hands, often strangers to the semiurban lifestyle and to industrial production, and to educate them to become reliable, morally and socially sound servants of the New South industrial machinery and its owners' fantasy—a paternalistically organized society. During the post–Civil War decades the mills and mill villages were built and managed by new men and money who were consciously working to create the new industrial South.[39] Yet the forces of custom and tradition helped to shape the mill villages into familiar southern social structures, complemented with generous, management-administered doses of both the new and old paternalism.[40]

The family labor system, where both parents and all able children worked in the same mill, provided an employer with a high labor output from every residence in his mill village. For recent arrivals from the mountains or rural sections of the Piedmont, mill villages and family labor systems alike provided a culturally meaningful way to continue their traditional, rural living and working patterns in industrial settings. Over time, mill villages evolved into almost self-sufficient communities, complete with stores, churches, schools, and baseball leagues, enforcing the workers' sense of community and belonging. As far as pocketbook issues were concerned, subsidized, company-maintained housing and utilities offered them affordable shelter, which were often superior to their previous living conditions.[41]

Mill villages, with all their shortcomings, were the foundation of hundreds of thousands of lives in the region. The popularity of the system remained strong almost to the very end. In 1945, 185,000 South Carolinians, or 17 percent of the state's white population, lived in the mill villages.[42] The disappearance of these communities was likely to trigger excitement at workers' ascent to the property-owning class, countered by nostalgia and occasional protests from workers disappointed at the terms of sale or the rapid disappearance of their inexpensive, subsidized, and paternalistically protected living spaces.[43]

In Spartanburg, as well as in scores of other communities in the South, the sale of mill villages helped to convert the town's textile workers into small-scale individual capitalists with a growing commitment to the place. Their culture and communities characterized by high mobility, textile workers had traditionally followed jobs throughout the Piedmont. The mill village system, as well as the interchangeability of jobs and regional mill village culture, had made physical movement easy. A "linthead carousel" had rolled for decades in the Southern Piedmont's textile area, as workers chased better opportunities from southern Virginia to northern Georgia and all places in between. The sale of mill villages played a substantial role in bringing an end to this movement, creating people with more tangible ties to the community and a growing commitment to capitalism in their small, home-owning way. The workers now had more vested interest in the success of their new town, making them at least somewhat more susceptible to the booster message of more jobs, an orderly community, and accumulating wealth for the entire community.

The changes affecting Spartanburg were not only local. The effects of the peace and the political, economic, and cultural changes it triggered shook all of South Carolina and the South. The pillars of regional culture, including proper political order and the post-Reconstruction concepts of racial hierarchy, were increasingly under strong and well-organized assaults throughout the South. The federal government's expanded role in the region and the increased exposure of veterans to the outside world gave young southerners confidence to go after the often exclusive and closed local power structures of their home regions. A series of GI revolts, political reform movements led and supported by the young, ambitious generation of World War II veterans, began to shake the entire South, accompanied by the NAACP's increasingly rigorous attacks against the most blatant expressions of racial inequality, even the principle of Jim Crow itself.[44]

In South Carolina the postwar efforts to reform the state's political culture focused heavily on the persons of Olin D. Johnston and, especially, Strom Thurmond. Thurmond was a state judge and a recently discharged war hero who had declared his candidacy for governor of South Carolina in May 1946. Thurmond's announcement speech repeated the shopping list of issues typical of GI rebels, including good government, expanded political democracy, industrial recruitment, and increased professionalization of public services.[45] The group of GI rebels rallying around Thurmond viciously attacked the status quo of the Palmetto State political culture, centered in a small group of aging power brokers known as the Barnwell Ring.[46]

The stakes were high. The election of 1946 was among the most antagonistic and important in the history of the state, determining not only South Carolina's postwar policies but also much of its administrative culture and the state's relation to the rest of the country. The significance of the election echoed in the harsh rhetoric of both parties, and Thurmond and his cohorts made perfectly clear what was at issue. It was not beneath the good judge to compare his opponents to Nazis: "I was willing to risk my life to stamp out such gangs in Europe," Thurmond declared on the stump. "I intend to devote my future to wiping out the stench and stain with which the Barnwell ring has smeared the government of South Carolina for, lo, these many years."[47] The progressivism of Thurmond's campaign received noticeable support among younger Carolinians, especially in the industrial Piedmont.

Spartanburg County, and especially its industrial and business-minded groups, were largely behind Thurmond. Walter Brown, a prominent businessman from Spartanburg, emerged as one of the closest friends and most active supporters of, and campaigners for, the candidate. The *Spartanburg*

Herald loudly supported Thurmond, praising his progressive stand against the Barnwell Ring and the rest of his platform for good schools, industrialization, and rural electrification.[48] In the Democratic primary on September 3, 1946, the de facto election in the state, Spartanburg County threw its support behind Thurmond by the margin of 3 to 2.[49] The results in the town of Spartanburg were a virtual draw, but the mill villages and Spartanburg County delivered local votes to Thurmond. His combination of business-minded progressivism and cultural conservatism—with more than dashes of old southern populism—was a good match with Spartanburg, offering a political reflection of its postwar values and aspirations.

Regardless of what its ideas about business and culture were, Spartanburg was not interested in maintaining the political status quo. Not even within the town itself did the Barnwell Ring find overwhelming support, even though the town traditionally was more elitist and had more vested interest in the status quo than its surrounding county. In general, Spartanburg was interested in partial reform, business-progressive renewal of the state's largely antiquated political culture and institutions. Additionally, the community was largely behind Thurmond's classic southern populism, Bilboite progressivism for white people only. Thurmond's brand of progressivism and populism was not anticapitalist, but it was not the Austrian free-market variety, either. Thurmond's brand talked about order and cohesion, change through reform rather than revolution. The government's role was to clean up and reform the unproductive vestiges of power in the state, improve the infrastructure, and shake up—but not revolutionize—the system. Thurmond's message echoed Spartanburg's visions, with its postwar map for prosperity and utilitarian communal solidarity.

Thurmond's message of modernizing the administration was complemented by the pro-labor populism of Olin D. Johnston, a former governor who had been elected to the Senate two years earlier. Since the 1930s Johnston, a full-blown New Dealer, farmer, textile worker, and the icon for thousands of South Carolina mill hands, had built a loyal following among mill workers and other blue-collar workers, a bond that would last until Johnston's death in 1965. Johnston combined the messages of labor-centered progressivism and improved public services, public works, and white supremacy, which gained him a dedicated following among white working-class Carolinians. As both governor and senator, Johnston systematically celebrated mill workers, spicing his economic messages with periodic proclamations of white supremacy.[50]

The majority of voters in Spartanburg supported both Thurmond and Johnston, and, despite these two men's obvious political differences, the town's acceptance of both candidates made perfect sense. In South Carolina's intrastate squabbles both men were rigorous opponents of the state's old machine politics. As a governor, Johnston had famously escalated a conflict with the highway department by calling the national guard to bring the recalcitrant office under his control.[51] Thurmond, on the other hand, made crushing the Barnwell machine and bringing political modernization to South Carolina his main campaign strategy for the governorship. In matters of race, both men combined their reformist spirit with dedicated opposition to African American suffrage and any attempts at social equality.

Both Thurmond and Johnston represented progress and administrative modernization, even if their emphases were different. Both also represented political renewal in a state historically dominated by political oligarchies, and their regional support rested heavily in the South Carolina Piedmont, with its industrial centers and growth-oriented culture. The political differences between the probusiness populist Thurmond and the pro-labor populist Johnston were obvious, but at a deeper level of cultural attitudes and the metapolitics of race, place, and identity, both men were surprisingly similar. The success they enjoyed in Spartanburg, occasionally among the same voters, was a telling symbol of the peculiar new politics emerging in the South Carolina Piedmont. The politics of class and economic identity, the theoretical Rosetta Stone for many classic interpreters of political orientation and voting patterns, was here complemented with new interpretations of mutual interests and community identity, which were increasingly shaping the political behavior and even identity among the region's workers.

The experiences of Spartanburg's African Americans did not noticeably differ from the wartime and postwar experiences of their brethren around the state. In matters of race Spartanburg was an archetypical South Carolina Piedmont community, with its blue-collar racism, condescending middle-class illusions of benevolence, and widespread white conviction that local African Americans were content with the racial system that prevailed in the region. During the war and its aftermath the demographic developments of the African American population of Spartanburg remained largely reflective of general population trends. In Spartanburg County and elsewhere in the region the black farm population was diminishing rapidly as urban or semiurban black communities burgeoned. The experiences of Spartanburg's African Americans differed little from the struggles of their counterparts in most other counties and towns around South Carolina.[52]

With the war and its aftermath, South Carolina's African American population began to awaken from the quiescence that had characterized it during the

Great Depression years. During the 1930s and early 1940s African Americans in the South and South Carolina had kept a noticeably low political profile. As unemployment, foreclosures, and payments for not growing cotton cut the number of jobs and, hence, the wages of black agricultural workers in South Carolina, sometimes to as little as 25 cents per day during the deepest Depression months, South Carolina blacks were too discouraged—and, no doubt, too busy trying to put food on the table—to raise issues of equality or even improvement. Migration to northern cities, despite their declining economic opportunities for working-class African Americans, continued to serve as the major release valve for frustrated blacks who could not tolerate the racial oppression of their home states. Almost half a million black southerners left for northern cities during the Depression decade.[53]

During the Depression decade the apparent passivity of southern blacks was so noticeable that some northern black intellectuals, led by Langston Hughes, had attacked their southern cousins with vitriolic condemnations in the pages of African American publications. In the *Crisis*, the NAACP's official magazine, Hughes condemned the low levels of student activity and progressive thinking in southern African American colleges, calling them "Jim-crow centers built on the money docile and lying beggars have kidded white people into contributing."[54] J. Edward Arbor, a young southern writer, published vitriolic attacks against the otherworldly passivity of his fellow African Americans, casting them as "hog-tied by the fundamentalist, do-nothing colored churches." Even black newspapers, Arbor commented tartly, heaped "praise on those who exploit them."[55] In South Carolina the accusations sounded at least partially credible in light of the statements by some of the region's black leaders, such as the director of the Charleston branch of the NAACP, John H. McCray, who, while claiming to speak for South Carolina's black residents, criticized attempts in the mid-1930s by liberal politicians and civil rights activists to enact federal antilynching legislation: "We are content to wait."[56]

During World War II patriotic fervor, democratic propaganda, and a sellers' labor market were instilling new confidence among blacks in the Palmetto State.[57] African American political activity and self-assurance reached levels not witnessed since the days before the state constitution of 1895 and its reenshrinement of white supremacy. As World War II was winding down, returning African American veterans were determined to carve more assertive and influential roles in Palmetto State life. And despite blacks' low profile during the 1930s, the decade had witnessed the rise of a new generation of leaders among the state's "race men" and women, who were eager and ready to join forces with veterans in their home state.[58]

Veterans, national sentiment, and even the state's legal system were not prepared or willing to return to the old days of open and unapologetic racism. The African American fight against racial violence and the most blatant examples of unequal legal treatment received support from some surprising sources. When Willie Earle, a black man, was lynched because of his alleged involvement in the February 1947 murder of a Greenville cab driver, Governor Thurmond astonished millions around the nation and violated an old regional tradition by pursuing the members of the lynch mob and helping to bring them to justice. Although the men were, predictably, acquitted at trial, the case nevertheless offered solid evidence that times were changing in South Carolina.[59]

Supported by the Truman administration and federal courts, African Americans in South Carolina worked through the NAACP and the state political machinery. Between 1939 and 1948 membership in the South Carolina chapter of the NAACP grew from eight hundred to fourteen thousand, and the organization began to show new vigor. Judge J. Waties Waring's monumental decision to outlaw all-white primaries in 1948 granted African Americans access to voting booths and, gradually, influence in the political decision-making process in South Carolina. In the 1948 Democratic primary, thirty-five thousand black Carolinians cast votes, providing a powerful testimony to the state's changing political realities.[60]

The racial atmosphere in South Carolina and Spartanburg remained subdued, with tensions brewing below the surface. Despite some well-publicized attacks of violence against African Americans during the late 1940s, black South Carolinians remained more moderate than the state's white population, according to one preeminent historian of the field.[61] By the early 1950s racial issues in South Carolina had been placed on the back burner, although Jim Crow remained alive and well in Spartanburg and elsewhere.

Partial accommodation and prevailing moderation kept the lid on most problems, especially from the perspective of the state's white inhabitants. As the experience of the 1950s would attest, South Carolinians hated to be lumped together with extremist, violence-prone states such as Alabama and Mississippi, preferring instead a polite, subdued handling and support of racial issues and segregation.[62] The state's white political leadership regarded the race issue as largely solved by the early 1950s, and South Carolinians began to elect moderate segregationists to the governor's office.[63] While the candidates for state or national offices—ranging from Strom Thurmond to Olin D. Johnston and Fritz Hollings—continued their modern bloody-shirt politics of maintaining the "dignity of the color line," their actions grouped them as moderate segregationists—at least when judged by the standards of the day.

Spartanburg's branch of the NAACP opened in 1944. Led by Reverend W. L. Wilson, the local NAACP addressed bread-and-butter issues affecting the middle-class African American communities in the urban South—from promoting higher teacher pay to demanding the hiring of black police officers.[64] As in many urban communities in South Carolina, African American protest in Spartanburg remained subdued, using the more widely accepted and moderate forms of social protest. Aggressive public demonstrations were practically unknown in the town, as much of Spartanburg's racial negotiation took place in private meetings between the leaders of its racial groups, not in the streets. Social protest was trumped by commitment to social progress, however moderate it might have been.

Spartanburg's leaders mastered the policies of maintaining racial control through partial accommodation. The opinion shapers of the town sought the proverbial middle ground by appealing to the Booker T. Washingtonian spirit of self-improvement and moderation among the community's blacks while encouraging its white citizens to denounce the Ku Klux Klan and other forms of racial extremism.[65] The hiring of two black police officers in 1950 and 1953, improved funding for the town's black schools, and periodic urban renovation projects touching black and white communities alike helped to instill at least some sense of progress and of blacks' stake in the community's development.[66] In elections Spartanburg's white voters joined most of the South Carolina Piedmont in supporting business-minded, moderate segregationists over the more dedicated, fire-breathing brand of white supremacists.[67]

Spartanburg's white establishment, including its newspapers, promoted "moderate" segregation and respect for order and authorities. The *Spartanburg Herald* preached the gospel of law and order, raising its voice against Klan and self-assertive civil rights activism alike.[68] It sought to support segregation whenever possible, but when courts sided with the civil rights movement, the paper called for respect for the law of the land and the decisions of the courts, no matter how ill informed or regrettable they might have been. In the paper's worldview the only good demagoguery was centered in peace and progress, economic advancement and creation, and maintenance of a cohesive, peaceful community.

The postwar era posed a challenge to the old orders and established elites around the country. Returning soldiers, the effects of the budding civil rights movement, labor union activism, and the massive economic boom contained forces potentially capable of challenging the status quo. Throughout the United States and the South, elites and socioeconomic hierarchies were toppled in a series of state- and community-level GI revolts, led by young, determined, and self-confident veterans of the Second World War. South Carolina itself saw one of the most substantial and significant changes in the South with the toppling of the Barnwell Ring and installment of Governor Strom Thurmond's neoprogressive regime. The new South Carolina was committed to business progressivism, modernized government, and facing economic changes and challenges head on. However, the developments in Spartanburg proved that determined, strong, and smartly managed communities could become capable of directing and moderating the powers of change. Spartanburg's economic decision makers largely succeeded in maintaining the old order through conciliation and appeasement, compromise and inclusion. Local textile bosses took the wind out of unions' sails by complementing their effective union-busting strategies with improved pay and working conditions. The political zeal of Spartanburg's African Americans was largely pacified by urban renewal, improved job opportunities, local condemnation of the Ku Klux Klan and other forms of white extremism, grudging acceptance of the black vote, and other modest gestures of white benevolence.

The appearance of inclusiveness and moderation set the stage for the development of Spartanburg. Community spirit, traditionally limited to middle-class townspeople, began to envelop the working classes. The gradual but rapidly accelerating disappearance of the mill village weakened the cultural demarcation lines. Mill hands, enjoying their share of the growing postwar prosperity, became culturally and geographically liberated from the confines of the mill village. As new property owners, their lifestyles, consumption habits, and improved standards of living pushed them ever closer to Spartanburg's middle classes. Property tied the workers to the community, transforming the mill hands' value systems and attitudes toward their immediate surroundings.

The leaders of Spartanburg succeeded in convincing growing numbers of local mill hands and other laborers that rejecting unionization and submitting to their vision of the community could serve everyone's interests. The sales pitch grew more effective with every passing year of growing prosperity. A largely nonmilitant working class with a growing commitment to the community's success was to play a crucial role in the economic development of Spartanburg. The stability of Spartanburg's socioeconomic order was perhaps the single most important selling point for the community as it courted outside investors in the years to come.

Within carefully set parameters Spartanburg continued to be welcoming to meaningful, limited reforms and outside individuals and influences. These forces, however, would eventually only strengthen local social and economic structures. The parameters of change were set by the early 1950s. By practicing moderate inclusion and closely managed growth, Spartanburg's chamber of commerce and its supporters secured the town's future as a community of stable growth.

CHAPTER TWO

Origins of the Latest South

By the mid-1950s the unwavering optimism in South Carolina and Spartanburg was giving way to something resembling a rapidly worsening case of economic personality disorder. The state continued to enjoy the benefits of the postwar boom, with all indicators and public forums touting the growing progress and prosperity. Beneath the surface, however, vague forebodings were emerging around South Carolina. The intensity of change surrounding their lives disconcerted many South Carolinians, Spartans included.

The newfound prosperity had not arrived with the promise of security. The traditional bulwarks of the state's economy and culture—foremost among them, textiles, mill villages, agriculture, and racial hierarchy—were disappearing or transforming rapidly. Changes in economic fortunes and structures could disrupt the order. Rapid riches could prove temporary or—perhaps worse—change the fundamental culture and social order of the community. The growth and new economic opportunities, combined with uncertainty and change, created openings for new individuals and economic strategies, but the entrenched elite in South Carolina and Spartanburg sought to control the changes, channeling them carefully within approved and preset parameters.

The need for economic modernization was obvious. The two foundations of the economy of Spartanburg County—agriculture and textile manufacturing—were undergoing comprehensive transformations. The status quo, even with diminished expectations, was not an option. Sharecropping, mule-powered subsistence farming, and even small-scale production for regional markets were disappearing options, leading to a diminishing and aging farm population. The changing nature of global textile markets, technological advances, and changing culture in the workplace were altering the local textile business. Especially after the recessions and import crisis of 1954–55, almost everybody associated with the industry understood that all aspects of their business were changing, from the disappearance of the mill village communalism to new types of factories and product lines.

The postwar decade had been very kind to South Carolina and Spartanburg. The enormous explosion of wealth had affected the entire nation, but in the South and South Carolina the years between 1945 and 1954 marked a golden decade of prosperity. While the economic progress of the United States was astonishing, the growth rates of the Palmetto State had surpassed even the national averages by a wide margin. South Carolina's rapid progress in fields such as finance and real estate offered solid, quantifiable evidence of a maturing economy that was responding positively to the postwar challenges. While the nation's finance, insurance, and real estate markets expanded approximately 36 percent during the 1950s, in South Carolina the growth rate climbed more than 133 percent, albeit from a much lower base. In construction, retail, and manufacturing South Carolina nearly doubled the national growth rates.[1]

Despite the advances in service industries, manufacturing and—to a rapidly declining degree—agriculture still formed the skeleton around which these new muscles grew. Manufacturing, especially in textiles, provided a steady supply of good news for South Carolina's laborers and capitalists alike. Textile factories were expanding, and some diversified industries, such as chemical companies and metal workshops, were entering the state. In the first half of the 1950s South Carolina received more than $509 million worth of new and expanded industry, which meant new payroll totaling $113 million.[2] Thanks largely to these substantial advances, the per-capita personal income of an average South Carolinian grew from $893 in 1950 ($7,689 in 2007 dollars) to $1,181 in 1955 ($9,143), a jump of nearly 30 percent.[3]

Between 1940 and 1952 the real income of the state's residents had grown a full 100 percent, compared with the national average of 51 percent.[4] The industrial Piedmont, with Spartanburg in its geographic and spiritual center, was home to the lion's share of South Carolina's industrial progress. Between 1947 and 1958 the total number of manufacturing establishments in Spartanburg County grew from 124 to 177, with the combined annual payroll climbing from $50,422,000 ($467,976,600 in 2007 dollars) to $77,749,000 ($557,421,600), a substantial improvement for the community.[5] From construction to population growth and general euphoria, Spartanburg's economic progress was visible to any casual observer. For most townspeople these were the halcyon days of new prosperity and optimism.

The numbers translated into conveniences and a sense of progress for ordinary Spartans that testified more vividly than any statistic to the economic progress of the Palmetto State. The entire state had secured a slice of the new prosperity, but no other region could match the rapid economic advancement of the Piedmont. The postwar decade transformed Spartanburg from a locally oriented community reliant on the textile industry, cotton, and peach farming into a regionally noticeable industrial and transportation hub. Looking back at this marvelous decade, a columnist for the Sunday paper, the *Spartanburg Herald-Journal*, wanted his readers to take a thorough and grateful look at their lives during the 1950s and asked them two simple questions: "Can you count the easy feeling of security? Does anybody keep an accurate count of the number of sirloin steaks he eats?"[6]

Readers of the paper had particularly good reasons for almost smug satisfaction. Both the population and industrial base of the town had been growing since the 1940s. Spartanburg in the mid-1950s was in the middle of a growth spurt that would push its population from 32,249 to 44,352 by the end of the decade.[7] Surrounding Spartanburg County was growing almost equally fast, with its population expanding from 127,733 in 1940 to 156,830 in 1960. The improved mobility of the car-owning working class was increasingly turning parts of Spartanburg County into an extension of the town, transforming the old cluster of mill villages and the downtown shopping and office complex into a modern suburban complex, complete with new suburban residences, strip malls, and some persistent pockets of poverty.[8] The demographic dynamics of the community were changing.

For a community that had built its economic destiny on low-paying work in the textile mills, the postwar prosperity triggered substantial changes in lifestyle. The growing affluence affected almost everybody, including the working class. Low-paying jobs at textile mills were gradually evolving into better-paid industrial careers, with corresponding effects on the workers' standard and quality of living. In the mid-1950s Spartanburg was in the middle of a ten-year infrastructural improvement and suburban transition that would increase the number of its households with electricity by 55 percent and number of motor vehicles by 90 percent.[9] For once, the traditionally rosy language of the town's boosters began to slowly—and at least partially—match the daily reality of its working class. Growing segments of the town population witnessed their lifestyle approximating that of the middle class of the prewar era, complete with modern conveniences and purchasing power that began to reach beyond bare necessities.

Considering the rapid growth in the number of industrial facilities, value added by manufacture, and total wages, the number of factory workers remained relatively stable. Spartanburg County received less than 1,000 new manufacturing jobs between 1947 and 1958, reaching 25,319 by the end of that period.[10] Even then, most of the growth took place during the first five or six years. Technical and managerial advances had increased the profitability and effectiveness of Spartanburg's factories. New industrial workers were more skilled, better paid, and numerically fewer than in the past.[11]

However, stagnant or even falling numbers of industrial workers did not mean that their importance to Spartanburg was in decline. The numbers did translate into a growing service sector and further diversification of the community's social structure, but factories continued to be the engine behind the growing wealth.[12] The town's working class was slowly beginning to break into factions; in its elite were industrial workers, while the rapidly expanding service sector offered the increasingly lower-paid, less prestigious jobs. Both the wages and prestige of industrial jobs were improving. The old disparagement of textile mill people as lintheads was gradually disappearing, as textile mill workers were increasingly incorporated into the main community.

Manufacturing brought in the capital that enabled Spartanburg to grow and evolve, but numerically the most impressive growth was in services and professions requiring a college education. The service industry began to establish itself as the town's second biggest economic sector. The changing economy also triggered a radical growth in the white-collar professions. The number of Spartanburg's professional and technical workers—including engineers, doctors, teachers, and the like—almost tripled during the 1950s, from 1,676 to 4,478.[13] The town witnessed the emergence of a new, urban, and educated middle class, which began to coexist alongside the old entrepreneurial groups of shopkeepers, lawyers, and other townspeople who had traditionally provided the small "middling sort" in a community dominated economically by mill owners and numerically by its textile workers.[14]

Agriculture provided a sobering reality check for the observers of Spartanburg's economy, with its aging and diminishing farm population and persistent poverty.[15] The troubles of southern farmers had been practically common knowledge since the Great Depression, and Spartanburg again provided almost an exaggerated picture of the trends within the region. War and European reconstruction had rapidly increased the demand for cotton, aiding South Carolina's farmers. Cotton prices, which had sunk as low as 9.46 cents per pound in 1930, reached an average of 31.9 cents per pound in 1947.[16]

The price increase, combined with technological advances, such as increased use of tractors and mechanical harvesters, briefly resuscitated the old single cash-crop system in much of the South, including the South Carolina Piedmont.[17] However, most South Carolina farmers continued to struggle below the poverty line. By 1949 almost three-quarters of South Carolina farms would sell only $250 to 2,499 ($2,170–$21,725 in 2007 dollars) worth of products annually.[18] Counties and communities that had tied their economic fortunes to agriculture saw their prospects decline, as farmers' access to industrial jobs began to separate "developed" from "underdeveloped" counties around the South Carolina Piedmont.[19]

Despite the problems in its agricultural sector, Spartanburg was not ready to fully abandon it. Reflecting the principles of the Depression-era "Balance Agriculture with Industry" (BAWI) programs, Spartanburg's boosters sought to help the community to continue its balancing act.[20] In the postwar visions of the chamber of commerce, agriculture, in a modernized form, continued to play a role in Spartanburg's economy. The boosters' vision, so enthusiastically promoted by the *Spartanburg Herald*, had encouraged dairy and cattle husbandry, truck farming, and other more nuanced, even niche, agribusinesses to replace the old cotton monoculture of the Piedmont.[21]

The number of farms in Spartanburg County declined nearly 60 percent during the decade, dropping to 3,108 in 1959. During the same period total farmland diminished rapidly, from 390,493 to 263,120 acres. The collapse in the number of farmers and families earning their livelihood from agriculture was even more drastic. The total number of farmers in Spartanburg County in 1959 was 3,108, barely one third of the number just nine years earlier. Extensive reliance on farming as the sole source of income grew increasingly rare. Sharecropping and other forms of nonproprietor farming were disappearing especially rapidly.[22]

The advances in the manufacturing and service industries were enough to offset the losses in agriculture. Still, perhaps the biggest loss associated with agriculture in Spartanburg County was cultural, not economic. The rapidly diverging fortunes of the two sectors settled the century-old competition between the county and town, farmers and mill people, to the advantage of the town and mill. In the new postwar era the economic future and dynamism of the region was concentrated in towns, not in villages or alongside rural vistas.[23] Industry established itself as the unquestionable engine for the county's development, supporting an exploding service sector that began to play an increasingly visible role in the new postwar Spartanburg.

The decline of agriculture finally ended the dual existence for thousands of Spartanburg's workers. For decades they had moved between farm and factory with relative ease. Even after generations in the mill villages, the workers' connections to the farm remained strong.[24] The workers had created an economic and cultural mode of existence that, much like the rest of Spartanburg County, kept one foot in the field and the other on the factory floor. Spartanburg had been an active participant in industrialization without fully surrendering to its whims. In contrast to the development of typical northern industrial communities, the modernization of Spartanburg had remained incomplete. Now, with the agricultural sector in decline, the town's future became inseparably linked to industrialization.

By any statistical measure the economic progress of South Carolina was visible, if not even astonishing. On a personal level quantitative measures translated into convenience and tangible improvements in the quality of life that few South Carolinians had experienced before. However, the security observed by the *Spartanburg Herald-Journal*'s writer—keen on measuring the number and quality of steaks enjoyed—was missing from the lives of most townspeople. Spartanburg did experience prosperity, but the security of rapidly accumulating wealth was not always enough to offset the emotionally and culturally unsettling forces that the postwar decades had unleashed.

Throughout the history of the Piedmont a desire for security had tempered the region's commercial impulses. Starting with its antebellum "safety first farmers," locals had tried to pursue growth without losing their traditional republican independence, to participate in a speculative economy without submitting their fortunes completely to its whims.[25] The commercial mentality of the region had held on to cotton and, later, to textiles with a dogged determination, seeking security and solace in the cultural and commercial predictability they had offered for so long. Now, whatever promises of prosperity the postwar era brought, its unpredictability seemed ominous. Simultaneously, the disappearance of the agricultural sector eliminated a traditional safety valve for Spartanburg's workers. They were now undeniably tied to the town and factory. Their jobs, property values, and professional careers were thoroughly intertwined with the destinies of the community. Spartanburg's workers were approaching a narrower definition of a modern, urban working class.

The fate of the rapidly disappearing mill villages and the changing nature of the textile industry were but two of the many forces of change shaking and transforming Spartanburg and the entire South. The war and its aftermath marked a departure for the region, pulling it away from its relative isolation and challenging its time-cherished traditions and prejudices. Like an estranged couple united by a common tragedy, the South and the nation had sought each other for help and moral support when the war started. A common enemy, massive federal investments in the South, and increasing physical contacts between Yankees and southerners had pulled the South into an increasingly closer interaction with the rest of the nation.[26] Peace was not enough to break the new bond. In fact, peace helped to intensify the movement of new men and ideas into the South and the South Carolina Piedmont.[27]

Much like the nineteenth-century migration associated with the formation and growth of the southern textile industry, the postwar migration to the South came directly from the North and was concentrated heavily in the managerial and professional classes. The pipeline of entrepreneurial capital, technology, and managerial talent from New England to the South was as old as the South Carolina Piedmont's textile industry itself, reaching back to the antebellum era.[28] This time, however, the movement was faster and quantitatively more substantial. The 1950s saw the humble beginnings of a mass migration to the South. For the next twenty-five years the South would be the fastest-growing region in the United States.

Within the Old Confederacy South Carolina would consistently remain the second fastest-growing state, behind only the emerging retirement haven of southern Florida.[29] No corner of South Carolina grew faster than the Piedmont, and the booming Greenville-Spartanburg axis expanded most rapidly of all. By 1960, 21,597 of Spartanburg County's 156,452 inhabitants had been born outside the state. While most migrants were part of the traditional "linthead carousel" of the textile belt states, a growing number of Yankees arrived, searching for amenities they had often learned to know and like during their stays in southern military camps.[30] This group of war veterans and other ambitious young men and women moved south to take advantage of the opportunities that this underdeveloped region, full of growth potential, could offer.[31]

The mingling of Yankees and Yankee-minded southerners gave rise to a new type of resident. The "organization man, a worthy successor to Ralph McGill's 'certain type, small town rich man,'" emerged to challenge the old rulers for a share of local economic power and prominence.[32] Like the Redeemers of the first Reconstruction, the organization men proved to be highly skilled and effective in gaining control of southern communities. Unlike the Redeemers, however, these men proved to be a formidable threat to the traditional southern way of life. Francis Pickens Miller's 1961 depiction of the organization men—glazed with southern romanticism, contemporary pathos, and anxiety—and their impact upon southern culture and politics is well worth repeating:

> His [the organization man's] appearance represents a complete break with the past. With rare exceptions there has never been anyone like him in the South before. He is an executive servant of the new industrial society. . . .

Because southern industrial development is still in its infancy and represents such a complete break with the past, these young men accurately reflect the values of the institutions and interests they serve. They show little evidence of what used to be called "southern culture." . . .

Men are seldom willing to admit that materialism is their philosophy of life, and that is true of these organization men. They prefer to take their stand on higher grounds of principle, and their principles are generally expressed in terms of free enterprise, fiscal sanity, states' rights and racial integrity.

They seem to me to be momentary men—individuals who have breadth, but no length or depth, men whose lives are like cross sections of history without reflecting any sense of continuity with the living stream of the past or with the living stream of the future. But they constitute the raw material out of which new political organizations in the South will be formed.[33]

Spartanburg had traditionally been relatively open to external influences, with more than its share of ideological forefathers of the organization men. Unlike their agribusiness brethren in the Black Belt, Spartanburg's small-town rich men looked to the factory and the markets and business partners in the North for most of their wealth. Local traditions were flexible and the newcomers' previous contacts with the region made their arrival easier to digest. The northern-born industrial tycoons and ambitious newcomers soon allied themselves with the local elites. Fred Dent, a Connecticut-raised scion of a wealthy textile family who owned Spartanburg's old Mayfair Mills, moved to Spartanburg in 1947 and rapidly became one of the most visible economic, civic, and political leaders in the community. Reeves Brothers, a New York–based textile conglomerate that had opened a finishing plant at Spartanburg's Fairforest village in the 1920s, moved its headquarters and its professional, largely northern-born managerial staff to Spartanburg during the early postwar years. Deering Milliken's growing role in Spartanburg's economy brought to town scores of Ivy League–trained northern professionals from managerial and scientific professions.[34]

Two Yankees in particular began to shape the community, acquiring local political and economic power and beginning to mold the community to reflect their vision of an emerging New South business center. Both newcomers, the textile magnate Roger Milliken and Richard Ellery (Dick) Tukey, head of the Spartanburg Chamber of Commerce, grew up in New York, in families originating in New England. Both had previous exposure to the South, but their business dealings and economic outlooks were essentially national. Their business values and personal aspirations were linked to the promise of the new New South. Their South was a blank slate, not the old Dixie burdened by

traditions and history. The New South of Spartanburg County, with its historical willingness to sell itself to the highest bidder and peculiar combination of
cultural persistence and flexibility in matters of money, appealed to them both
personally and professionally. Spartanburg was an ideal incubator for their
business aspirations and social visions.

In the mid-1950s Roger Milliken was a young and energetic textile boss,
a tall man with an aristocratic manner and bright red hair. On a hot June
afternoon in 1947 he had suddenly inherited one of America's most important
textile corporations, Deering Milliken. In the middle of a round of golf on
Long Island, Gerrish Milliken collapsed and died in the arms of Roger, his
oldest son. Roger had joined the family business soon after graduating from
Yale in 1939, where he had majored in French history. When his father died,
Roger, who was being groomed to take over the firm, was thirty-two and had
worked for the company for seven years.[35]

Gerrish Milliken's death sped up the transition, and the young CEO was
forced to mature on the job. Roger Milliken showed an impressive commitment to his work and the family corporation. Although he had been born and
raised in New York City and the Hamptons, and schooled at Groton and Yale,
Roger Milliken decided to become a full-time Spartan because the company
was doing so much business in the area. In 1954 Milliken, his wife, Justine
(née van Rensselaer Hooper), and their five children settled into a comfortable
but far from ostentatious house at 627 Otis Boulevard.[36] Milliken was obsessed
with maintaining strict control of his operations and favoring an excessively
hands-on management style; his move to the town put him closer to the new
geographic heart of the family's businesses.[37]

Like numerous other textile companies with roots in New England and the
Middle Atlantic states, Deering Milliken had gone through a gradual southernization, a shift that escalated in size and scope during the first half of the
twentieth century. The company had begun as a small sales and marketing–
centered textile interest that used local capital and know-how and became a
national producer with rapid expansion in the South. It had been lured by the
cheap labor and proximity to raw materials that had dragged dozens of northern textile entrepreneurs below the Mason-Dixon line between the Civil War
and World War II. Moving the company's headquarters to Spartanburg also
was dictated by the growing importance of regional markets and the South's
rapid economic emergence as America's leading growth center.

Deering Milliken's first contacts in the South Carolina Piedmont reach
back to the 1880s, when Roger's grandfather and the founder of the family
business, Seth Milliken, built a plant in Pacolet. During that decade the

company rapidly boosted its presence in the South by buying interest in forty-two mills around the region. During the Great Depression, Deering Milliken, now led by Roger's father, Gerrish, acquired numerous bankrupt southern textile mills and played an important role in the consolidation and reorganization of the entire southern textile business.[38] By the end of World War II, Deering Milliken, a Maine-born and New York City–raised business, was essentially a South Carolina corporation, with Spartanburg in the geographical and spiritual center of its continually growing business.

Roger Milliken's move to the South was, like almost everything he did professionally, a practical move with substantial ideological repercussions. He brought to Spartanburg his business, commitment to conservative ideology, willingness to bankroll conservative causes, and his peculiar combination of community involvement and hermitlike reticence. Once in Spartanburg, Milliken started rapidly to reshape the town, the Piedmont, and even the South according to his political and economic beliefs. He soon became involved in a variety of conservative causes, ranging from the global to the unabashedly trivial, from supporting the nascent South Carolina Republican Party to assisting in the fight to prevent the entry of coeds at Wofford College, Spartanburg's leading male educational institution.[39]

Blessed with money, well-established connections, patrician charisma, and seemingly boundless energy, Milliken was welcomed into Spartanburg's elite. He picked up memberships in local organizations, including a seat on Wofford College's board of directors, creating an aura of presence and influence while shunning public visibility. Milliken's name repeatedly surfaced in association with Spartanburg's public beautification and educational programs, but he guarded his person with almost obsessive privacy.[40] For the media Milliken proved to be an elusive presence, always there but hardly ever accessible. As the decades passed, people in Spartanburg would learn to understand and appreciate the man and his manners, his participation and deep involvement with the community that left a trace of actions and achievements but rarely a record of visible public presence.

In business Milliken played a crucial role in the modernization of Spartanburg's textile industry. In 1945 he had launched the Deering Milliken Research Trust, a modern research and development institution, to help devise new products and methods of production for the company. In 1958 the trust, now renamed the Deering Milliken Research Corporation, relocated from Connecticut to Spartanburg, filling an ultramodern, carefully manicured, and immaculate industrial campus on the north side of town, right next to where Interstate 85 would be built.[41]

The sizable research facility demonstrated Milliken's commitment to quality, research, and innovation in securing the future of his business in the highly competitive textile industry. Milliken, a fiercely competitive and secretive businessman, demonstrated surprising openness with his promotion of a new approach to research and quality in local textile production. Milliken helped his colleagues in Spartanburg's textile industry to see that bulk production with low wages was a rapidly dying industrial strategy, even in the South. During the next several decades he would play a crucial role in convincing the Spartanburg textile industry to revamp its operational model, with aggressive investment in technology, research, and development.[42] Milliken would also help the community to fight unionization and recruit new industries, in the process molding the future of Spartanburg's business and culture.

Milliken's close associate in shaping contemporary Spartanburg, Richard Ellery Tukey, came from the opposite end of Yankee society, the plebeian to Milliken's patrician. While Milliken carried the air of old money, Ivy League education, and reserved East Hampton prestige, Tukey was a brash, expansive man with thinning hair and a persistent weight problem. He enjoyed publicity and skillfully played the role of an impulsive, cigar-smoking, straight-to-business salesman for national and international media. Tukey's style was all New York, and his education characteristic of an ambitious lad from the northeastern middle class. He was a born salesman, full of energetic impatience and back-slapping buoyancy, prickly confidence, and sincere commitment to the community he worked to enrich. In the end, Tukey's contributions to Spartanburg equaled, if not surpassed, those of Roger Milliken.

This key player in South Carolina's economic history hailed from Brooklyn, New York, of all places. Born in 1918 to Frank and Mabel Tukey, a bed salesman and a homemaker originally from Massachusetts, Richard was substantially younger than his two older siblings and the only member of the family born in New York. After Richard's early childhood in the bustling, multicultural urban borough, Frank moved the family about twenty miles north, into a suburban community and home at 64 Davis Avenue in White Plains, Westchester County.[43]

White Plains in the 1920s and 1930s was a rapidly growing suburban community, full of the half-satisfied aspirations of the first generation, self-made *démi-success*. It was a determined neighborhood of self-made men and their offspring, an upwardly mobile community of arrivistes with will and drive but still light in bourgeois gentility. The neat and unimpressive houses were homes to salesmen, civil servants, and small businessmen and their families. The majority of the inhabitants were refugees from the five boroughs of New

York City, but White Plains also housed substantial immigrant communities. Large groups of Germans, Scots, and Irish, complemented with some Swedes, Russians, Italians, and smaller groups of other Europeans, mingled with their native-born, northeastern neighbors.[44]

The Tukeys managed to ride out the Great Depression relatively unscathed. Frank Tukey switched his job from a bed salesman to sales manager with an insurance company, and his oldest son, Norman, soon following him into the business. Despite the hard times, the family found enough money to send young Richard to college. He attended Bowdoin College in Maine, preparing himself for a career in journalism. After college Richard returned home to become a writer for the *White Plains Daily Reporter*, but his career was soon interrupted by World War II.[45]

Like millions of young northerners of his generation, Dick Tukey had his first direct contact with the South during military service. Soon after joining the army in 1941 Tukey became a public relations man, a job he performed both in the field and in Washington, D.C. After two years in the service he was transferred to Fort Benning in Columbus, Georgia, where he served as a public relations officer until his honorable discharge in 1946. Tukey decided to stay in the area and accepted a job as the director of the chamber of commerce in Columbus. Two years later he moved back to New York to take a job as an assistant to the president of the Cigar Institute of America, a public relations job that required him to split his time between Los Angeles and New York. The position taught him valuable skills in dealing with influential businessmen and also expanded his economic horizons. Continuing his pattern of fast and numerous early career moves, Tukey left the Cigar Institute a year later to become a vice president of operations for the Ettinger Company, a New York public relations firm, a job he held until his move to Spartanburg in the late summer of 1951.[46]

Readers of the *Spartanburg Herald* learned about the selection of Richard Ellery Tukey to be CEO of the new Spartanburg Chamber of Commerce on June 9, 1951. The story, which ran on page two, introduced a young and eager man who tried to sell himself to the community with self-deprecating humor and a penchant for clichés, describing his main challenges as getting his feet wet while trying to get dry behind the ears.[47] The nomination capped a two-month search for the new chamber's director; its previous CEO, Opie L. Shelton, had announced in late March that he had decided to move to Baton Rouge to head the chamber of commerce there.[48] The lure and promise of the New South and Spartanburg were apparently strong in Tukey's mind: He took a sizable pay cut to take the job in Spartanburg.[49]

On the surface the thirty-three-year-old New Yorker was a curious choice. Tukey was neither a southerner nor a thoroughly seasoned industrial recruiter. He had won the support of the chamber's board of directors despite his noticeable New York accent, young age, and relative unfamiliarity with the South Carolina Piedmont. His previous exposure to the Palmetto State was limited to one wartime incident. He had first landed in the South Carolina Piedmont by parachute. While stationed in Fort Benning, the young public relations officer had to bail out of an airplane that was faltering over the northern part of South Carolina. Tukey and his parachute ended up on a field somewhere near Walhalla, in the northwest corner of the state.[50]

Unlike Milliken, whose pedigree and sizable personal wealth would make him an immediate presence in Spartanburg, Tukey spent years working to assimilate himself, gathering influence and support for his economic agenda. His early career was relatively undistinguished, filled with efforts to get to know the community and desire to work within the community's traditional frame of industrial recruitment, with heavy emphasis on controlled growth and recruiting northern textile corporations. His recruiting strategy and plan for securing Spartanburg's economic future through industrial diversification would take more than a decade to evolve, requiring a sense of crisis and decline before it was embraced by the community.

Disappearing mill villages, changing dynamics of race, generational changes in the leadership, and growing irreverence for the complex set of attitudes and customs that had defined the southern culture were not the only changes affecting the South Carolina Piedmont. By the mid-1950s very real economic threats began to emerge alongside more ethereal cultural concerns. The postwar textile boom evidenced the first signs of slowdown in early 1953. A short recession had hit the textile business during the first half of the year, but the industry had largely recovered within months. The brief drop had affected Spartanburg's small, nonintegrated textile mills the hardest, while larger textile concerns continued to perform at a high and profitable level.[51]

Less than a year later the textile industry saw another decline, but this time it was a full-blown recession. Excessive production and declining military purchases had bloated inventories, dragging prices down across the board, squeezing profit margins, and hurting especially the more antiquated factories. Unlike a normal, temporary slowdown associated with full inventories, this state of overproduction seemed to be structural. J. P. Stevens Jr., chair of the J. P. Stevens textile giant, suggested: "The textile industry can produce more goods than it can sell."[52] The crisis provided clear evidence that a new round of consolidation, managerial modernization, and, especially, continued automation were crucial to the survival of the local textile economy.

Another new threat, foreign competition, aggravated the crisis. In July 1955 the Japanese began to export their cotton textiles to the United States. The move, blessed by President Dwight D. Eisenhower, was an economic carrot to solidify Japan's commitment to the Western bloc in the cold war.[53] The Japanese, who had rebuilt their textile industries with the dual blessing of the latest technology and cheap labor, jumped at the opportunity to sell their textiles in the United States. While the White House viewed the Japanese imports as politically necessary and economically acceptable, their arrival triggered loud and outraged demonstrations from the textile states and regions, most notably South Carolina.

The relatively modest quantities of Japanese imports sent South Carolina into a near hysteria. South Carolinians were stunned to discover that somebody could actually produce textiles less expensively than they could. Amazement soon turned to anger and outrage. Loud cries of "unfair competition" and criticism of foreign "slave labor" echoed around the state, making the imports into the hottest political and economic issue of the day. Politicians jumped to condemn what was happening and tried to stop it. By early 1956 the South Carolina legislature had pushed through, without a debate, the Hart-Arthur Act, which required all establishments selling Japanese fabrics to hang up a sign, in large and visible letters, stating: "Foreign Textiles Sold Here."[54]

During the same session the legislature's Fiscal Survey Commission delivered its report on the state's economy to the state House of Representatives. After celebrating the impressive economic advances and demonstrating how the previous twenty-five years had formed what may have been the most prosperous quarter century in state history, the committee nevertheless concluded with a gloomy assessment: "[U]ntil there is some effective handling of the textile import situation, the future of the textile industry will remain under a cloud of uncertainty as will the future economy of South Carolina."[55] Any real or perceived threat to textiles was enough to trigger hyperbolic reactions among South Carolina politicians and their constituents.

In Spartanburg the textile crisis united the community behind the protectionist cause. The sense of shared interests, combined with the good employment situation and constantly improving wages, had helped to maintain relatively peaceful industrial relations in the community since World War II. By turning down their union suitors during the Operation Dixie years, Spartanburg's industrial workers had, in essence, decided to cast their lot with their employers, guided by calculations that the bosses could offer workers more security and prosperity than an absentee union could. Or, at least, they had determined that the potential benefits of union were not worth the hassle or the associated risks. The shrewd strategy of many bosses, to increase wages and benefits of nonunionized factories to match those of unionized companies, combined with varying degrees of coercion and intimidation, had helped to keep the CIO at bay, despite the organization's sizable investments of money and effort in the South Carolina Piedmont in the postwar years. Now, the comity of bosses and workers, created during the sunny days of South Carolina's textile machine, was to be tested by an external threat.

Their opponent was a two-headed monster, an unholy alliance of the U.S. government and Japan, the enemy scores of Spartans had died fighting just a decade earlier. Spartans, and South Carolinians in general, became persuaded that by some twisted logic of a new global economic order, Washington's loyalties were turning upside down. Instead of helping its own citizens to survive in the world of reawakening global competition, the federal government was removing its protection from Spartans and giving it instead to a recent military enemy.[56]

The reactions to the foreign import crisis in the South and South Carolina were understandable, and the crisis itself had been relatively easy to predict. Soon after the war the Marshall Plan had included loans to Europeans to buy inexpensive American cotton at heavily subsidized export prices. Additionally, an emergency assistance program for textile mills and apparel factories in occupied Japan and Germany provided yet another major market for heavily subsidized American cotton. From England to Japan foreigners bought southern cotton to provide raw material for restarting their textile industries.[57] It appeared to South Carolinians that their own government had revived their competition—and then invited the Japanese into the U.S. market to sell textiles at prices that the home team couldn't match.

For thousands of working men and women of Spartanburg, Washington's indifference to their problems and the Eisenhower administration's support of the recent enemy were shocking. Spartans felt that they deserved their prosperity, even that the government *owed* them support and protection for their newly acquired wealth. The people of Spartanburg had struggled for decades with declining agricultural markets, the economic destitution of the Great Depression, and the hardships of the war. They could not accept or understand the federal government's decision to sacrifice the prosperity and security of Spartanburg and South Carolina.

Spartanburg found itself the victim of Eisenhower's global economic policies. The move to liberate trade was consistent with both the economic and
national defense policies of the Eisenhower administration. The Eisenhower
White House had systematically promoted economic interaction within the
capitalist-democratic bloc, seeking to "obtain, in a manner that is consistent
with our national security and is profitable and equitable for all, the highest
possible level of trade."[58] The principle of promoting economic growth in
the underdeveloped regions of the newly free world ranked high among the
administration's foreign policy objectives.[59] The administration was committed to opening the U.S. economy and devising methods for reducing
tariffs while also working to make Americans more receptive to imports.[60]
After the Soviets had managed to win the sympathy of many intellectuals
and the majority of the European peace movement, free commerce and
increasing prosperity around the Western bloc became an even higher pri-
ority in the U.S. strategy of gathering and maintaining support for its cold
war policies.[61]

The official White House position not only promoted the rapid liber-
alization of foreign trade but encouraged imports to the United States and
movement of U.S. corporations and dollars abroad. A 1955 Department of
Commerce study sought to devise ways to encourage and accelerate private
U.S. investments throughout the Western world.[62] The administration thought
it important to continue fostering European and Japanese development and
recovery but preferred to use private capital and direct investments, supported
by the resources of the Departments of State and Commerce.[63] Whenever
private businesses had the requisite skills and resources, Eisenhower favored
letting them handle European reconstruction. The administration actively
encouraged both U.S. companies and foreign governments to internationalize
their economic outlook.[64]

The attitude and efforts of the federal government were in line with the
economic and political wisdom of the day, but South Carolinians were not
prepared for the blow to their main industry. The South had been warned
about the changing nature of global markets and federal priorities. In 1951
a study by Calvin B. Hoover and B. U. Ratchford of the South's role in the
world economy, *Economic Resources and Policies of the South*, emphasized the
importance of open U.S. markets for global recovery. Foreigners needed U.S.
dollars to buy U.S. products so that they could avoid the recession and ensuing political instability that had occurred after World War I. However, Hoover
and Ratchford predicted a nationwide reaction against inexpensive foreign
imports, including protests in the textile regions of the South: "It is quite likely

that this sentiment may develop in the South in case the competitive situation between our textile manufacturers and those of countries exporting to our domestic market should become difficult."[65] Even in Spartanburg, the local newspapers had published sporadic warnings about the rising textile empire of the Far East, attempting, half-heartedly and rather unconvincingly, to prepare their town for what was coming.[66]

The fears surrounding textile imports reflected an important transition in the traditional internationalism of the South and Spartanburg. The rest of the nation had grown accustomed to viewing the South as the most internationalist, avowedly pro-free-trade region in the United States. From promoting U.S. involvement in foreign wars to defending free markets for the Sunbelt's agricultural products, southerners had systematically defended active, multilateral U.S. involvement in world affairs. However, the classic assumption of southerners as ideologically committed proponents of internationalism came increasingly under attack during the 1950s.[67] Industrialization had somewhat muted the old southern preference for low tariffs, especially in the textile regions, but the true test of southern free-trade principles had not yet occurred.[68]

The Eisenhower administration refused to sacrifice its principles and cold war strategies to intervene on behalf of the South Carolina textile industry. The stakes were too high, the State Department concluded, and granting special protection to textiles was certain to exacerbate the demands for protection from other industries.[69] In the end, it was the Japanese who gave in. Fearing potential damage to trade relations with the United States, Japan agreed to impose voluntary quotas to restrict its textile exports to America. The immediate threat of the "one dollar blouse" had passed, but the specter of a much more competitive future had entered Spartanburg's consciousness. The White House had been blunt in its defense of open markets. Spartans understood that they had achieved only a partial victory, a defensive delay in the fight for survival in the global economic transformation.[70]

The psychological fallout of the import crisis proved to be much more important for Spartanburg than the direct economic impact of the relatively small amount of Japanese imports. In 1954 the total amount of Japanese imports, 17 million square yards, amounted to less than one half of one percent of all U.S. production. One year later the total value of all Japanese textile imports was $30.4 million, dropping to $18.1 million in 1956, the first year of voluntary Japanese quotas. There was not exactly a balance of trade. In 1956 alone the Japanese bought $217.3 million worth of raw cotton from the United States.[71]

In light of trade balances and the overall character of U.S. trade with Japan, textile protectionism was very difficult to defend.[72]

The recession and import crisis marked the end of the long stretch of happy days for South Carolina's and Spartanburg's textile machine. Between 1939 and 1957 the annual output value of the state's textile industries had increased from $263 million to $1.85 billion.[73] Textiles had benefited from the war and a substantial decline in foreign competition from war-torn European and East Asian countries. By the mid-1950s this unnatural advantage had passed. The growth of output value continued but was substantially slower, as Spartanburg found itself unable to sustain the exceptional growth rates of the previous two decades.[74] The new booms would periodically occur, but the aura of invincibility was gone. For experts and average Spartans alike, the signs of the slowed growth were obvious by the mid-1950s.

The Japanese textile crisis had three lingering major ramifications for Spartanburg. The crisis marked the end of the postwar optimism and unforeseen economic boom. The town's economy continued to grow but not with the astonishing speed and corresponding euphoria that had characterized the first postwar decade. Additionally, the crisis gave new life and credibility to the calls for industrial diversification and modernization of the remaining textile industries. As the community was finally forced to face the vulnerability of its industrial monoculture, its earlier lackluster reaction to periodic calls for diversification gave way to more intense concerns and commitment to economic reform.

Finally, the federal government's apparent coziness with Japanese textile industries eroded much of the local trust and affection for Washington. The budding warm relationship between Spartanburg's working class and the federal government, conceived and nurtured during the New Deal years, passed rapidly. After the textile crisis Spartanburg's workers ceased to look at the federal government as an ally in their quest for a better tomorrow. While Washington had fostered what they regarded as unfair competition, the working classes of Spartanburg saw their bosses speaking against that unfair competition in no uncertain terms.[75]

The crisis strengthened the budding coalition of Spartanburg's textile workers and their bosses. From the perspective of many mill hands, textile bosses, even with all their imperfections, were at least occasionally beginning to look like more useful allies in pursuing wealth and security than those unpredictable, ideologically driven folks up in Washington. Spartanburg's workers and bosses would continue to fight, push, and challenge each other, but in the foreign import crisis the bosses had turned out to be solid and respectable allies. As far as workers were concerned, the vision of Spartanburg's economic future as set by local bosses made more sense than the federal government's—at least here, at least now.

The phenomenal growth accompanying optimism was coming to an end. Textiles no longer carried an air of invincibility in the eyes of Spartanburg's men and women. The calls for industrial diversification, a persistent Greek chorus in Spartanburg since World War II, intensified again after 1955, especially among workers and urban middle class, who had vested interests in the further development of the community.[76] More segments of the community were ready to search for new economic survival strategies and adapt more willingly to any changes they might have to make.

Technological improvements had decreased the industry's dependence on human labor, and Japanese competition and the rising cost of domestic labor had forced the mill owners to improve their factories. Changes in the nature of the industry were beyond Spartanburg's control. If local textile companies wanted to survive, they had to adjust by automation, Tukey and the textile industry representatives told residents. "Whenever textile industry has become stagnant, it has died," said Frederick B. Dent, the president of Mayfair Mills and, until recently, a Yankee. "Look at New England."[77] New England had shipped its jobs and optimism to Spartanburg; now the dying northeastern textile industry stood as a clear warning for everybody in the community: Don't resist change—accept it and adapt to it or die.

Moving to the South had not solved the problems of the U.S. textile industry. The number of U.S. textile mill workers declined from the 1947 high of 1.28 million to fewer than 1 million seven years later and never reached the million mark again.[78] Financial investment in the new mills continued to decline during the 1950s as well, as new factories required less personnel and were more efficient and less expensive to build and run. A fever for modernization ran through Spartanburg's textile business. The old admiration for huge factories, large labor forces, and a plethora of spindles was gradually being replaced by smart and more economic production. The old, two- or three-story factories began to disappear from the town's landscape, replaced by sleek one-story industrial halls with quiet and well-manicured campuses. Even the old factories began to house new, more effective, and sophisticated machinery.[79]

Concerns about the community's future made Spartans look for new solutions. As the community grew more serious about pursuing diversification, Dick Tukey's stock began slowly to rise. The young chamber of commerce

CEO and his message of industrial diversification began to resonate with the community's economic leaders. Earlier attempts to promote diversification, such as Spartanburg's postwar "11-point roadmap for the future," had tended to lose luster with every record year for textiles. This time, Tukey and his cohorts emphasized, Spartanburg could ill afford to wait for a new rising tide in the textile industry.[80] The lip service to diversification, combined with a half-hearted hunt for small metal shops or retail ventures, was not enough. A large-scale investment in attracting major new manufacturers had become a necessity.

The first major coup for diversification proponents in Spartanburg was Kohler. The Wisconsin-based maker of bathroom porcelains, sinks, and other household plumbing hardware was seeking to expand its operations through-out the 1950s and find a location that was closer to the growing southern markets. After a series of visits and the help of long and intense lobbying from the Spartanburg textile boss Walter Montgomery; Governor George Bell Timmerman; Charles Daniel, who was both a Greenville construc-tion magnate and a U.S. senator; the South Carolina State Resources and Development Board; and former governor James F. Byrnes, Kohler decided in 1955 to build a $5 million factory on a 260-acre lot near Camp Croft in eastern Spartanburg.[81]

From the outset Spartanburg's recruitment strategy had concentrated on nonunionized corporations. Diversification posed new challenges, as incom-ing nontextile interests operated in a different industrial culture and under the influence of new and alien unions. Local industrial leaders and recruiters, committed to maintaining the community's neopaternalistic, nonunionized industrial character, emphasized carefully controlled growth and proac-tive union-busting measures. Kohler was a good match with Spartanburg. Kohler's owner and boss, Herbert V. Kohler, was a dedicated enemy of trade unions and eager to speak publicly against the "violence and coercion" that unions brought to the workplace. He railed against the closed-shop practice with vigor and candor rare for an executive of a northern, largely unionized, corporation.[82] If, despite Herbert Kohler's rhetoric, any in Spartanburg's old textile guard entertained suspicions about a manufacturing company from "pink" Wisconsin, they were eradicated by the long closed-shop dispute by the United Auto Workers (UAW) over at Kohler's Wisconsin plant. By the time Kohler had publicized its plans to come to Spartanburg, the strike had contin-ued for more than a year.[83]

Some other nontextile establishments followed Kohler. The Landrum Manufacturing Company and the Spartan Metal Products Company started operations in 1956, followed by a steady trickle of small and midsize metal shops, food-processing companies, and other diversified factories.[84] Despite these arrivals, the relative importance of textiles as an employer barely changed, with the percentage of Spartanburg's industrial workers involved in textiles and apparel holding steady at about 75.[85] But the newcomers gave reason for optimism and even some excitement. Nonetheless, the community celebrated diversification cautiously, with some in leading positions preferring to see existing plants and industries expand rather than court entirely new businesses.[86]

As the chamber of commerce went after new types of businesses, local business interests grew increasingly worried about losing their control of the community's labor pool. New corporations often brought with them a threat of unionization, even if the company bosses had impressive antiunion credentials. When Kohler had announced its decision to start a factory in Spartanburg, a union representative at the company's Wisconsin factory had allegedly promised that "the union will be on hand to greet Kohler" when the company opened the Spartanburg plant.[87] Preventing unionization required a more aggressive and proactive approach.

Spartanburg leaders felt the need to build new organizations for fostering and directing the growth. Existing institutions might have been experienced in and capable of industrial recruitment, but screening for recruits, monitoring and managing Spartanburg's labor activities, maintaining functional relationships between Spartanburg and Spartanburg County, and managing the town's physical growth and increasing sophistication and modernization required new commitment and organizational improvements. Spartanburg's citizens responded by organizing themselves into clubs and organizations, representing various levels of social hierarchy and uniting different strata of the community into horizontally organized clusters of social ideals and economic interests. The economic leadership of Spartanburg organized itself more effectively in order to prevent the workers from following their example.

The organizations ranged from the Spartanburg Community Development Program, a voluntary grouping of neighborhood beautification clubs that began in 1954, to the Spartanburg Development Association and the Spartanburg County Development Association, organizations formed to present positive images of the community. Also in 1954 the Spartanburg County Planning and Development Commission started operating with a $150,000 grant from the state; the commission was charged with helping to direct and attract growth to Spartanburg County. Run by leaders representing a wide array of Spartanburg County businesses and civic organizations, the commission was authorized to buy, lease, and rent land and utilities around the county to promote its vision of growth and agricultural, industrial, and commercial development.[88]

Even long-time municipal organizations saw their activities revitalized, as the City Planning Commission and other related offices enjoyed new attention and multimillion dollar funding for infrastructure improvements and urban beautification projects, designed to convert Spartanburg from an old mill town into a modern community.[89] Industrial progress, urban beautification, good government, and civic pride were understood to represent different branches of the same tree.

The most powerful of the new organizations was the Spartanburg Development Association. Established in 1959 by textile bosses and well-known antiunion crusaders, the official credo of the Spartanburg Development Association was to "encourage good management practices and promote industrial relations conducive for economic growth," but almost everybody familiar with the organization understood its true nature. The SDA was from its birth an awe-inspiring antiunion machine. It combined soft coercion with rigorous screening of potential industrial recruits, protecting the loyal workers of Spartanburg from aggressive, greedy, and disruptive unions.[90]

The inner workings of the SDA remained a source of mystery and speculation, a font of endless rumors about its decisions and industrial screening operations. A more visible and openly discussed aspect of the SDA's operations was its human resources training programs, which sought to spread modern, conciliatory labor management practices among Spartanburg's employers.[91] The organization sought to steal the unions' thunder by protecting the sense of comity, an approach that had guided the elite's vision of Spartanburg's postwar industrial development and labor-management relations.

Despite increased efforts at and steadily growing demands for diversification, the leaders of Spartanburg were not completely sold on the idea. Control and careful planning became the watchwords of Spartanburg's approach to industrial growth and diversification. Toward the end of the 1950s, growth slowed substantially. Indeed, the gatekeepers had preferred slow growth to fast but uncontrolled growth. Their recruitment efforts were highly selective. Spartanburg's economic leaders had sought to maintain their town's strong linkages to the textile industry.[92] Unlike Atlanta or even neighboring Greenville, with their developers, construction companies, and more open competition between different industries, Spartanburg did not want to explore radically new fields. Diversification was a good word in speeches but not for real life.

Many of the companies that were coming to Spartanburg, chemical factories and transportation firms, were symbiotic extensions of the county's textile industries. The new chemical factories largely produced raw materials for the community's textile mills, and the machine shops, transportation companies, and other incoming businesses were often directly dependent on the mills for their business. As far as Spartanburg's elite was concerned, ideal companies were nonunionized, willing to be molded according to the local business culture, and respectful of local traditions. If possible, they offered moderate diversification without establishing a noticeable threat to the dominant textile industries.

Although Spartanburg leaders were receptive to the principle of change, they were eager to influence its size and direction. Even if they were willing to adjust their management practices, they were very hesitant to share control. The next decade would prove that Spartanburg's managers could find recruits that were almost ideal, but they would come from a surprising source. Foreign corporations proved to be almost exactly what the leadership desired.

The economic progress of the South, South Carolina, and Spartanburg was potentially revolutionary, but the town's leadership worked to contain and direct its force. Revolutions by definition include rapid changes and transformations of power, the emergence of new leaders and classes as stewards of society. Spartanburg welcomed a new group of men but they complemented the old elite. Workers witnessed substantial improvements in their standard of living, but growing wages did not automatically translate into a greater say in the affairs of their community. But their improved wages and the profit margins in the textile industry increased workers' consumption power, which contributed to the rapid expansion of the town's professional middle class. As a result the "revolution" in Spartanburg during the 1950s was a thoroughly conservative one, led by the old forces and individuals closely attuned to their old values.

The periodic desires of local workers to unionize, their growing self-confidence, and their increased willingness to assert their independence did not disappear or even weaken, as they continued to pursue their self-interests with dogged determination. However, their new status as property owners made workers more connected—and tied—to the community, contributing to their growing interest in the continued growth and development of the town. Additionally, the shared concern about foreign imports at least temporarily united workers and local textile bosses.

As the textile industry began to lose its air of invincibility during the mid-1950s, Spartanburg's workers and bosses began to look at each other as potential allies in the fight against imports. The battle was fundamentally local, concerning local jobs and economic success. The fight against imports further united people of diverse social and economic strata. As the economic challenges continued, picking up more speed in the 1960s, Spartanburg's sense of community would be tested.

CHAPTER THREE

The Roots of International Recruiting

The first foreign corporations came to Spartanburg relatively quietly in the late 1950s and early 1960s, and by the late 1960s their presence had turned into a major force shaping local culture and economy. The first European companies in Spartanburg were highly specialized textile machinery makers that arrived to serve the region's dominant industry and corporations. As relatively small operations working in a business-to-business sector, their effect on Spartanburg's economy remained largely hidden from casual observers. Their arrival, however, created the foundation for the town's future efforts to recruit foreign corporations.

As the number of foreign companies started to grow, Spartanburg's boosters began to develop more systematic methods and strategies for going after foreign investors. Increasingly confident in dealing with foreign corporations, Tukey, CEO of the Greater Spartanburg Chamber of Commerce, tuned his international recruiting operations into an impressively smooth machine. Once almost an afterthought, the recruiting effort became a sizable, carefully managed strategic program. Tukey and his allies realized that globalization and the increasingly free flow of companies and capital across national borders could work to Spartanburg's benefit. International recruitment became one of the most important aspects of the operations of the Spartanburg Chamber of Commerce.

With European economic recovery from World War II nearing completion by the late 1950s and early 1960s, the unnatural postwar boom in the United States started to erode. The battle for markets grew tighter on both sides of the Atlantic. U.S. military commitments abroad, changing currents in international trade and tourism, and international investment flows all contributed to a growing problem of gold and dollars flowing out of the country. The economic miracle and unwavering sense of growing prosperity of the 1950s was slowly giving way to a creeping malaise.

In a nation and region struggling with intensifying foreign competition and growing balance-of-payment problems, Spartanburg's plan promised to turn globalization to the town's advantage. Spartanburg became a pioneer in systematically going after foreign investments. The Spartanburg example grew to influence the economic policies of the state, which added international recruitment to its agenda. Spartanburg's plan gradually became the plan not only of South Carolina but the entire South.

The arrival of foreign corporations in Spartanburg is inextricably linked to Roger Milliken, who opened the gate for the transformation of the community, albeit largely unintentionally. By the late 1950s Milliken's factories had begun to rely increasingly on Swiss and German textile machinery. New European machines had features that were not available in the United States—at least not at such a good price and fine quality. Europeans had, for example, started the cost-effective production of the then-fashionable double-knit years before their U.S. competitors. The reliability and refinement of European machinery further increased their competitive edge.[1] Like most producers of the day whose business strategy focused on quality, Milliken grew increasingly reliant on his European suppliers.

Textile machinery is sensitive. Spindles, looms, boppers, and other intricate pieces of the mill apparatus are full of small parts, flying staccato over miles of cloth every day. Their complexity and heavy use causes machines to wear and break easily, making them dependent on a reliable supply of spare parts and regular maintenance. For a large producer with multiple factories, physical proximity to skilled maintenance and spare parts can become a crucial factor in ensuring competitiveness. To prevent expensive interruptions in his company's production, Milliken suggested that two of his largest machinery suppliers, Rieter Corporation and Sulzer Ruti, both of Winterthur, Switzerland, open sales and service operations in Spartanburg.[2] Milliken was a large customer, and his suggestion received careful consideration in the boardrooms of both corporations.

Rieter already had a U.S. branch office in New Jersey, but the location had outlived its usefulness with the demise of northeastern textile industries. After Milliken made his request, Rieter contemplated bringing its operations closer to its customer base, to the new centers of the textile industry. After conducting a four-month study of "every hamlet from Atlanta to Greensboro," Rieter's U.S. representative met with Richard Tukey. Tukey delivered his sales pitch, and Spartanburg became the location that Rieter's representatives recommended to the home office.[3] Rieter moved its U.S. operations to the town in 1962, shortly before Sulzer, which had never had a U.S. office.[4] In 1965 another textile machinery manufacturer, Karl Menzel Maschinenfabrik GmbH & Co. of Bielefeld, West Germany, decided to improve its competitive situation by opening a plant in Spartanburg and became the first European textile machinery company to start manufacturing in Spartanburg County.[5]

After Sulzer Ruti and Rieter set up shop, the arrival of foreign corporations turned into a steady, consistent movement.[6] Their arrival pushed local economic boosters to start considering a comprehensive and conscious strategy of recruiting foreign corporations, but the idea took years to evolve into a full-fledged campaign. Although the presence of Sulzer, Rieter, and Karl Menzel reflected the evolving nature of the textile business and new trends in international investment flows, their direct economic impact in Spartanburg was relatively small as they employed only a few people.

The more far-reaching, systematic decision to woo foreign corporations developed as a combination of coincidence, innovation, and mounting economic necessity. The growing trickle of foreign corporations into Spartanburg convinced Tukey and other key members of Spartanburg's chamber of commerce of the enormous economic potential of foreign direct investment. Automation, sluggish growth in the labor markets, and the community's longtime contacts nudged Spartanburg to look at international investment markets as an untapped and promising source for economic growth.

From time to time after World War II some Americans had broached notions of recruiting industry internationally, but it remained a theoretical possibility; no one floated a real plan for doing so. In the 1950s North Carolina governor Luther Hodges, an inveterate traveler who was determined to modernize his state's economy, had entertained some vague notions of recruiting foreign corporations.[7] It complemented his vision of transforming North Carolina into a technologically driven postindustrial state, as exemplified by his ambitious plan to turn the cow pastures, farmland, and small groves between Raleigh and Durham into a modern high-tech research park.[8] Hodges saw North Carolina's future as increasingly intertwined with the global markets and multinational corporations, even if his vision remained somewhat blurred and his actual efforts and achievements in foreign recruitment limited.

Soon after Hodges made pioneering international recruiting efforts, his young counterpart in South Carolina, Ernest F. "Fritz" Hollings, began to explore international trade—and even recruitment—as potential means of improving the economy of his state. Ever since the Japanese textile import crisis of the mid-1950s, increased competition and technological advances had gradually pushed South Carolina officials and businessmen to prepare their state for changes in its economy. With the recent technological advances and the growing foreign competition in textiles, many South Carolina business leaders realized the need to search for alternative routes to prosperity. By 1960 the thirty-eight-year-old governor was determined to deliver, demonstrating an unwavering commitment to pump up the state's recruitment efforts. Hollings was also committed to seeking investors outside the conventional sources.

Elected in 1958 as a staunch young segregationist and a defender of states' rights and the southern way of life, Hollings as governor (1959–63) was nevertheless more concerned about the state's economic progress and prosperity than defending it from agents of the civil rights movement or maintaining the integrity of the color line.[9] When southern traditions conflicted with the state's economic interests, Hollings consistently sided with the pocketbook. If the economic situation required him to do so, he was willing to challenge local social and fiscal traditions. Additionally, Hollings had the initiative and imagination to look in new places for solutions to the state's economic problems.[10]

Like many of his predecessors, Hollings emphasized the importance of recruiting industry and heaped praise upon communities and business people who had excelled in the field. However, Hollings radically expanded the state's recruiting activities, added new targets, and updated his state's tools. Initially, his targets were largely in the Northeast, the traditional hunting ground for industry-hungry southern governors, but by 1960 Hollings had expanded South Carolina's recruiting ground to cover the entire Western Hemisphere. In an address to South Carolina's General Assembly in the winter of 1961, Hollings commended a group of South Carolina business leaders who had traveled twelve thousand miles to visit four South American countries in pursuit of new business opportunities. Even more important, Hollings himself had flown across the Atlantic to initiate the state's recruiting efforts in Europe.[11]

Hollings's exploratory trip was short in direct achievements but rich in symbolic significance. He worked to make people on both sides of the Atlantic aware that his state was eager to cooperate with industry. In his remarks to European audiences Hollings worked to familiarize Europeans with the rapid economic progress of his state and the South in general, comparing its poor and war-torn past and its recent affluence to the war and *wirtschaftwunder* (economic miracle) shaping Western Europe since World War II. He waxed poetic about the enormous growth and potential of the South, regaling his listeners with statistics about the size and scope of the Sunbelt boom, the most remarkable demographic and economic shift affecting North American markets. South Carolina was firmly in the middle of the boom, Hollings said. He repeated the familiar mantra of growing markets, dedicated labor, and a good transportation infrastructure that had helped to convince scores of northern companies to relocate in his state, stressing the location of Charleston harbor in the heart of the state's transportation system and its role in international trade for the entire region.[12]

Hollings's pathbreaking recruitment efforts demonstrated his new approach to business in South Carolina. Influenced by Strom Thurmond, Hollings emerged as a more refined version of the prototypical southern business-progressive populist after World War II. The burden of economic and social traditions rested lightly on his shoulders. Rather than protecting and celebrating his state's traditional economy, with romantic defenses of agrarian traditions and the industrial republicanism of the Piedmont's textile crescent, Hollings sought change and new dynamism, simultaneously directing much of his economic message not only to the state's boosters or business people but also to its workers. Although his postwar predecessors, most notably Thurmond himself, had been actively interested in modernizing the state's economy, Hollings's efforts were more powerful and visible. He demonstrated more concern about increasing the number of jobs and opportunities for workers than protecting the interests and power of the state's industrialists. Hollings mostly began to view issues of race as annoyances that took time from his true calling, namely, recruiting industry and modernizing the economy.[13]

During Hollings's tenure the South Carolina State Development Board went through a radical rejuvenation. The board grew from five to fifteen members, and its budgets more than doubled from their mid-1950s levels.[14] In education Hollings radically improved South Carolina's technical training program, expanding it into an impressive statewide network of technical schools that provided carefully tailored industrial education to serve the needs of South Carolina–bound industries.[15] These efforts laid the framework for a more aggressive pursuit of new industries, demonstrating to both potential recruits and South Carolina communities alike the state's new commitment to industrial growth and modernization. Inexpensive labor had long been one of the state's most important assets. Now, Hollings wanted to use education to increase the value of the state's human capital, making it more prepared and responsive to the needs of modern industries.

Hollings's governorship marked an important phase in the growing professionalism of South Carolina's efforts to recruit industry. By the 1950s the state's early recruiting efforts had evolved into systematic and suave sales campaigns. The professionalization of the state's bureaucracy, a mantra in Columbia since Thurmond's stint as governor (1947–51), had been thorough and rapid, with improvements in industrial recruiting and economic development leading the way. When James F. Byrnes, a forty-year public servant and very much a product of the old Carolina and its administrative culture, was governor in 1951–55, he was surprised to find younger state officials asking, even demanding, his participation in the state's efforts to recruit industry.[16]

The South Carolina Research, Planning, and Development Board, later shortened to the State Development Board, saw its budgets grow, as the state's top elected officials recognized the importance of its efforts. Between 1948 and 1959 the annual budget of the office grew almost 500 percent, from $109,696 to $537,258. The improved funding allowed the agency hire more personnel and to stabilize and professionalize its staff. [17] Now the State Development Board's recruitment missions were armed with political support, increasingly sophisticated economic data, and sizable expense accounts.

The new salesmen of the South succeeded so well that their presence and practices began to attract the interest of the nation's scholars and the ire of New England politicians. For northern workers and politicians alike, southern recruiters came across as little more than well-organized industrial privateers, systematically looting the North of its industries with their suave sales pitches and state-supported, quasi-corporatist promises. The emerging debate was emotional on all fronts, with politicians pulling businesses in both directions, and academics siding with their regions, working to lend an aura of scholarly credibility to their highly partisan research.[18]

As Hollings's term was reaching its end, South Carolina's recruiting machine was a smooth, well-oiled operation. Generous funding and cooperation between different communities, state agencies, universities, and civic organizations created synergies and resources unforeseen in the state and rare in the entire nation. The University of South Carolina had contributed by establishing the Bureau of Business and Economic Research in January 1954. The bureau provided the state's economic apparatus with increasingly sophisticated and persuasive data to support its economic aspirations.[19] Communities worked with the state bureaucracy, receiving effective support, such as gubernatorial lobbying and carefully constructed market analyses for their recruitment efforts.[20]

The work bore fruit. Despite periodic recessions in textiles and increasing foreign competition, South Carolina throughout the 1950s and early 1960s continued to steam ahead as one of the fastest-growing economies in the nation. Its recruiting successes were complemented by native expansion in services and educated professions. The rapid economic growth of the Palmetto State had begun to gather the attention of national business magazines, which noticed the growth and construction mushrooming around the state. National media and business gurus began to acknowledge the potential of the South and South Carolina, paying particular attention to the Piedmont, South Carolina's historical industrial center, which was now further strengthened by the construction of two interstate highways through the region.[21]

Spartanburg complied with Hollings's message of growth and industrial recruiting but only partially. It participated in and celebrated industrial expansion and recruiting successes with hyperbolic language. Local newspapers continued to wrap Spartanburg's economic advances and advantages in a message of economic manifest destiny, but in reality the community did not put its full effort into recruiting until the latter half of the 1960s—Tukey's efforts and occasional successes aside.[22] While the more diversified, construction-company-driven Greenville had charged ahead in population growth and business activity, Spartanburg continued to cling to textiles. Despite numerous warnings and occasional scares associated with automation and foreign competition, the town had continued to serve King Cloth with minimal preparation for succession, and few voices were raised to urge such preparation.

The town had acquired the tools and infrastructure necessary for industrial modernization and diversification. Spartanburg's Technical Education Center, a local branch of the statewide network of technical schools that Hollings had initiated, opened its doors in 1963. The school began to feed Spartanburg's expanding factories and its new ones by training their current and future employees in welding, electronic design, machine shop, and other arts required by local industries.[23] Soon after its birth Spartanburg TEC expanded its size and educational offerings. The school grew and evolved rapidly, offering night classes for students already in the workforce, training managers, and creating courses in response to the evolving needs of new local businesses.[24]

Spartanburg boomed and suffered with textiles, and the periodic expansion and growth was usually just enough progress for the town's tight-knit textile elite and its associates. Textile mill expansions and modernizations were the most numerous and visible economic good news for the town.[25] "During recent years the area has had no spectacular boom but has enjoyed a steady substantial growth, which is better," opined James F. Byrnes, a native son, in an essay for the *Spartanburg Herald* in 1960. He may have been alluding to his old hometown's neighbor and traditional rival, Greenville, adding, "Much of the development has come from the expansion of existing industry, which is most desirable because in those industries management and employees are already a part of the life in the area."[26] Byrnes's essay reflected the mind-set of affluent Spartans, who were set in their ways and feeling secure with the textile industry, which had repeatedly managed to crawl back to prosperity after periodic cycles of recessions, depressions, and escalating competition.

In the heavily cyclical textile industry, markets suffered during the early 1960s, then climbing back up and reaching a nearly overheated state by 1966. Spartanburg's textile industry, struggling under foreign competition and declining orders just a few years earlier, saw perhaps its tightest labor market and a flurry of mill construction during the mid-1960s.[27] As the periodic recessions turned into better days and occasional booms, the business pages of Spartanburg's newspapers were filled with stories about expanding mills and rapidly growing wealth and wages.[28] Until the late 1960s, despite repeated warnings and continued worries, the prosperity had always returned. For the chamber and its supporters in local media, this circumstance was familiar, free from undesirable, disturbing alterations in the economic and political character of the town. During the 1960s only one truly large company emerged to compete with textile mills for labor, but most in the community welcomed it wholeheartedly. The recruitment of the Hoechst-Hercules chemical factory and its arrival in Spartanburg had a strong influence on the community. From that point on, Spartanburg's recruiting of international corporations evolved into a highly profitable and sizable economic strategy.

Spartanburg's early experiences in international recruiting of industry had not been part of any larger, systematic economic strategy. Roger Milliken's invitation to Swiss textile machinery manufacturers coincided chronologically with Hollings's ventures in Europe, but the efforts were independent, springing from different mind-sets and motives. Milliken had recruited the Swiss to serve an immediate and concrete need. Hollings, on the other hand, had looked at the larger picture, but his efforts did not target particular companies or even industries. After several years had passed and the arrival of Hoechst-Hercules had awakened Spartanburg to the riches it might gain from a concerted effort, Spartanburg and South Carolina emerged as the leading players in the growing competition for foreign investment.

In 1966 American Hercules and Hoechst, a German chemical giant, formed a joint venture to operate a chemical factory in the United States that would produce raw materials for polyester, a manufactured fiber increasingly used by clothing manufacturers because it was inexpensive and didn't require ironing. The planned factory was a large project for any community, worth hundreds of new jobs and approximately $115 million ($755 million in 2007 dollars) in capital investment. At the time of the announcement the location of the factory had not yet been determined, with the company representatives scouting sites up and down the eastern seaboard. When Dick Tukey heard about Hoechst-Hercules's plans, he and the Spartanburg Chamber of Commerce launched a frantic twenty-six-day campaign to snare the factory for Spartanburg. They harnessed the full energies of the chamber and the cooperation of the entire community.[29]

Preparing to make his case for Spartanburg, Tukey contacted the Germans, who appeared to be leading the site search. Demonstrating a keen understanding of the concerns of foreign executives, Tukey and the chamber focused on convincing the Europeans of the cost-effectiveness of locating the factory in Spartanburg. The Germans heard how land in Spartanburg cost only a fraction of what it would cost in the more densely populated industrial Northeast. Tukey demonstrated how skilled labor, energy, and water were abundant in the South Carolina Piedmont and how effortlessly Hoechst-Hercules products and raw materials could move within U.S. and global markets using the interstate highways and Charleston's expanded and modernized port.[30]

By emphasizing the bottom line, Tukey and his team convinced Hoechst's executives and, later, other recruits, of the fiscal wisdom of basing their U.S. operations in Spartanburg. Tukey's Sunbelt pitch of inexpensive and nonorganized labor, good infrastructure, growing markets, and a favorable corporate tax structure persuaded the Germans. Additionally, South Carolina by the mid- to late 1960s could boast—in regional comparison—of a relatively peaceful racial atmosphere.[31] Tukey presented Spartanburg as the epitome of the New South and South Carolina, a city of possibilities, with infrastructure, community, and mind-set supportive of growth with stability.

Hoechst-Hercules decided to build its factory in the northern part of Spartanburg County, on a spacious lot bordering Interstate 85. The deciding factor turned out to be American Hercules's previous business ties to Spartanburg County and the county's geographic location.[32] According to the calculations of one Hoechst executive, approximately 80 percent of all U.S. textile manufacturing took place within a 250-mile radius of Spartanburg.[33] However, Tukey's sales pitches were also effective and well targeted. Spartanburg's ability to provide workers, land, water, and power for the factory's needs, which was the heart of Tukey's message, distinguished the South Carolina Piedmont and Spartanburg in the calculations of the German executives.

Although Tukey's selling points focused on the bottom line and profitability, he laced his sales calls with information about noneconomic factors. He worked to ease the Germans' concerns about the local quality of life, ranging from the quality of Spartanburg's schools to the availability of dark bread. Tukey convinced local grocers to stock European delicacies, hoping to impress the visiting Germans of the community's commitment to their emotional well-being and Spartanburg's ability to provide the same amenities they would find in bigger and more cosmopolitan U.S. communities.[34] One delegation of Spartans after another crossed the Atlantic, distributing information and taking care of problems that the Germans had not yet even thought about, such as arranging convenient housing for company executives. The Germans had other suitors, of course, but a high-ranking Hoechst executive described Spartanburg's presentation as in "a league of its own."[35]

The recruiting campaign did not end with Hoechst-Hercules's announcement that it was coming to Spartanburg. Tukey's team continued to work to make the newcomers feel welcome, helping the new arrivals to become part of the community and educating them about American styles of living and doing business. Soon after Hoechst-Hercules announced its location plans, Tukey and his wife flew to Frankfurt to thank company representatives for their choice. In addition to attending formal business meetings, the couple, armed with catalogs from J. C. Penney and Sears, organized a crash course in American consumer culture for the wives of Spartanburg-bound Hoechst personnel.[36] The follow-up and other assistance, cleverly organized on the Germans' home turf, helped to publicize Spartanburg in a new territory, introducing the community to other companies and their executives. The visit by the Tukeys put a human face on the community, showing the Germans the southern hospitality they could expect when they got to Spartanburg.

As the mid-1960s textile boom slowly began to fade, Tukey and the chamber of commerce beefed up their recruitment program, this time determinedly and systematically going after foreign industrial investors. Tukey and his team began to concentrate a rapidly growing share of their attention and recruiting resources on foreign corporations, focusing on central European companies, especially textile machinery manufacturers and other textile-support industries. A steady trickle of companies answered the call. Bruckner Machinery Corporation of West Germany arrived in 1965; Mahlo KG of West Germany came to town in 1968, Swiss-German Zima and Austrian J. Zimmer Maschinenbrau in 1969. The flow of companies gained speed and momentum, as other multinational textile companies responded to their competitors' moves and established a more visible presence in the textile center of the South Carolina Piedmont.[37]

Spartanburg quickly perfected its international recruiting efforts. The message was built on the same foundation they had used to secure Yankee investors: inexpensive and docile labor, natural resources, low unionization, and growing markets.[38] Now they were ready to expand the strategy. However, Tukey understood that taking on an entire continent would be a challenge even for a man blessed with his energy and optimism. He let state officials in on what Spartanburg was up to, which had the effect of combining Spartanburg's know-how with the state's resources.

Spartanburg was only one of many South Carolina Piedmont communities that enjoyed the same pocketbook advantages. The differences in the economic infrastructures of Spartanburg, Greenville, Anderson, or Rock Hill were relatively small, save perhaps Spartanburg's position at the intersection of the state's two main interstate highways and railroads. To put Spartanburg at the head of the pack, Tukey's group planned to sell the entire community to international visitors; the home team was aware that some might have limited knowledge of the region and even some suspicions about the quality of life in the South—and that what they did know was often shaped by televised images of a cultural backwoods engulfed in racial turmoil. Dispelling stereotypes and demonstrating the friendliness and stability of the community became crucial aspects of Spartanburg's sales presentations.

The campaign that landed Hoechst became the model for Tukey and the chamber's future international recruiting efforts, focusing on Spartanburg's far-reaching commitment to the economic and emotional well-being of the newcomers, a strategy designed to retain Hoechst and others and to attract other firms to town. Tukey's motto was, "I'll do anything to get them here and help 'em get in the black. Then word of mouth does the rest."[39] In public Tukey liked to emphasize the practical, profit-driven messages, which were effective in countering stereotypes of the South's business culture. But Tukey was not oblivious to the importance of soft factors.

When potential foreign investors came to town, their hosts took them on tours of Spartanburg's hospitals, country clubs, and neighborhoods. If the visitors expressed any concerns about their children's education, Tukey was quick to take them to local schools and give them generous amount of information of the high quality of Spartanburg's public school system. Spartanburg's sales brochures advertised its quality of life, especially its attractive, secluded neighborhoods and spacious houses.[40] Spartans worked hard to show off their community. Key business and political leaders were apprised of imminent visits by European delegations, and hundreds of other residents were involved to some degree in the recruiting effort. Visitors were entertained at the private homes of Tukey and chamber of commerce members, where the Europeans had a chance to get to mingle with Spartanburg's economic leaders and other socially prominent residents.[41]

If there was opposition to the recruiting effort, it was largely invisible. Spartanburg's newspapers were downright zealous in their embrace of the program. Bringing foreign investment to town became the widely approved goal of the local booster elite and something of a personal crusade for Tukey. By 1967 a coherent and extensive strategy was in place.

No matter what their relationship was with boosters and community leaders in other matters, labor unions were not going to stand in the way of intensified recruitment efforts. Witnessing the growing diversification of neighboring communities and states, some South Carolina labor activists were appalled at their state's continuing attachment to strict economic control and its old economic monoculture. "Once again our leaders are giving us the short end of the stick!" South Carolina Labor Council AFL-CIO President Jim Adler declared in a letter to affiliates. "They are discouraging Philip Morris from building in S.C. because their pay scale is too high! A giant Volkswagen plant was to be built here and the same thing happened! That plant is now in Pennsylvania. . . . Our textile industries are discouraging this [new plant location] because it will mess up their playhouse. . . . Let's not stand by and let them change South Carolina to South America!" Adler finished his letter with a passionate plea for a grassroots lobbying campaign for new and diversified industries: "Tell your neighbor. Tell him he has no say in who's invited to locate in his state. Inform that his tax-supported State Development Board caters to vested interests, sacrificing new trades and new leaders!"[42]

Tukey and the chamber continued to refine their community-centered recruitment strategy, paying attention even to the smallest details. Chamber representatives worked with local grocers, convincing them to further expand their selection of foreign wines, sausages, and cheeses to keep the newcomers happy. Local real estate agents received a stern warning from the chamber not to overcharge the incoming home buyers. Tukey worked with local schools to send American schoolbooks to the children of Spartanburg-bound Europeans.[43] From private businesses to civic organizations, municipal bureaus to private citizens, all of Spartanburg was invited—or coerced—to participate in the recruiting effort. As Tukey saw it, Spartanburg was selling itself, and everybody was a potential salesperson.

Tukey's other favorite slogan, "We don't sell South Carolina's magnolias and moonlight. We sell economic justification," became the punch line for local boosters, who repeated it faithfully in interviews and business meetings on two continents.[44] Simultaneously, however, Tukey sold the southern hospitality of Spartanburg, which now proffered itself as a massive country club, a semisecluded community where business and pleasure mingled without outside interference, a place where the needs of its industrial bigwigs were met with a servile smile and friendly nod from the staff and fellow members of the club alike.

With the exception of Hoechst, the incoming corporations were not big enough to pose a serious threat to Spartanburg's textile mills in the competition for labor. And the textile bosses gave even Hoechst a warm welcome. After all, this chemical factory, built to provide polyester for local textile factories, offered Spartanburg partial diversification, and Hoechst had an interest in the continued well-being of the local textile firms. Additionally, Hoechst's executives largely shared Spartanburg's values for labor management and order, which emphasized rapid settlement of any conflicts and blamed bad management for any unionization that occurred.[45]

Spartanburg's early experiences with international recruiting were mostly positive for the entire community. From textile machinery manufacturers to Hoechst's polyester plant, the incoming companies brought jobs, an appropriate dash of diversification, and products and services that helped keep Spartanburg's textile mills running smoothly. Most companies were directly or indirectly involved with textiles. The incoming companies were also culturally flexible, as their transferred personnel proved eager to assimilate and were largely declared to be devoid of the arrogance, real or perceived, that was sometimes associated with Americans whose companies had relocated to Spartanburg from northern states. The presence of German- and French-speaking newcomers became a point of regional pride and excitement.[46]

As Spartanburg's recruiting efforts began to gather national and even international attention, Tukey's prestige grew both home and away. Publicity gave Tukey a bully pulpit, converting a once relatively anonymous booster into a local celebrity and a man with substantial power in determining the future direction of the town. Tukey now took a seat next to the town's traditional industrial leaders, even mildly challenging the textile bosses for control of the future of the town. He promoted his vision of Spartanburg, sometimes even against the wishes of the community's old leadership. Many Spartans liked Tukey, but even more feared and respected him.[47]

The town's new push to woo foreign industry to Spartanburg began in the fall of 1967, during a trip to Europe by Tukey and John C. West, then South Carolina's lieutenant governor.[48] Tukey and West visited Basel, Switzerland, where they encouraged Swiss participation in the Greenville international textile machinery show in 1969. West proved to be a highly valuable ally for Tukey. They shared the same persistent commitment to industrial recruiting and modernizing the state's economy. The role of salesman is a natural for any politician, and economic development was West's main commodity. Tukey found West's values and objectives to be strikingly similar to his own, and it was at this point that Tukey decided to invite West into his master plan. As they were returning home, Tukey shared with West his idea of recruiting internationally and its catchy working title: reverse investment plan.[49]

By "reverse investment" Tukey meant simply to reverse the trend, the direction in which investment funds were flowing, and get marks, gilders, and kroners streaming toward Spartanburg. It was a clever term, responding perfectly to the crystalizing worries about the economies of the state, region, and country. Since the mid-1950s economists and foreign policy professionals had become increasingly concerned about the flow of investments and money out of the United States. American currency flows, still the mercantilistic stick that most observers used to measure the economy, began to stay consistently in the red zone. The United States was beginning to suffer balance-of-payment deficits—it was sending more money abroad than it received in return.

This deficit was an understandable and—some analysts thought—even a desired side effect of a national policy that had been in place since the end of World War II. Every U.S. president since FDR had systematically promoted technology transfer, U.S. foreign aid, and direct investment abroad, believing that global recovery would benefit the United States both economically and politically. The policy was essentially a cold war measure designed to keep cooperating countries in the capitalist camp.[50] Between 1946 and 1953 the United States had transferred, in loans and gifts, $33 billion ($255 billion in 2007 dollars) worth of goods and services to other countries.[51] The rest of the world promptly spent most of this money on U.S. products and services. The transatlantic cycle of dollars had served both the nations recovering from the war and U.S. manufacturers. The win-win formula met almost universal approval in Washington, as well as in corporate boardrooms and union meeting halls throughout the nation.

Eisenhower's foreign economic policy focused on the active participation of private businesses and consistent promotion of free trade. At its core was the conviction that recovery should be led by private investments rather than by direct government aid. The policy even had a catchy slogan, "Trade, not aid," and both the White House and the State Department supported the program and provided resources.[52] The postwar boom enabled the foreign economic policy experts to operate in a financial Never Land, free of demands of equilibrium and other restrictions associated with operating in normalized markets. Eisenhower's policy basically called for the United States to spend its way to wealth, helping Europe and Asia in the process. Rather than worrying about trade balances and U.S. competitiveness, Eisenhower's economic advisers during his first term were busy creating and marketing programs that would accelerate the flow of U.S. investments abroad.[53]

By the mid-1950s the ripples of the European recovery were beginning to cause Eisenhower's Council on Foreign Trade Policy to adjust its thinking. While some cold warriors and State Department officials continued to promote U.S. investments abroad, their colleagues at the Treasury Department began to raise an alarm about the rapidly escalating flow of dollars and gold out of the United States.[54] Europe's rapid and successful industrial recovery began to tighten the economic competition. By the mid-1950s Americans could no longer count on Europeans spending their aid dollars and income to buy American goods. Instead, Europeans were beginning to consume domestic goods, selling their dollars back to the United States, which, according to the principles set forth during the Bretton Woods Conference in 1944, were convertible to gold at the preset price of $35 per troy ounce.

U.S. trade balances continued to be favorable but not favorable enough to offset the balance-of-payments inequities caused by massive U.S. military expenditures, Americans' growing taste for international travel, and private U.S. investments abroad. From 1945 to 1955 Americans were almost unchallenged in global trade, but the U.S. economic hegemony was showing signs of erosion by Eisenhower's second term. In 1957 U.S. trade balances were $6.4 billion in the black, but by 1959 that figure had dropped to $1 billion.[55] European goods, ranging from industrial machinery to sports cars and stereo systems, began to compete for American consumers. The combination of the U.S. government's international spending commitments and the changing consumption habits of Europeans and Americans alike resulted in a steady flow of dollars and gold out of U.S. vaults and into the central banks of European nations.[56]

Protectionism was not an option, politically or economically. The White House continued to support the expansion of open markets, even in the face of trade deficits. Leading policy makers regarded protectionism as a threat to U.S. foreign policy. Geopolitically, the notion of balanced trade continued to be the "orphan of the U.S. foreign policy," as some members of the Senate Finance Committee lamented.[57] Foreign policy leaders continued to fight protectionist impulses and any other efforts that might sacrifice cold war diplomacy to the limited perspective of short-term economic gains.[58]

By the early 1960s stories about the real and imagined decline of the U.S. economy were beginning to emerge as standard fodder for popular business magazines and academic publications alike. Sporadic waves of protectionist sentiment, such as South Carolina's Japanese textile import crisis of 1955, stirred both Capitol Hill and communities hit by foreign competition. Congress and the White House engaged in a tug-of-war over protectionism marked by well-publicized but fairly ineffective challenges that arose whenever debates about developments in foreign trade and American job markets became more intense.[59]

However, the White House and Congress decided to stay the course and fight the growing balance-of-payments deficit with more internationalism. John F. Kennedy and Lyndon B. Johnson both followed Eisenhower's example. The Johnson administration systematically promoted the principle and policy of lowering trade barriers, even during the GATT's contentious Kennedy Round of negotiations, held between 1964 and 1967. Even when Europeans and Japanese pushed their agricultural protectionism, the United States caved in rather than gamble on the future and success of the entire negotiation— free trade remained a cherished principle and an important tool in the U.S. cold war arsenal.[60]

Soon after the signing of the Kennedy Round agreement, which generally reduced global industrial tariffs by 36 to 39 percent, President Johnson called the document the "most successful multilateral agreement on tariff reduction ever negotiated."[61] The document undoubtedly pleased cold warriors, but the Kennedy Round was a monumental failure. U.S. trade negotiators failed to get concessions from Europeans regarding their heavily protected agriculture. Japan kept its domestic markets almost completely closed to foreign competition. Led by Brazil, South Korea, India, and other developing nations, seventeen industrializing nations negotiated a contract that did not require reciprocity, and forty-four nations refused to participate in the Kennedy Round in any way.[62] But the round opened U.S. markets to even more foreign products.

The second arm of Johnson's foreign economic policy was designed to attract money to the United States by making foreign investment in the country more attractive. Originally put forth by the Kennedy administration, the Foreign Investors Tax Act of 1966 was approved by Congress after a lively debate. Its opponents thought the bill so favorable to foreign investors that they nicknamed it "the Christmas tree bill." The measure allowed foreign investors to separate their personal and investment incomes for tax purposes and permitted them to stay in the United States for as long as 183 days a year without having to pay capital gains taxes on their U.S.-earned income.[63]

Wall Street, which attributed much of the mid-1960s strength of domestic utilities, oil exploration, mining, and food markets to the presence of foreign investors, liked the new law.[64] Europeans were slowly buying U.S. buildings and food-processing companies and investing in the construction plans of the enormous U.S. telephone and power companies.[65] Foreign manufacturing firms, increasingly confident and willing to try their luck and skill across the Atlantic, joined the movement.

Although Wall Street was well familiar with foreign investors by the mid-1960s, much of the rest of the country was not. Before the Foreign Investors Tax Act took effect, the British were the largest investors in the United States with $2.7 billion. The Dutch followed with a stake of $1.2 billion, and the Swiss were third with $825 million. By contrast, in 1966, United States investments abroad were estimated at almost $60 billion.[66]

In essence, Tukey had devised a strategy to help the economy of the entire state of South Carolina by recruiting industry internationally, so that other parts of the state could benefit as Spartanburg had with the incoming Swiss and German textile companies and Hoechst. Tukey was undoubtedly curious to see whether he could duplicate that feat, and if officials in Columbia got excited about the project, it would probably would mean bigger budgets, the use of state resources, and the gravitas and prestige that state involvement would lend to the effort. Although South Carolinians were experienced recruiters of northern corporations, foreign recruitment was still a radically new and alien concept to most residents of the state, and the strategy's long-term success was far from guaranteed.

Tukey had guessed correctly when he told West about his idea. Columbia liked the idea, and South Carolina state officials rapidly began to apply the lessons from Spartanburg's experience. The state's flagship university was gently recruited to lend its intellectual imprimatur and an aura of academic credibility to South Carolina's international recruiting efforts. When Richard E. Stanley, an associate professor of marketing at the University of South Carolina's College of Business Administration, published his plan for international trade missions in 1967, he was merely documenting what Spartans had already practiced for years and amending it by promoting a more high-level political involvement.[67] West began to drum up political support for the state-level industrial recruiting missions, and he convinced Governor Robert E. McNair to fly abroad for a three-week, five-country European tour in September 1969. In a nod to Tukey and Spartanburg, the tour was called South Carolina's First Reverse Investment Mission.[68]

West became an especially avid student and promoter of Tukey's vision, adopting it as a cornerstone of his successful 1970 run for governor.[69] With West as governor, Spartanburg's plan became South Carolina's plan. West became the indispensable leader of international recruiting, directing the campaign from the front lines in Columbia and Europe. He also worked to convince his constituents of the sanity of spending millions of dollars to convince foreign corporations to open branches in South Carolina. If anybody in the legislature or the editorial offices of South Carolina newspapers questioned the reasons for going after foreign investors, West had a four-word stock answer: "Jobs, jobs, jobs, jobs!"[70] He backed the reverse investment plan with significant funding and administrative support. When West was sworn in as governor, the South Carolina State Development Board's operating budget for fiscal year 1969–70 was $1,368,683. When he left office four years later, the budget had grown to $2,412,552, with approximately $60,000 earmarked for running the state's brand new recruiting office in Brussels, Belgium, in the administrative heart of the new, uniting Europe.[71]

The state's enthusiasm was invaluable to the recruiting efforts of individual communities. High-level attention to courting foreign corporations meant that the Spartanburg Chamber of Commerce now had ready access to the data and analytical resources of the University of South Carolina. The faculty helped arm the recruiters with statistics and new talking points for marketing the state abroad.[72] The participation of the governor and other high-level state officials ensured a cordial reception when South Carolinians called on foreign corporations. The Spartanburg–state joint venture proved to be a highly profitable symbiosis, with Tukey bringing the vision and experience, and the state bringing prestige and capital resources to the table. Reverse investment became an enduring term in South Carolina's political and economic lexicon, and it would play an important role in the careers of South Carolina politicians and the economic destinies of communities throughout the state.

The strategy that Tukey laid out gave communities a way to defend themselves against foreign competition. Spartanburg had been aware of the problems associated with the nation's balance of payments, but the town had also seen the positive side of increased trade and globalization.[73] Spartanburg knew from experience that smart states and communities could turn the flow of money and investments to their advantage. As Tukey sold his program to South Carolinians, the very word *reverse* signaled a correction, a turnaround of an unfavorable trend affecting their community and nation alike.

In Spartanburg reverse investment was an easy sell for the town's workers, who of course were excited about any expansion of the town's job market. And Tukey had no trouble convincing the elite of the wisdom of his plan.

During the late 1960s and early 1970s Tukey turned essentially into an international recruiting specialist. Under his guidance the Spartanburg Chamber of Commerce adopted a decidedly international outlook on recruitment and economic development. The sizable investment of time and money that Spartanburg put into recruiting foreign corporations marked a departure for the community. The clubby textile mill owners, the traditional keepers of the community, even showed a surprising willingness to welcome and accept the newcomers. Mill owners had traditionally guarded "their" labor supply jealously, working assiduously to keep excessive competition, high wages, labor unions, and other "agitators" out of the community. Ensuring low-cost and cooperative labor had been the central principle of their economic planning.

During the 1950s and 1960s, modernization—that is, automation—had began to reduce the textile industry's dependence on labor. Spartanburg's textile bosses had worked hard to convince the community and the workers of the necessity of transforming their factories from labor-intensive sweatshops into modern industrial facilities, even at the expense of some jobs.[74] Although many mills continued to do well and even added jobs, they no longer had the incentive to prevent Spartanburg from widening its economic base.

Tukey's plan gave the old guard an opportunity to ensure the vitality of its community and diversify its industrial base. Moreover, recruiting European textile machinery manufacturers and chemical companies brought to town businesses that provided products and services essential for their textile mills. Additionally, recruiting foreign corporations could help the elite retain control of the community. The newcomers' relative lack of knowledge of American culture and business practices could be an advantage. Perhaps these incoming foreign companies could be taught southern business and social traditions with more success than northern businesses and executives, whose knowledge of American business culture, labor relations, and politics had made them immune to such lessons in the past.

Although Spartanburg had outgrown the mill owners' "selective growth" policies, they had a positive side: as the 1960s ended, Spartanburg had an adequate labor pool accustomed to the routines of industrial work, plenty of industrial land, and significant other resources to attract new industry.[75]

CHAPTER FOUR

The Maturing of Foreign Investment in Spartanburg

As Spartanburg's international recruiting machine matured, the community became more sensitive to changes in international trade and politics. Developments in global markets, shipments of gold across the Atlantic, international trade, and even European election returns began to influence the economy of the South Carolina Piedmont. Throughout its history Spartanburg, like the rest of South Carolina, had been connected to global markets for raw materials and manufactured goods, but now the relationship was growing more complex. Local understanding of foreign economic policy evolved from concentration on import-export issues to include an interest in global investment flows, changes in the balance of payments, and a more nuanced understanding of tariffs, industrial developments, and economic policies in other parts of the world.

Just when Spartanburg had laid the groundwork for transatlantic industrial recruiting, President Richard Nixon's New Economic Policy created a surprising boom in international investing in the United States. When the wave of foreign direct investment and the ensuing feverish recruiting battles hit the United States with full force, Spartanburg had a crucial head start on most of its competition. Arrivals accumulated rapidly, as the foreign presence in the community evolved from a curious local detail into a substantial force shaping the life and economy of the entire South Carolina Piedmont. Spartanburg and the world took their relationship a step further, with both parties showing a visible long-term commitment to their future together.

For the locals Spartanburg's redefined character and new relationship with the rest of the world was an exciting and well-publicized development. The arrival of foreign corporations in the community was a source of pride and optimism for most residents and Spartanburg's economic leadership alike. Yet the rapid and substantial changes surrounding the arrival of foreign individuals and corporations also posed challenges for the community. The new money and the people who controlled it were potentially powerful enough to topple the old social order and change the region's carefully managed character, including the town's economic control, social structures, and cultural traditions. Spartanburg welcomed the arrivals warmly, but the local leadership understood the importance of educating the newcomers in local ways of living and doing business. The fresh elephants had to be trained to dance to the music of the old circus.

During the 1960s the pressures on the U.S. economy and its ubiquitous symbol, the dollar, continued to accumulate. The problems that had first emerged during the Eisenhower administration, including growing international economic competition and, especially, a negative balance of payments, had not gone away. War in Vietnam created yet another enormously powerful vacuum, sucking billions of dollars out of the economy and into the cities and jungles of Southeast Asia. The outward flow of dollars deepened the political and economic malaise that was descending upon the United States.

By the end of the decade America's problems with its balance of payments were growing too big to correct with the limited, largely voluntary measures that the Johnson administration had favored since its early years in office. As Johnson's term was creeping towards its end, the rapidly mounting deficits forced the administration to acknowledge the seriousness of the situation and react to the growing political calls for more drastic action. While the president continued to promote open trade vigorously in public, the administration kept a close eye on the flow of dollars out of the country. In private, Johnson and his advisers considered various new methods for curbing the flow, ranging from imposing a tax on international tourism to even creating some last-source tariffs to protect industries hurt by excessive foreign competition. The change in attitude was obvious in Johnson's public economic addresses. In 1966 Johnson recognized World Trade Week with a thoroughly optimistic, positive celebration of open trade, but his 1968 address honoring the same event was much more ominous, including a gloomy meditation on the future of the Bretton Woods agreement, the backbone of the noncommunist world's economic system.[1]

As Richard Nixon began his presidency, the problems surrounding the balance of payments and gold reserves had grown politically almost unbearable. The Kennedy Round and the increased competition for American goods both at home and abroad had eroded the trade surplus, the great equalizer of the dollar traffic during the two previous decades. U.S. trade balances declined from a six-billion-dollar surplus to zero by the turn of the decade. In 1971 the United States experienced its first trade deficit since 1893. The feeling of failure and disappointment spread, as even U.S. industrial production could no longer shore up the U.S. balance of payments.[2] Faith in the progress and wisdom of increased globalization began to erode across the party lines, as European industrial prowess and agricultural protectionism, cheap Japanese textiles and electronics, and other fair and unfair competition affected America's bottom line.[3]

Frustrated with both the domestic economic problems and difficulties in international economic cooperation, Nixon announced on August 15, 1971, that the United States had taken itself off the gold standard and that it would impose a 10 percent surcharge on all dutiable imports. In effect, the statement marked the death of the economic system that had guided the noncommunist world since the end of World War II. Shocked by the announcement, the Group of Ten, an advisory board of the capitalist world's major economic powers, met four months later at the Smithsonian in Washington, D.C., to negotiate a new economic system for the Western world. The Smithsonian meeting averted the crisis. The United States agreed to limit its devaluation of the dollar to 10 percent and to drop the surcharge, and the rest of the Group of Ten agreed not to retaliate against the dollar devaluation.[4]

The agreement helped to secure the survival of economic internationalism by preventing a major trade war. Additionally, this new arrangement at least partially helped to salvage the U.S. economy by forcing Europeans to realize that even America's fiscal resources and patience with budget deficits had limits. Termination of the Bretton Woods agreement was a drastic and dramatic event, but international economic cooperation managed to bounce back. The wounds healed surprisingly fast, as the most important trade partners and political allies of the United States learned that the move was necessary to keep the American economy afloat, and a strong American economy, even with the growing prominence of Europe, was still the locomotive to which the rest of the Western world had hitched itself.[5]

The termination of Bretton Woods had curious effects upon both U.S. manufacturing and international investment flows. Within two years Nixon's fundamentally nationalistic move turned into a major catalyst for increased internationalization of the U.S. manufacturing scene, especially in areas that operated in fields dominated by international trade and competition. The tariffs and taking the United States off the gold standard affected global trade but did little to diminish the U.S. appetite for foreign goods or foreign determination to hold on to U.S. customers.

By the late 1960s the rapid economic growth of Europe, the continuously worsening balance-of-payments situation of the United States, the maturing of European multinational corporations, and even European political developments had created an environment that was increasingly conducive for foreign investing in the United States. A number of companies with a dominant market position, such as the Swiss and German textile machinery manufacturers that had entered Spartanburg almost ten years earlier, had previously sought to satisfy a specific U.S. demand for European products in fields where Europeans had a substantial competitive advantage, but by the end of the decade a more macroeconomic collection of motives emerged to foster the growth of foreign businesses in the United States.[6]

As Europe and Japan shook off the devastation of war and rebuilt their economies, their large corporations had gathered the skills, confidence, and resources to expand beyond national borders. The rapid growth of the European and Japanese economies, combined with mergers and acquisitions that reshaped their industrial landscapes, gave their corporations the muscle to enter U.S. markets.[7] By crossing U.S. borders, foreign multinationals sought economies of scale, political stability, a foothold in the biggest market in the world, and an opportunity to improve their performance by learning modern management and marketing techniques from the presumably superior U.S. executives.[8]

There was little question that Americans liked foreign products. European exports grew 600 percent between 1960 and 1974, with a healthy chunk of these goods traveling to the enormous U.S. markets.[9] Reducing transportation costs and delivery times to their U.S. customers emerged as important considerations when foreign corporations contemplated manufacturing in the United States. Finally, rapidly growing European labor costs, heavy government regulation, and even a series of sizable and significant socialist election victories throughout Western Europe convinced a rapidly growing number of European multinationals to seek new opportunities and capitalist asylum in the United States. To a continent still shaken by the Parisian spring of 1968, the possibility of a socialist or communist revolution was more than a mere paranoid fear or theoretical threat. Even if the revolution failed to materialize, the growing power of the labor movement, and the continued dominance of leftist and left-centrist governments, ensured that the tighter regulation and higher labor costs were not going to disappear from Europe any time soon.[10]

The stage for almost exponential growth in foreign direct investment in the United States was set, and Nixon's New Economic Policy provided the catalyst. The landscape of foreign investment in the United States changed drastically after the sudden death of the Bretton Woods agreement. The devaluation of the U.S. dollar, combined with the tariffs, made foreign direct investment in the United States attractive—and often a necessity—for those foreign corporations whose business depended upon U.S. trade.[11] The tariff wall and the changes triggered by the fluctuations of the U.S. dollar provided these corporations the impetus to rethink their old ways of reacting to and dealing with international currency and investment flows. Opening a branch in the United States became an increasingly attractive strategic alternative.

After the devaluation the enormous dollar assets of the European central banks, accumulated over decades of negative U.S. balance of payments, were ready to return to the United States with gusto. This mountain of cash, the undervaluation of U.S. corporations, and the availability of relatively inexpensive and skilled labor led many European investors to view the United States as the latest Xanadu. "It is a joke, isn't it," marveled one young British investment banker to a *Forbes* interviewer. "Europe is flooded with all those Eurodollars that you paid for our businesses. Billions and billions. The answer for us is to lap up those dollars and buy into America. I am in El Dorado. It's like getting Harrod's at half price."[12] U.S. stock prices, depressed during the bear markets of 1969–70 and 1973–74, combined with the rapid decline of the U.S. dollar vis-à-vis the currencies of major foreign investing countries, reinforced the impression that the United States was for sale at bargain prices. Between Nixon's termination of the Bretton Woods agreement and the end of 1973, U.S. stock prices dropped more than 30 percent for European buyers.[13] In 1972 foreign corporations invested $900 million in the United States. Two years later, when the effects of Nixon's New Economic Policy was fully felt throughout the country, foreign investments totaled $4.8 billion, consisting of both foreign takeovers of businesses listed on the New York Stock Exchange and brand new industrial investments.[14]

The United States entered the post-gold-standard era suddenly. The rapid and large-scale arrival of foreign investors in the United States surprised most American observers, including officials in Washington, D.C. While European investors now had American fever, neither Congress nor the executive branch had a clear plan for dealing with these investors, nor did Washington demonstrate any noticeable interest in promoting foreign investment in the United States. When U.S. representative John C. Culver, a Democrat from Iowa and chair of the Subcommittee on Foreign Economic Policy of the House Foreign Affairs Committee, held hearings in 1972 on the adjustment assistance program to ease pressures to protect U.S. markets, not a single witness or member of Congress even mentioned the idea of encouraging foreign investment in the United States as a way to improve domestic employment and the economy in general.[15]

Indifference was further accompanied by organizational disarray, which further hindered the birth of effective, concentrated visions regarding the foreign investment in the United States. More than sixty federal agencies had at least some say in international economic issues.[16] As far as foreign investments were concerned, the proverbial left and right hands acted autonomously, occasionally pulling in contradictory directions. While most agencies or political offices were either oblivious to or not even concerned about foreign direct investment, after 1971 the Department of Commerce gave limited funding for multistate investment missions abroad under its "Invest in the United States" program, which sought to improve the depressed U.S. economy through foreign investments.[17]

Despite federal inertia and occasional hostility, the value of foreign investments in the United States skyrocketed under Nixon's New Economic Policy. A Commerce Department study estimated that at the end of 1972, the value of foreign investments in the country was $14.4 billion. An independent study put their value as high as $38 billion, almost three times the Commerce Department number.[18] Regardless of the research method or the study's sponsor, the value of foreign direct investments in the United States was exploding. By 1975 even the Commerce Department's traditionally conservative estimates put the value of FDI at $50 billion.[19]

The federal government not only failed to promote foreign investment; some members of Congress even saw it as a potential threat to U.S. economic sovereignty and national security. Increased foreign ownership led the alarmed Congress to search for ways to learn about the size and scope of foreign investment in the United States or even limit foreign ownership of U.S. land, buildings, and production facilities. While balance-of-payments deficits and U.S. corporations that were relocating abroad had worried the American public, the idea of foreigners acquiring U.S. assets did not appeal to economic nationalists either. Globalization was accompanied by an emerging and increasingly persistent strain of full-blown economic xenophobia.

Since the late 1960s the "creeping expropriation" of U.S. assets and increased foreign competition had worried the public and some politicians, especially when the new owners spoke Japanese or Arabic.[20] Congress authorized the secretary of commerce to begin a thorough study of foreign direct investment in the country and its impact on the United States and its economy, a task that took almost two years to complete. The massive, nine-volume study demonstrated that when it came to foreign investments, Americans often reacted with emotion rather than reason. While the growth of foreign investment in the United States was substantial, it nevertheless represented only a minuscule fraction of the total investment capital floating in U.S. markets.[21] Additionally, U.S. investment abroad continued to surpass the size and scope of foreign investments in the United States.

A new form of economic nationalism began to shape American thinking about foreign ownership. Loss of economic autocracy and other fears associated with foreign acquisition of American land and corporations, ranging from purchase of the Good Humor ice cream company by Anglo-Dutch Unilever to massive land purchases around the nation, triggered laments and protestations from the public and the politicians alike.[22] The tables had turned. In 1967 Jean-Jacques Servain-Schreiber's book *Le Défi Américain* (American Challenge), a nationalistic prediction of economic doom and gloom under the American threat to French economic sovereignty, had developed into a big hit in continental Europe. The book predicted that by 1982 the world would be divided into three economic superpowers: the United States, Soviet Union, and U.S. investments in Europe. Less than a decade after its publication, the United States was learning firsthand the same confusing but powerful emotions associated with foreign direct investment that had shaped the economic thinking of its European allies for more than a decade. For millions of average Americans the U.S.-sponsored international economic network was both the cornerstone of U.S. hegemony and the biggest threat to it.[23]

The southern states did not share the growing concerns in Washington about foreign investors. Contrasting attitudes of the South and the federal government toward the foreign money and investors invading the nation, one *Forbes* journalist concluded, "However people might feel in the rest of the country, nobody in South Carolina is hoisting 'foreigners-go-home' placards."[24] That was true throughout the South. As the scale of the investments increased, other regions joined the competition, which turned into a major brawl. From governors to chamber of commerce officials, recruiters developed a new-found interest in studying foreign languages and business cultures, showing new eagerness to find common cultural and economic ground with their new recruits.[25]

Spartanburg and South Carolina discovered that other states and communities were getting into the game they had largely invented. The effects of foreign direct investment were felt the strongest at the state and local levels, and boosters and employees alike were pleased. Despite the harrumphing in Washington, most communities graced with foreign investment saw the development as positive, not a threat.[26]

States rushed to compete for foreign investors and other industrial immigrants. From Florida to Washington state, communities gussied up their main streets and beautified their industrial parks to lure Euro-dollars. Chambers of commerce readjusted their industrial recruiting machines to accommodate foreign corporations and executives. Boosters, workers struggling with the sluggish economy and job market of the 1970s, and local businessmen all dreamed of brand new factories, with names and logos that lent either old European prestige or the mystique of the Japanese economic miracle.[27]

The states and communities greeted foreign investment as a capital and job-creating development. The oil dollars of the Saudi Arabians and Kuwaitis helped to finance impressive resort-projects on the South Carolina coast.[28] In Atlanta city officials and local businessmen were enthusiastic about the Saudis and Japanese who were pumping money into their aging downtown, buying apartment complexes and skyscrapers and developing world-class hotels, a trend that continued to escalate throughout the 1970s and much of the 1980s.[29] The big prize of the foreign investment sweepstakes, however, was the manufacturing corporations. Manufacturing represented stability and growth, and factories brought the most desirable, high-paying jobs. Foreign manufacturing in the United States was experiencing an upward swing. Hundreds of international corporations wanted to penetrate the new tariff wall and establish themselves firmly in a competitive position, in case the fickle Americans got some crazy new ideas about tariffs or currency manipulation.

In the growing competition for industrial immigrants, southern states more than held their own. Since the late 1960s ten states, including South Carolina, had begun to invest substantial amounts of money and effort in recruiting foreign corporations.[30] Additionally, foreigners recognized and reacted to the demographic developments and other market changes taking place in the United States. When European executives considered opening branch operations in the United States, they turned out to be savvy investors, thoroughly informed about the investment flows and shifts in the economic geography of the United States. They had noticed the Sunbelt movement, and the same factors that lured companies from Boston, Detroit, and New York to the South persuaded the business executives in Frankfurt, Clermont-Ferrand, and Zurich to give the region a careful look.[31] Foreigners liked the low wages, large labor pools, subsidies, growing regional markets, and the absence of unions just as much as any red-blooded American capitalist.[32]

In many ways the arrival of foreign corporations was an extension of the Sunbelt phenomenon, the intercontinental extension of a well-documented domestic movement. The foreign plants built a strong presence in the South and the Southwest. Of the $66.785 billion in productive physical assets that foreign corporations owned in the United States in 1977, $21.869 billion was located in the states of the Old Confederacy. South Carolina's $2.137 billion in foreign assets competed with and chased the old northern industrial powers of New York ($2.845 billion), New Jersey ($2.963 billion), and Illinois ($2.582 billion).[33] The new manufacturing efforts continued to concentrate in the South and Southwest at a speed and scope that occasionally puzzled northern industrial interests.[34]

No American state experienced the immediate effects of Nixon's New Economic Policy more than South Carolina did. The Palmetto State benefited immensely from the foreign investment because it was in the process transforming itself from a textile state stuck in cultural and economic nostalgia into a modern, diversified and cosmopolitan state. Motivated by their economic needs and influenced by the tangible benefits they had realized from foreign investment in recent years, state and local officials in South Carolina had developed substantial skills in dealing with foreign investors, which gave South Carolinians crucial advantages in the growing competition for foreign dollars. In its extensive analysis of the international investments in the United States, the *Economist* applauded southern efforts and success in foreign industrial recruiting, naming South Carolina in particular as "the most skilled angler for foreign investment," thanks to the "blend of southern charm and northern hucksterism" evidenced by the state's representatives in Europe.[35]

Taking their cue from Spartanburg, South Carolina officials now practiced the same attention to potential recruits' smallest wishes, made personalized contacts, and proffered excessive hospitality. Moreover, state officials had the resources to give their industrial prospects an even more impressive welcome than the Spartans had managed to put together. In a speech to other industrial recruiters from around South Carolina, Caleb C. Whitaker of South Carolina's State Development Board said: "We try to give them very personal attention, from the Governor on down. We invite them to our homes, to our clubs, to our resorts on the weekends, et cetera. We give them personal hospitality and in almost all cases, they reciprocate when we visit them in their countries, and many times introduce us to other prospects."[36] During the 1970s the recruitment battle turned into a red-carpet extravaganza that featured stretch limousines, private jets, and exclusive retreats, as the states attempted to outdo each other in pampering foreign executives.[37]

South Carolinians were benefiting not only from their recruiting skills but also from the peculiar social psychology of foreign investors. The early contacts of South Carolinians and, especially, Spartans were more beneficial than probably even they understood at the time. As far as business logistics, labor, and other market factors permitted, the early foreign investors tended to settle in states that were both geographically and culturally closest to their home countries, a phenomenon that became known as the "border effect."[38] Canadian companies formed a noticeable presence in the upstate New York and midwestern border regions, Japanese corporations favored California, and European investors settled in the states on the eastern seaboard, most noticeably from the mid-Atlantic states of Maryland and Delaware down through Virginia and the Carolinas.[39]

The rolling hills, proximity to the mountains, and orderly Protestant character of South Carolina's Piedmont were more than a bit similar to central German and Swiss culture and geography. "It was not too far from the sea, close to the mountains, a healthy environment—much like Switzerland," Luciano Cont, a local director of Sulzer, said of the company's decision to locate in Spartanburg.[40] Often, business is also culture. Textiles formed both a common commercial interest and a culturally unifying factor for upcountrymen and German-speaking textile bosses.[41] As the flow of foreign investments intensified, new foreign companies wanted to settle near their compatriots in the United States. This proved to be a strong lure for numerous German executives, especially when it was working in conjunction with more tangible business motives.[42]

Europeans were also highly likely to rely on word of mouth from and the example of their immigrant predecessors. Smaller companies often took their cues from larger corporations with enough resources to conduct thorough location searches and market and labor analyses. After Michelin, the French tire-manufacturing giant, opened several production facilities throughout the South Carolina Piedmont in the 1970s, including a factory in Spartanburg in 1974, one prospective French investor told a Columbia publication, "If Michelin, owned by the meticulous capitalist François Michelin, chose South Carolina, there was no need for other smaller French companies to scour the nation looking for a better business climate. If it is good enough for Michelin, it's good enough for them."[43]

The antiunionism and probusiness corporatism were also attractive to European companies like Michelin. The publicity-shy, fiercely private tire concern fit easily into a region where the most visible government involvement in business was usually the doling-out of financial incentives and assistance in keeping out labor unions.[44] For the conservative Europeans and South Carolinians, finding a common business language did not prove to be difficult.

South Carolina's earliest international manufacturing contacts were with the British, Swiss, German, and some French corporations. These early links and the continued importance of the textiles continued to pull in companies mostly from German-speaking central Europe. While some isolated Japanese, Canadian, Dutch, and South African companies had also opened offices in South Carolina, central European companies formed the backbone of the state's industrial immigration. Swiss and German textile, textile machinery, and metalworking companies became an especially noticeable part of the landscape of Spartanburg and the rest of the Piedmont.[45]

By November 1973 more than fifty foreign-owned plants were either operating in or rising around the state, representing approximately an investment of $432 million ($2.140 billion in 2007 dollars).[46] In 1974 alone, foreigners invested $313 million ($1.316 billion) in South Carolina industries, representing almost 47 percent of all industrial investment in the state.[47] Foreign money emerged as a major force in building wealth and factories throughout the state, but especially in its northwestern industrial corridor, the 107-mile stretch of Interstate 85 that cut through the South Carolina Piedmont, connecting it to national and international markets. More than 50 percent of all international investment in South Carolina took place in the greater Greenville-Spartanburg area, making it the uncontested leader in foreign direct investment in the state, if not the entire nation.[48]

Spartanburg continued to be both the prophet and the biggest beneficiary of the state's international capital inflows. Despite growing competition throughout the South, Spartanburg still managed to land almost all the foreign companies it could handle. Bruckner Machinery Corporation of Germany began operations in Spartanburg in 1965. Erhard + Leimer and Mahlo America, also from West Germany, opened Spartanburg offices in 1968. Zimmer Machinery of Austria arrived in 1969, and Otto Zollinger of Switzerland started operating in the town in 1970.[49]

The peculiar emergence of an international business community in the foothills of the Blue Ridge Mountains began to draw even international attention. Shameless self-promotion has always been a crucial aspect of the South's industrial recruiting efforts, and Spartanburg's publicity machine was highly impressive, especially for a community of its size. Spartanburg's increasingly cosmopolitan image developed into a regional anomaly, and local officials exploited the image to the best of their abilities.

The conspicuous success of this small Piedmont town in attracting international corporations became a source of fascination for both the European and the American press. Publications from two continents sent their journalists to Spartanburg to cover the extraordinary story of the international economic marvel taking place there. From London's *Sunday Times* to America's own *Reader's Digest*, writers reported, with varying degrees of surprise and condescension, the story of the rising cosmopolitan business community in the boondocks of the Piedmont, which had refused to whither away with the region's declining textile industries.[50]

The stories tended to be formulaic, describing an isolated Piedmont community on the periphery of urban sophistication that, thanks largely to a few energetic locals and faceless global economic forces, suddenly found itself in cultural contact with the rest of the world. Writers exaggerated the effects of industrial relocation in the community, describing the foreign newcomers in colorful and caricaturized forms, using language influenced by Spartans' skillful media manipulation and traditional business-reporting hyperbole. Because of these foreign corporations, the stories said, Spartanburg had become a community of unforeseen prosperity, a great place to shop for quality foreign beers and cheeses. Articles painted contemporary Spartanburg as a place that groups of French, Swiss, and Germans had turned into a multilingual, culturally aware hotbed of European-influenced sophistication.[51]

Spartans used the publicity well, taking partial credit for the exaggerated image of their community that was spreading on both continents. Dick Tukey, the one-time newspaperman and publicist, understood the nature and character of journalism and journalists. As he spouted solid facts, he delivered the one-liners that journalists love and happily include in their articles. Spartanburg's media strategy was rooted in boosterism that touted its economic, political, demographic, and geographic advantages. It mixed truth and wishful thinking creatively, rarely resorting to outrageous inaccuracies while presenting Spartanburg the way everyone hoped that it was.

For all its success, South Carolina did not have a systematic approach to the domestic and/or foreign press, save the State Development Board's routine press notifications whenever a new foreign corporation decided to locate in the state.[52] South Carolina communities maintained substantial control of the shaping of their images, supported by the State Development Board's larger efforts to market the entire state. Spartans made sure that their message, characteristically local, dominated the cacophony of sales pitches echoing around the marketplace. While rich in facts and information, Spartanburg's public message was personality driven, with Tukey and happily transplanted foreign executives at its fore. Business was good in Spartanburg, but business was built and conducted by people, not faceless impersonal forces.

Spartanburg used the European-born business executives and other members of the community to reel in more business. Once newcomers were comfortably settled, Spartanburg's salesmen began to court their participation in the town's international recruiting efforts. Foreign-born executives received invitations to join the board of the Greater Spartanburg Chamber of Commerce. Motivated by both good business sense and their personal interests, several locally established European executives began to join Tukey and his team in wooing foreign factories and other operations to Spartanburg. Spartanburg's Germans, Swiss, and French were eager to both grow their ranks and to show their allegiance to their adopted community.[53]

A multilingual line of communication developed between Spartanburg and Frankfurt, Zurich, and other European business centers. Foreign corporations heard speeches, in both English and their native languages, about the benefits of locating in Spartanburg. "The word has spread that Hoechst has been treated well here," Günther I. O. Rübcke, the company's head honcho in Spartanburg, told *Trends* magazine in 1975. "Since our arrival, a number of multi-national companies engaged in highly specialized fields decided to locate in the Spartanburg area."[54] Foreigners became assimilated to Spartanburg's social and economic structures, evolving rapidly into willing boosters, with vested professional and personal interests in their adopted community's further development.

The strategy worked on two fronts. First, the participation of Spartanburg's foreign community in their adopted community's recruiting efforts helped Tukey and his assistants to sell Spartanburg abroad. European executives were often much more responsive to their fellow countrymen's presentations than to the blandishments of a professional recruiter.[55] Additionally, their participation in Spartanburg's international recruiting efforts strengthened their ties to the community and their cooperation with its socioeconomic power structure. Spartanburg's European executives were welcomed into the local economic elite. As these Europeans put down new roots in Spartanburg and as their number grew, their role in the community gave them a stake and a role in running the affairs of their adopted home.

By the early 1970s the arrival of foreign corporations and individuals had evolved from a peculiar local characteristic into a noticeable economic force. Over the years the number of foreign corporations and individuals grew so high that the foreigners ceased to be a curious detail in the local economic landscape. The economic weight of the Spartanburg-based foreign corporations became substantial enough to warrant some reevaluations of local socioeconomic hegemony. Spartanburg's leaders had to determine where these newcomers stood in the social hierarchy of their town.

Newcomers lacked connections and social capital when they landed in Spartanburg. And, unlike Roger Milliken, Fred Dent, and some other high-profile arrivistes, the foreigners were not rich enough to warrant automatic social entrée. Many newcomers were men at midcareer, well-educated corporate professionals who were rising stars. They were, for the most part, in their thirties and forties, up-and-comers all, but men whose current status would not warrant invitations to join Spartanburg's elite.

However, these men were the face behind the factory. Unlike earlier absentee owners, who had shared the language, culture, and citizenship of the native Spartan elite, the executives at corporate headquarters were an ocean away. Foreign executives carried more weight and autonomy than did average mill executives, whose leashes could be followed to their holders in the Northeast. Often there was no clearly identifiable man behind the man in Spartanburg. Thus the foreign executives in Spartanburg represented and personalized their corporations, much as local textile families had personalized their mills. This factor was not without significance in a community with strong, paternalistic, exclusive, and highly personalized business traditions.[56]

These newcomers become powerful and important factors in Spartanburg's economic planning. Their well-being mattered enormously, as foreign executives and managers controlled important links between Spartanburg and other potential industrial immigrants in Europe. Their comments and impressions might translate to billions of dollars in lost or acquired investments. As the Spartanburg Chamber of Commerce capitalized on these new-found business connections to Europe, the personal testimonies of foreign executives and managers became crucial to the success of Tukey's reverse investment plan. Corporate headquarters and fraternal business organizations in Frankfurt and Zurich became important unofficial forums for spreading Spartanburg's message.[57]

Finally, human curiosity, community image, and personal relations also shaped the social status of foreign immigrants. In a town that had always been relatively placid and culturally homogeneous, foreign individuals triggered curiosity, even pride, among residents. Local inhabitants and media paraded "their" foreigners as symbols of the new and cosmopolitan Spartanburg. The polite, exotic, and powerful Europeans served as living testimonies to the new, more visible role in the world of their community and state.[58]

The foreigners were no longer few in number. By 1970 Spartanburg County was home to more than 2,600 people of foreign nationality, including more than 700 native speakers of German, almost 400 who spoke French at home, and even 125 Italians.[59] The total number of foreigners had more than tripled since the 1960 census. Organizations such as the Swiss-American Society of the Piedmont emerged to help Swiss families make the transition by acquiring friends among Spartanburg's natives.[60] New services and traditions, such as Franz Kastner's European Deli and annual Bastille Day festivities and other foreign celebrations brought much-wanted cultural diversity and color to the community's daily life. In Spartanburg's stores and restaurants, European languages mixed with the accents of the southern Piedmont.[61]

Spartanburg's leadership emphasized the forging of close personal relationships between members of the host community and the executive transplants. Incoming executives were rapidly invited to contribute to the very fabric of the community. I. O. Rübcke, executive vice president of Hoechst, was invited to join the board of Wofford College. Rudolf Mueller, manager of Menzel Machinenfabrik, served on the board of the Tolstoy Foundation, which helped Asian refugees to relocate in the United States. Kurt Zimmerli of the Zima Corporation began to play a highly visible role in various benevolent organizations in Spartanburg, giving back to the community that had welcomed him and other Europeans "with open arms."[62] Paul Foerster of Hoechst joined the board of the Greater Spartanburg Area Chamber of Commerce in 1970, only four years after arriving from Germany.[63] In the words of one transplanted German executive, "Spartanburg gives foreigner a feeling that you belong."[64] Such inclusion not only created a better community but was effective policy, helping to create happy transplants with a vested interest in their new community and ensuring that locals got along with the newcomers.

In a matter of years foreign managers became essential, natural participants in Spartanburg's economic and social life. Tukey's insistence that Europeans should not move into ethnic suburban ghettoes and should instead locate throughout Spartanburg's upper-middle-class neighborhoods helped to prevent the creation of foreign social cliques separated from the mainstream of the community. Despite the town's noticeable international presence, Spartanburg maintained its American and southern character, spiced with appropriate—but not dominant—foreign flavor.[65] The local business community accepted the newcomers. Occasional complaints about the South Carolina Piedmont's depleted workforce aside, the industrial newcomers caused little or no tension within the local business community.[66]

Europeans also learned to adapt to the American form of welfare capitalism. For example, the concept of corporate donations to good causes in their
host communities was alien to Europeans, who were more accustomed to generous government funding for various pro bono projects. After a few years in
town Hoechst's Spartanburg-based executives started to propound corporate
benevolence at company headquarters in Frankfurt, eventually managing to
convince the company's leaders of the importance of voluntary giving.[67] By
participating in fund-raising for various projects in the community, Hoechst
and other European corporations became even more rooted in the local community and its traditions.

Spartanburg successfully avoided the conflicts that had plagued some
poorly managed international relocations, such as the conflicted relationship
with German Korf Steel Mills and the community of Georgetown on the
South Carolina coastal plain. Korf's attempts to make labor comply with a
strict and highly hierarchical German managerial culture, rather than adapting itself to southern labor relations, had triggered severe community-wide
resentment and negative national publicity. While Germans in Spartanburg
were usually beloved, warmly welcomed, and eager to adopt to local customs
of business and pleasure, their countrymen in Georgetown were seen as rude
and inflexible intruders who showed no respect for the old, deeply rooted ways
of the workplace and the community.[68]

In regard to their employees, foreign corporations differed little from local
corporations, save perhaps the accents of the bosses. Many European companies operating in Spartanburg had chosen the town and the South Carolina
Piedmont largely for its inexpensive nonunionized labor.[69] Michelin had
resisted unionization in France, and in the South Carolina Piedmont it found
a region that shared its values. For those who had not thought about labor
practices too much, learning local ways of doing business included learning
how to deal with the workforce. The Spartanburg Development Association,
a local association of business owners and an awe-inspiring antiunion organization, helped newcomers to learn to navigate Spartanburg's labor markets.[70]
Much as in other matters business and social, Spartanburg's foreign corporations assimilated their labor policies to the degree that they were largely indis-
tinguishable from those of native-born companies.

During the late 1960s and early 1970s Spartanburg became increasingly aware
of its new economic connections with the world. Spartans saw clearly that the
effects of international economic developments were not limited to the presence of foreign corporations and individuals in their community, but their

community was connected to the world with new bonds. The local understanding of Spartanburg's economic connections with the world grew from a pipeline that ran from import to export into an intricate and complex web of international economic causes and effects. Spartanburg was now not only trading with the world. It was of the world, closely connected to the trends, ebbs, and flows of international commerce and manufacturing.

International economic news took up increasingly more space in local newspapers. The business pages began to notice the economic effects of European elections, as the cold war–centered international news coverage began to give way to business-minded news and notes from the international scene. The trend corresponded with a general growing awareness throughout America of the changing realities of international business and global competition, but in Spartanburg international news was now local.

Although Spartanburg continued to celebrate the arrival of foreign corporations and individuals, the community had not changed in any substantial degree. It entertained many of the same economic prejudices and values that it had held dear before the economic transformation. Foreigners were invited into the community, but the fundamental character of the community remained largely intact. Spartans continued to entertain notions reeking of protectionism and outright economic xenophobia but made distinctions for "their" foreigners. Demonstrating remarkable skills of seeing only one side of the argument and equating personal advantage with truth and justice, they learned to simultaneously welcome foreign jobs and reject foreign competition.

With the noticeable foreign presence came a veiled threat. Spartanburg was developing a power vacuum. The textile business was seeing managerial and technological changes: old families were moving out of the business, and bankruptcies and other closures—antiquated textile factories were closing or moving abroad—were wreaking havoc with the community's stability and socioeconomic structure. As the number and size of foreign corporations continued to grow, foreign industrial leaders gained even larger roles in Spartanburg's economy and social leadership.

CHAPTER FIVE

Change and Continuity
in Spartanburg

On Thursday, July 26, 1979, the front page of the *Spartanburg Journal* signaled a dramatic end of an era for the community. Richard Ellery Tukey,
Spartanburg's leading recruiter and the CEO of its chamber of commerce, was
dead at sixty-one. A rapidly advancing prostate cancer had claimed Tukey's life
the previous day. City officials lowered all the flags on Spartanburg's public
buildings. In front of the Greater Spartanburg Area Chamber of Commerce
Office Building, a colorful palette of international flags hung at half-mast, in
a telling symbol of both Tukey's life and death.[1]

After a somewhat restless early career, with numerous relocations and job
changes, this native New Yorker had found a home in Spartanburg. Tukey
had left a permanent imprint on the community, steering and influencing
it during an era of potentially volatile change. He had declined numerous
more prestigious and better-paid job offers to stay in his adopted home.[2] His
untiring work for Spartanburg's economic progress, urban development, and
educational improvement testified to a deep affection and commitment to the
community, reaching well beyond the requirements of his job as Spartanburg's
leading salesman. Tukey had played a crucial role in introducing Spartans to
the world and vice versa, and the community owed him much of the worldly
confidence it demonstrated in the global marketplace. Befittingly, an international group of Spartans served as pallbearers, including Paul Foerster, a long-
time Hoechst executive; Kurt Zimmerli, a Swiss-born textile boss; Hubert
Hendrix, editor of the *Spartanburg Herald*; and Rudolf Mueller, another powerful business transplant.[3]

In Spartanburg Tukey had found the South that he had learned to love
during his military career, but his second entry into the region had been
marked by a combination of change and assimilation. By the end of his life
Tukey had spiced Spartanburg with touches of the cosmopolitanism of his
Brooklyn and White Plains childhood, making Spartanburg more polyglot and
sophisticated, if still not to the degree of the North of his youth and the South

of his visions. Spartanburg was perhaps the archetypical New South industrial community before Tukey's arrived. At his death the town had evolved into a regional and even national leader as the United States adjusted to competing in a climate of international recruitment and far-reaching globalization. Thanks largely to Tukey, Spartanburg had learned to see its existence not only in regional or even national terms but also in international terms.

Tukey was dead, but Spartanburg's globalization effort lived on. Whatever worries Spartans might have harbored about the survival of the community's industrial growth after Tukey, they were rapidly eradicated. Tukey's work continued to bear fruit even after his death. The stream of international corporations to Spartanburg did not stop or even slow down, as the town's now solid reputation and earlier arrivals served as magnets for the further development and continued internationalization of its economic life. Developments in international investment markets, U.S. foreign policy, and domestic economy continued to favor the aggressive inflows of international investment, in Spartanburg and the nation alike.

The nature of international investment markets was changing during the first half of the 1980s. The monetarist revolution, which had begun with President Jimmy Carter's nomination of Paul Volcker to lead the Federal Reserve and escalated during President Ronald Reagan's early years in office, received an enthusiastic reception from investors both at home and abroad.[4] Before 1980 foreign investments in the United States were heavily cyclical, linked directly to the value of the U.S. dollar. When the dollar was cheap, foreign investments were flowing in, and as dollars got more expensive, investments slowed substantially. By the early 1980s global confidence in the U.S. economy, triggered by deregulation and the demise of stagflation, returned with gusto. From 1982 onward the investment inflows seemed almost immune to short-term fluctuations in the value of the U.S. dollar.[5] Foreign corporations were betting on the United States, securing their share of the increasingly rigorous American markets by moving substantial parts of their operations, manufacturing included, to this side of the Atlantic.

The growth in foreign investments had escalated throughout the 1970s. During the five-year period between 1978 and 1983, the investment inflows had grown more than three times faster than during the previous five-year stretch, turning the balance of international investment flows to America's favor.[6] Between 1982 and 1986 the value of foreign investments in the United States shot from $124 billion ($266 billion in 2007 dollars) to $209 billion ($395 billion).[7] The upward spiral would continue, as national economies of the Western world continued to amalgamate into a big polygamous family, with rapidly weakening borders, spiritual and physical alike.

The changes in foreign direct investments in the United States were both quantitative and qualitative. Operations expanded in both number and size. The role of manufacturing continued to grow, as foreign auto manufacturers and other heavy industries continued to respond to the growing U.S. market for Japanese and European cars and other goods.[8] By 1987 more than 3.2 million Americans from coast to coast received their paychecks from foreign-owned conglomerates. Large states with major markets, administrative headquarters, and distribution centers were home to the biggest number of such workers, including the more than 300,000 New Yorkers and Californians who worked for foreigners. But, given the size of their economies and populations, southern states fared remarkably well against their competition. Additionally, the South was particularly successful in attracting factories, the most capital- and labor-intensive investments. Of the 3.2 million jobs at foreign-owned corporations, 1.02 million were below the Mason-Dixon line.[9]

The stream of foreign investments to South Carolina continued without signs of slowing down. International investment flows provided the state with some of its best economic news throughout the 1970s. In 1977 the value of foreign investments in South Carolina totaled $2.13 billion ($7.287 billion in 2007 dollars), providing jobs for 35,000 South Carolinians. Three years later the value of foreign investments had grown to $3.87 billion ($9.74 billion in 2007 dollars), and the number of foreign-provided jobs surpassed 54,200.[10] In 1987 at least 75,700 South Carolinians were working directly for foreign-owned corporations.[11]

International recruitment had become a major part of the job for governors and lieutenant governors during the 1970s.[12] Ever since the then–lieutenant governor John C. West had promoted the idea in Columbia during the late 1960s, South Carolina officials had rung up hundreds of thousands of frequent flyer miles in numerous annual recruiting trips to Europe, Asia, and Latin America. By the 1980s such trips were routine for the state's economic development professionals, who had learned to follow economic developments around the world closely, reacting to the news and economic trends with swift and decisive action. When she started to read stories about the Scandinavian economic boom and severe labor shortages in the late 1970s, Lieutenant Governor Nancy Stevenson arranged for a tour, and State Development Board officials quickly made a trip to Scandinavia an annual event.[13]

Maintaining active contacts with potential industrial recruits and touring the world on often long and arduous recruiting trips became a mandatory part of the job of any successful South Carolina governor. The state's chief executives sometimes spent weeks in Europe, hopping from country to country, wooing new companies, and thanking those that had already established operations in the Palmetto State.[14] The rapidly growing size of foreign investments had increased the intensity of the competition for foreign plants and dollars. To keep up with the competition, states, including South Carolina, had to focus more resources on courting foreigners. South Carolinians were no longer alone on the international recruitment trail.

Ever since West had shared South Carolina's reverse investment plan with other governors in 1971, other southern states, most notably Georgia, had jumped in.[15] By the end of the decade foreign recruiting had become a heated fight, with the states reallocating resources and defining new strategies to separate their sales pitches from the tens of state- and community-level messages echoing throughout Asia and Western Europe.[16] Thanks to the skills of South Carolina's team, the shape of the message was not the problem anymore, but getting fresh ears to receive it was. European investors were increasingly overwhelmed by invitations from states and individual communities to attend their investment seminars and sales pitches.[17]

Despite its undeniable and well-publicized success in attracting foreign industries, by the late 1970s South Carolina was losing its edge in the competition. Foreign investors, increasingly confident and at ease in the U.S. cultural and economic landscape, slowly became more open to different factory locations. The psychological factors that had directed the early arrivals to follow their compatriots to the same states and communities began to show signs of erosion. Additionally, the subsidy packages offered by the states had become increasingly attractive. During the 1980s South Carolinians gradually realized that their competitors were gaining on them.

In 1977 only North Carolina surpassed South Carolina in the number of foreign-company-provided jobs in the South. Three years later both Georgia and Florida had passed South Carolina, and Tennessee and Louisiana were breathing down its neck.[18] They had learned the same tricks that South Carolina had pioneered a decade earlier, supplementing them with their own ideas and techniques. Georgia had opened its European and Japanese sales offices during Jimmy Carter's gubernatorial years, and the state was learning to outhustle even South Carolinians for foreign investments. "I wouldn't call it hand-to-hand combat," one Georgia official said, "but every southern state wants every foreign company it can get."[19] By 1978 Georgia's complement of

328 foreign corporations, including one hundred manufacturing facilities, was big enough to trigger awe even among South Carolinians.[20] Georgia offered many of the amenities that South Carolina did, and Atlanta was emerging as an increasingly cosmopolitan international business center and the leading transportation hub for the entire Southeast.

The competition continued to intensify throughout the 1980s. By the early 1990s an AP reporter viewed the new industrial landscape as a contemporary battlefield that could determine the future of the entire country. "The first war between the states was fought at Manassas, Gettysburg, Vicksburg, and Shenandoah. The New Civil War battlefields have a similar ring: Spartanburg, Indianapolis, Arlington, Ypsilanti, Hoffman Estates," the writer observed: "This is a war—but it's a war fought with incentives, not bullets. A war waged over taxes, not territory."[21] Southern governors had pioneered the concept of governor as a salesman and international recruiter, but by the 1980s the rest of the nation had caught up with the South. A study of state-of-the-state addresses by thirty governors showed that economic development, including international recruitment, was the leading subject of their more recent orations.[22] In 1970 only four states had overseas offices; in 1990 forty-three states operated 163 industrial recruiting offices abroad.[23]

In various state capitals across the nation, the escalating size and significance of foreign direct investments translated into growing willingness to offer incentives. U.S. and foreign corporations alike began to pit states against each other, and companies considering a new location made state officials work hard for every new job and investment dollar they brought in. While the states hustled to put together increasingly generous subsidy packages, companies soon learned to prolong their location decisions until, as Governor Wallace Wilkinson of Kentucky said, "[T]hey were sure they had squeezed every drop of blood out of every turnip."[24]

Throughout the 1960s both South Carolina and Spartanburg officials had largely rejected the notion of offering tax breaks and other concessions, emphasizing publicly the positive business culture and long-term commitment to economic progress over temporary deal sweeteners, such as state-compensated labor.[25] South Carolina and Spartanburg concentrated on companies that were likely to make a long-term commitment to the region. They sought and offered stability, steering away from any that looked like they might be fly-by-night operators or industrial hustlers, which had occasionally managed to con some southern states and communities.[26]

But as the competition for the rapidly growing amounts of capital floating in the international investment markets heated up, the states began to offer

goodies. While subsidies had by no means been absent from southern industrial recruiting efforts in the past, the scale of the offerings now expanded
radically.[27] The competition for foreign corporations saw states offering
increasingly outrageous tax breaks, free land, and other pot sweeteners.
Buildings built on speculation to attract potential industrial immigrants rose
throughout the nation. The smorgasbord included business incubators, community loans for improving factory facilities, donations of free land for corporations, subsidized job training programs, lengthy tax forgiveness arraignments,
and even direct monetary grants. Foreign corporate executives, for their part,
now began to hire industrial location consultants to assist them in milking the
situation to their maximum advantage.[28]

South Carolina had to respond to the increasing competition and changing rules. The state had pioneered a job-training program and used it successfully in individual recruitment efforts, but the job-training program alone
was not enough. By the early 1980s South Carolina was offering industrial
immigrants a variety of perks, including some tax concessions. In 1981 alone
the state's localities issued $271.3 million ($618 million in 2007 dollars) worth
of industrial revenue bonds to finance the creation of new business ventures
around the state. A new tax system allowed corporations to write off corporate
assets, enjoy a moratorium from county property taxes for all new or expanded
manufacturing facilities for up to five years, and receive an exemption from
property taxes for all manufacturing inventories.[29]

Foreign trade zone status, granted to Spartanburg by the U.S. Department
of Commerce in 1978, further reduced the tax load of Spartanburg-bound foreign corporations. The foreign trade zone designation allowed the customs-
free transfer, storage, assembly, and exhibition of international goods. The
zone, located in eastern Spartanburg County, close to the township of Greer,
marked a substantial incentive and improvement for international industrial
production, supporting Spartanburg's efforts to market itself as a growing
center for international production and trade, not just as a stepping stone to
the U.S. and southern markets.[30]

These new incentives worked in conjunction with the factors that had
always made Spartanburg an attractive place to locate, the supply and cost
of labor, stable government, and livability of the community.[31] Spartanburg's
most effective attraction was structural and, considering the community's
rapid advances, surprisingly persistent. Regardless of the rapid growth of
the town's population and its substantial economic progress, the labor in
Spartanburg continued to offer potential employers their dream trifecta:

Spartanburg's workers were relatively skilled, not prone to unionization, and inexpensive.

In the early and mid-1960s, at the dawn of international recruiting in Spartanburg, the wages and fringe benefits in Spartanburg and Greenville were low even by southern standards. In general, workers in the Greenville-Spartanburg area earned less, worked longer hours, and received fewer paid holidays and vacation days than their colleagues elsewhere in the South.[32] The wage differentials were the largest in low-paid, low-skill positions, but as the comparison moved up the administrative and professional ladder, the differences between the Greenville-Spartanburg area and the rest of the nation shrank, making the region very attractive for the management and ownership in charge of the location decision.[33]

Low wages in Spartanburg proved to be a persistent characteristic of the town's labor market. Despite the town's rapid economic advances and well-publicized industrial expansion, the declining textile employment and effective labor-cost management through antiunionism had kept local wage rates down. In 1969 Spartanburg's per capita annual income of $2,969 ($16,787 in 2007 dollars) was well below the national average of $3,813 ($21,559). Even after two decades of intense international recruiting, rapid growth, and well-publicized industrial progress, local wages continued to lag far behind the national averages. In 1989 the town's per capita annual income had reached $14,597 ($24,407), but the nation's per capita average had climbed up to $17,690 ($29,570).[34] In other words, despite all its progress, Spartanburg's wage rates had not caught up, or even substantially narrowed the gap, with the national averages. Even more significant was that in the late 1980s and the early 1990s, total personal income in the Greenville-Spartanburg axis grew more slowly than in most other parts of South Carolina, including Charleston, Columbia, and Sumter, even Florence. The Greenville-Spartanburg area's income growth rates were even slower than the state's nonmetro averages.[35] Apparently, the service- and tourism-centered counties of the coastal lowlands had outperformed the industrial Piedmont.

Low wages and suave salesmanship helped Spartanburg to maintain its economy's rapid pace of internationalization. Despite the growing competition, Spartanburg continued to attract a disproportionate share of the South- and South Carolina–bound foreign corporations. Between 1975 and 1990 Spartanburg pulled in at least fifty-three foreign corporations, with their home bases stretching from Canada to Mexico and Sweden to Taiwan.[36] Foreign corporations became a natural part of Spartanburg's economy and cultural landscape. Considering the ominous predictions about the future of U.S.

textile industries, foreign companies sometimes seemed more rooted in the community than some of its barely surviving homegrown textile factories.

While the Greater Spartanburg Area Chamber of Commerce, Spartanburg Development Association, and private citizens and corporations with vested interests in the process were busily recruiting foreign corporations and celebrating the community's successes, a more ominous understanding of globalization continued to spread among the town's textile workers and executives. The textile industry in Spartanburg was battling for its life. Since the 1950s the textile executives had occasionally predicted gloom and doom, warning that the industry might not survive in Spartanburg. By the late 1970s locals began to sense that these predictions were uncomfortably accurate. What had originally been a largely propagandistic tool to gain more federal protection and other favors was now becoming a self-fulfilling prophecy.

After the last sustained boom of the mid-1960s, the textile mills had begun to fail. The first to go were the old smokestack factories—outdated family mills that mostly produced equally antiquated coarse cloth. Locals were accustomed to the cyclical nature of the textile business, but this time the virus of failure did not seem to stop after killing the weak and the old. The economic germ started to bring down even modernized, reasonably well-managed companies. Clifton Mills, a local institution, changed owners in the 1960s, then closed in 1971. Butte Knitting Mills, an immensely successful maker of double-knit leisure suits, collapsed spectacularly during the latter half of the 1970s. Draper, a huge textile machinery manufacturer, ran into trouble in the same period, finally closing in the 1990s.[37] In most of the surviving factories the latest technology emptied the production halls of most of their remaining workers.

Spartanburg's textile workforce reacted to the failures by blaming foreign competition and the lack of effective federal protection. During the early 1980s the protectionist impulse began to regain some traction in the town. Sentiments of economic nationalism had periodically swept the textile regions, ascending and descending to the rhythms of the textile business cycles. Protectionism in Spartanburg, much like in the rest of the nation, had remained for the most part a reactionary and emotional movement, providing a largely verbal outlet for the growing fears of the textile workers.

By the 1980s the failures of Spartanburg's historical textile corporations caused textile interests to turn their grumbling into action. The campaign was national, but it received the most attention throughout the old textile regions, from nearly all groups involved with the textile industries. In

Spartanburg the movement united the factory owners and their workers and pitted them against U.S. retailers, the determined antiprotectionists occupying the White House, and all competing textile countries and companies around the globe.

The textile industry has traditionally been among the most protected industries in the United States. Its wide geographic reach, large labor pool, and historical importance to the U.S. economy had made textiles a powerful player in state legislatures and Washington, D.C., alike.[38] Members of Congress from the textile states, especially Georgia and both Carolinas, had often joined forces across party lines in defending the interests of their most important industry.[39] This well-organized and skilled protectionist machine was now put to a serious test. In the 1980s the battle over imports and protectionism geared up for what many viewed as the decisive round of textile trade negotiations. The result was widely expected to determine the future of the entire industry in the United States.

In 1980 Ronald Reagan had won the South Carolina Republican primary by making generous promises to protect the state's main industry. Writing to Senator Strom Thurmond in 1980, Reagan had acknowledged the importance of "2.3 million vitally needed American jobs" that textile, apparel, and textile-related fiber manufacturing provided and promised that he would "make sure that these jobs remain in this country."[40] Reagan's message of competitive capitalism and deregulation, mixed with a commitment to protectionism for textiles, was exactly what the textile regions wanted to hear. South Carolina and, especially, Spartanburg went for Reagan in both the Republican primary and the general election.

By 1980, according to textile industry representatives, foreign cotton and wool textiles and apparel had captured 25 percent of domestic U.S. consumer markets, with no slowing of the trend in sight.[41] In a later study American textile interests claimed that textile and apparel imports to the United States grew from 4.8 billion square yards in 1980 to 10.2 billion in 1984.[42] The imports were destroying their industry, textile people declared. In 1983 textile manufacturers, politicians from the leading textile states, many citizens of the textile-producing regions, and textile unions got together to fight the evils of Asian competition, claiming that the Chinese were illegally subsidizing their textiles and shipping their finished products to U.S. markets. Now they demanded Reagan take quick and decisive action.[43]

The industry wanted to cash in on Reagan's textile pledge. To prevent Chinese "dumping" and to exercise better control of the quantity of the imports, the Reagan administration agreed to a careful monitoring of the imports and promised to impose automatic quotas in the case of sudden import surges from underdeveloped countries.[44] Textiles, happy with the White House's cooperation, interpreted the deal as a modest victory and an opening for future concessions. Industry leaders, textile state politicians, and labor unions began a spirited, multifront assault on imports that was aimed at both Washington politicians and U.S. consumers nationally.

In a peculiar political twist of self-interest and conflicting loyalties, in Spartanburg the organized movement for implementing protectionist measures was led largely by Roger Milliken. By the 1980s Milliken, the same man who was largely responsible for the arrival of the first foreign companies in Spartanburg and a noted customer of foreign machinery, began to direct his considerable resources, energies, and organizational talent toward pumping new life into the protectionist movement. Milliken had a long history of both open and clandestine involvement in protectionist movements. Strong rumors and several journalists had connected him and his wallet with protectionist-minded lobbying of politicians throughout his career.[45] By the mid-1980s Milliken was being open about his lobbying campaigns, giving the movement in South Carolina a surprising face: his own.

The contradiction between Milliken the importer of textile machinery and Milliken the textile protectionist had not escaped the Spartans.[46] Some locals had pointed out the inconsistency of his behavior since he had first started buying machinery in Europe in the early sixties. Milliken had systematically defended his machinery purchases as regrettable exceptions to his patriotic consumption habits, necessitated by foreign competition and by the superior quality of the European machinery.[47] As the barriers to trade tumbled, Milliken grew increasingly adept at both resisting and adapting to globalization, often simultaneously. His remarkable ability to equate self-interest with a rhetoric of justice resonated positively with Spartanburg's workers and politicians alike, as they gathered the legions behind Milliken's leadership.

Milliken had continued to buy foreign machinery and expand his operations internationally, while he simultaneously intensified his protectionist campaigns.[48] In 1984 Milliken and other textile men from various branches of the industry created a national publicity and marketing campaign, "Crafted with Pride in the U.S.A.," designed to stir the patriotic feelings of American consumers and encourage U.S. retailers to buy from American manufacturers.[49] The campaign had an operating budget of $11 million and Bob Hope, Diahann Carroll, and Don Johnson among its highly visible spokespersons. It used interviews and TV and radio advertising to deliver its message to the American public.[50] In Washington, D.C., "Crafted with Pride in the U.S.A."

became a political organization lobbying for textile protectionism. At home Milliken, a devout recluse, suddenly grew eager to spread his protectionist message through media.

Milliken spoke in ideological, even historical, terms. The survival of American civilization was linked to the survival of American textiles, Milliken preached to the people of Spartanburg, drawing dramatically ominous comparisons between the United States in the 1980s and the declining Spanish Empire of the sixteenth century. To secure the future of the United States, Milliken wanted to reject "the entire free-trade dogma which conditions Americans to accept the decline of our manufacturing sector as a natural process in the evolution of economic system which should not be rejected."[51] For him, free trade was a "God no other nation worships," and blind obedience to it meant that the practical economic nationalists of the Far East were likely to succeed where the Communists in the Kremlin had failed. [52]

The protectionist campaign made Milliken, a vicious opponent of unionization, a peculiar local hero for Spartanburg's textile workers. They aligned themselves behind the Crafted with Pride campaign, with thousands donating money, refusing to buy foreign textiles, and promising to patronize the stores that carried only U.S.-made apparel. Milliken's aggressive protectionism resonated among people who had either lost or were in danger of losing their textile jobs to foreign competition. Support for Milliken appeared in editorials and letters to the editor alike, lavishing high praise on his integrity and leadership against the attempts to kill the U.S. textile industry by the economic traitors from Washington, D.C.[53]

In the end the campaign failed. The campaign to recognize and patronize the retailers of U.S.-made goods, the television commercials, the protests in Spartanburg's Morgan Square, the textile workers' letter-writing campaign to President Reagan, the fierce lobbying by Spartanburg and South Carolina elected officials, and the unified front of workers, textile bosses, and labor unions were not enough.[54] Having won reelection and secured the support of the textile region with the 1983–84 moves against Chinese textiles, President Reagan and his economic advisers were increasingly hesitant to grant the industry new favors. From the White House's perspective protectionism was both ideologically wrong and unnecessary for the industry—it appeared that the production of textiles was doing just fine, even if textile employment was not.[55] The Reagan administration found little political or coherent ideological reasons to expand, or even extend, the federal protection for American textiles at a time when antiprotectionism was increasingly popular in the United States.[56] In 1986 Reagan vetoed a bill that would have limited textile imports and Congress failed to override, signaling the futility of relying on federal protection as the rescuer of technologically obsolete jobs.[57]

Indeed, Reagan was right: the U.S. textiles industry had not only survived but had actually grown between 1950 and 1990. During the 1960s it had increased its output by 43 percent.[58] For most of the 1970s and 1980s textile production grew at an average annual rate of 0.45 percent, while the annual production growth rate for apparel industries had passed 1 percent. The production growth rates were nowhere near the boom of the 1960s, but it was growth nonetheless.[59] The true villain behind declining textile employment was the industry's own technical effectiveness, made in large part possible by technology that Milliken himself had been buying overseas since the late 1950s.

By the late 1980s the point was rapidly becoming moot. Textile jobs, and many of the old textile companies, were largely gone. The remaining textile factories continued to hum quietly along, operating in almost empty production halls, attended by quiet lab-coated technicians who paced between unattended, automated machines. The textile monoculture in industrial Spartanburg was gone.

Milliken continued to rally Spartans for the periodic campaigns against the General Agreement on Tariffs and Trade, the North American Free Trade Agreement, and other laws and organizations aimed at promoting free trade, but the gestures looked increasingly symbolic.[60] Textiles survived, but the textile jobs were all but gone, the factory whistle permanently silenced. Spartanburg continued to be a textile town, but the textiles were separated from their makers and, increasingly, from the community. A steady stream of trucks continued to enter and leave the new, sleek industrial buildings, but small parking lots, the absence of people, and the strange silence surrounding the factory buildings were a striking contrast to the textile town of yore.

The decline of textiles forced Spartanburg's leaders to rethink the character of the entire community. From the disappearing mill villages to the demolition of the old factory buildings, from the steady erosion of textile jobs to the bankruptcies of Spartanburg's industrial stalwarts, Spartanburg's traditional textile culture had both crawled and leaped toward its own demise.

For decades, the leaders of Spartanburg had promoted a very organic understanding of local citizens' relationship with their city. They had sold the community to outsiders and townspeople as a place with a soul, a good investment for the money and heart alike. The character of Spartanburg was linked to its industries and its people. To increase its value, town leaders had for decades worked to turn both the physical appearance of the community and its self-image around with endless urban renewal projects, community pride campaigns, and neighborhood involvement programs.[61] Now the town had to redefine its identity and character to correspond with its changing economic realities.

Perhaps the biggest postwar challenge had been changing the community's self-image. A town historically dominated by social division between mill and town; broken geographically into mill villages; divided by class, race, and culture, Spartanburg after World War II had willed itself into a new, more consensus-oriented community.[62] The project had largely succeeded, as the mill people had integrated with the townspeople. Now, with the decline of textiles, the community had to transform its character again, preparing for a new industrial culture or, perhaps, even for a postindustrial existence.

The town had arduously transformed its public image. The gospel of planning and civic education had begun to bear fruit in the late 1950s, as the town's mayor, Neville Holcombe, celebrated its new image: "[O]ur community spirit has changed. We are beginning to think [of] Spartanburg as the fine city it is."[63] Dick Tukey had also noticed a substantial improvement in Spartanburg's self-perception: "When I came here 12 years ago, it hit me between the eyes. There was a negative community attitude in many regards. A community has a personality and a community can be sick. It has to be administered just as a person who is sick must be attended."[64]

Spartanburg's success and marketability depended on its infrastructure and an improved sense of community and internal cohesion. Starting from the end of World War II, Spartanburg's leaders had repeated the mantra of unity and conflict avoidance to the town's bosses and workers alike. After decades of proselytizing, the message finally sank in. The old paternalism of mills and mill villages slowly evolved into the carefully marketed image of participation, team work, and community cohesion, which promised prosperity for every individual and social class.[65] The unspoken subtext was that if workers resisted unionization and did their part in maintaining a positive business climate, industrial immigration would continue.[66] By cooperating with the community and the corporate vision of an orderly Spartanburg, workers would have jobs, better schools, and neighborhood improvement programs.

Urban renewal in particular became an ideological touchstone for Spartanburg. Since the days of mill villages, waves of urban beautification and downtown revamping had periodically washed Morgan Square, the rest of the downtown, and the surrounding neighborhoods, especially those most visible to visitors.[67] Urban renewal and infrastructure improvements offered effective ways to enforce the sense of community, improve the town's marketability, and help struggling downtown retail businesses. Additionally, investment in libraries, concert halls, and other public spaces helped to convey an image of urban sophistication and intellectual growth, as the community sought to become a more modern industrial town, suited for the postindustrial future of the nation and the region.

The community was in large part built and rebuilt with private money. Spartanburg had a long tradition of philanthropy. College and hospital buildings carried the names of the community's leading industrial families, old and new alike. The level of giving and commitment to noblesse oblige was one of the leading determinants of an industrial leader's position in the community. With the decline of textiles, urban renewal and generous giving to the public good gained more urgency. Community leaders donated money and their administrative skills to the town. Dick Tukey worked to land for Spartanburg a campus of the University of South Carolina and helped to launch a local public television station, which took his initials, as its call letters. WRET 49 finally went on air in September 1980, a year after Tukey's death. And, partly as a result of Tukey's efforts, a small, local nursing school became a four-year college, part of the University of South Carolina system, in 1975.[68]

In the 1960s Spartanburg's leaders also began to emphasize more structural renewal of the entire city. Urban renewal became an essential part of its campaign to recruit the "right type" of industries.[69] As the chamber of commerce and city officials saw it, renovating the city's dilapidated ghettoes and revitalizing its sagging downtown were mandatory. The marketplace—not even benevolent capitalism—was not enough to solve the infrastructure problems plaguing the community.

Since the 1950s Spartanburg had been afflicted by the problem of "creeping slums," often created by a mix of bad zoning practices and inadequate public facilities.[70] City officials were also becoming actively concerned about the visible deterioration of downtown buildings and economic hardships faced by long-time businesses. In 1957 the City Planning Commission had called for hiring a planner to address Spartanburg's infrastructure problems, which were threatening to become very real economic difficulties for the downtown and eventually would hurt Spartanburg's recruiting efforts and economic development. Tukey and the chamber of commerce repeatedly emphasized the connection between urban renewal and economic success.[71]

After decades of periodic efforts to pump life and economic vitality in the downtown through market mechanisms and minor aid programs, by 1967 Spartanburg was ready to search for nonmarket solutions for the downtown's problems by seeking federal assistance for a substantial rebuilding project. The chamber of commerce, local media, and Spartanburg's leadership committed to meeting federal requirements, even if that meant giving up some of their cherished local control.[72] In November 1966 local voters approved a referendum that gave city officials the right to condemn private properties and sell them to private developers if that meant that its future use would be more beneficial to the community than what the long-time owner envisioned.[73] When the progress of the community was at stake, the sanctity of private property was a secondary consideration.

Decade after decade waves of urban renewal and downtown redevelopment continued to periodically emerge and shake Spartanburg.[74] Downtown redevelopment was but one aspect of Spartanburg's urban renewal frenzy, tied closely, if not fused, to industrial recruitment.[75] From labor to lifestyle Spartanburg had sold itself to industrial investors. Eradication of the town's ghettoes was a gesture of benevolent paternalism. Improving local housing and polishing Spartanburg's commercial venues provided clear evidence of progress for established residents and newcomers alike.

As the old textile culture and economy disappeared, Spartanburg had to readjust its recruiting strategy to correspond with its physical transformation. By the 1980s the focus on attracting some supporting industries for the town's textile mills had outlived its usefulness. The town had to be rebuilt physically and mentally. It needed new, larger, and completely nontextile-related companies to secure its future. Coincidentally, this saving grace was to be found abroad as well.

Persistence of Place

The growth in Spartanburg was a potentially challenging, even dangerous, development for the county's boosters and employers. Spartanburg's economic leadership had approached the growth as it had almost every other aspect of the community's life: by planning and careful presentation. The town had sought development but not at any price. Spartanburg had witnessed its neighbor and rival, Greenville, grow and bypass Spartanburg in size, with no apparent concern. Spartanburg's leadership had been content with its own pace of growth, demonstrating no desire to risk its carefully constructed and maintained position with a reckless pursuit of expansion. Growth was good, but control and familiarity were better.[1]

Spartanburg's newspapers greeted their neighbor's progress largely without visible envy. Local media and other commentators celebrated their own hometown's sense of community. Ever since the end of World War II, the Spartanburg papers, chamber of commerce, and a loose coalition of numerous community activists and business leaders had attempted to transplant the sense of community from the organic, close-knit mill villages to the entire town of Spartanburg.[2] They defended the town's sense of community, basing their approach at least partially on an emotional foundation, but maintaining their idea of communal spirit and character carried clear and undeniable economic benefits for Spartanburg's elite.

Nonetheless, steady growth arrived. According to the 1990 census, Spartanburg County's population had grown to 226,800.[3] The growth had translated into substantial improvements in the town's urban character and soft-factor marketability through improved schools and a growing variety of services, but the growth posed challenges for the people determined to maintain the community's wage structures and its competitiveness as an industrial relocation site. The ambivalence toward the change and concern about the challenges associated with the growth did not go unnoticed by prospective relocators. "The city fathers are afraid they're going to become an Atlanta. And then again, they're afraid that they're not," as one relocated observer commented.[4]

Throughout most of its history, southern manufacturing has been a labor-intensive operation, characterized by low profit margins and a lack of technological sophistication. To succeed requires a labor force willing to work for low wages, which has traditionally discouraged companies from locating in the region's larger cities, with their higher wages and more intense competition for skilled labor.[5] The South Carolina Piedmont's industrial textile monoculture had defined much, if not most, of the South's industrial character. Its string of small towns and proximity to Appalachia meant a steady supply of potential mill hands willing to work for low wages.

For those who had shaped Spartanburg, an important element of Spartanburg's success had been its ability to grow in size and influence without changing its small-town identity and economic culture, which included tightly controlled wages. Despite the carefully promoted impression of stunning economic progress with benefits to all, Spartanburg's blue-collar workers did not witness a particularly rapid economic advancement. Their wages grew, but when compared to national or even state-level statistics, the growth of wages in Spartanburg was not all that impressive, keeping roughly at par with the general development in the state and the nation. Nationally, the average hourly wage was $6.83 in 1979, whereas it was $5.34 in South Carolina, and $5.35 in Spartanburg. By 1989 the average hourly wage in the United States was $10.33; in South Carolina it was $8.51, and in Spartanburg it was $8.34.[6] Tourism, services, the knowledge industry, and other growth sectors seemed to provide growth and benefits nearly at par with the state's old industries. Some scholars had predicted the transformation, suggesting that maintaining growth in the South was not possible without substantial improvements in the quality of the region's labor force.[7]

The standard macroeconomic factors, such as scarcity or surplus in the community's labor markets, could explain Spartanburg's wage developments only partially. Textile employment in the town had started its steady decline in the mid-1960s, with the mills releasing approximately 10,000 workers between 1966 and 1990.[8] Employment in the apparel industry peaked in 1972, with 6,612 Spartans working in the industry, but by 1990 that number had declined to 2,500.[9] The new factories and other employers were in a position to handpick motivated, eager staffers from the large pool of laid-off textile workers and custom-trained young applicants coming out of Spartanburg's Technical Education Center.

However, despite the high number of laid-off textile workers, throughout the 1980s unemployment rates in Spartanburg were lower than they were statewide. Among South Carolina Piedmont counties in the path of Interstate

85, Spartanburg's unemployment rates were the second lowest, trailing only its booming neighbor, Greenville.[10] Local labor markets were not saturated.

Much of the reason for Spartanburg's wage structures was careful management. Spartanburg's leadership had wrapped its antiunionism in the rhetorical clothes of tradition, orderliness, growth, teamwork, and community spirit. The public language of the community's economic and political elites was filled with appeals to avoid conflict and work toward the mutual goals of a harmonious community, bourgeois prosperity, and a good life that, they said, characterized the values of Spartanburg's bosses and workers alike. Although the culture of harmony and consensus was often real and tangible for Spartanburg residents, those promoting it were the elite, and Spartanburg's workers had little to say about it, especially in the matter of wages. While a new and promising method of securing industrial peace, labor-management cooperation committees, gained popularity throughout the Midwest and Northeast, discussions about the future of Spartanburg took place almost exclusively within managerial circles.[11]

Local corporations carefully maintained the traditional individualistic, direct relationship between staff and managers. The same emphasis on the individuality of each worker, simultaneously a tool of control and an acknowledgment of regional culture, continued to describe Spartanburg's employer-employee relations. Incoming foreign corporations rapidly learned to share local managers' appreciation for direct interaction between the company and its labor force, untarnished and uncomplicated by the presence of a third party—the union.[12]

From Hoechst to Michelin individualized personnel management and paternalistic labor relations had been a soft sell. François Michelin, the leader and visionary behind the company's growth and expansion to Carolina, opposed unionization with Milliken-like rigor and principle-driven conviction. Demonstrating paternalistic skills that would have made old Spartanburg textile patrons of the past nod in approval, Michelin tied some of the company's benefits, such as company-provided housing for employees, to their abstinence from union activities. Michelin refused to even acknowledge the unions or admit their legitimacy by negotiating with union representatives.[13]

Their dislike of labor unions aside, Spartanburg's corporations, including recent European immigrants, wasted little time in organizing themselves into tightly knit and powerful industrial associations. The community's economic leadership was actively united in defining and defending Spartanburg's economic character, including its wages and labor climate. In the mid-1970s the velvet fist of the antiunion Spartanburg Development Association had begun to receive help in managing the labor community from the Spartanburg Area Personnel Association, a grouping of local businesses created to promote a "better understanding among companies with the same 'people needs.'"[14] The monthly meetings of the association allowed corporations to exchange information about trends in pay, benefits, and other important developments in local labor markets.[15]

Spartanburg's international corporations became willing participants in the personnel association. Within a year of its founding many of Spartanburg's largest and most valued industrial immigrants had become members. Hoechst and Michelin were accompanied by smaller but regionally important companies, such as Sulzer, Hergeth, Tietex, and numerous others, which seized the opportunity to share information and learn from the more rooted Spartanburg businesses.[16] The organization helped the newcomers to save money by synchronizing their pay scales with local standards, and the newcomers earned important goodwill and cooperation from the community's more established corporations, even as they avoided triggering more intense competition for workers in the region.

The Spartanburg Development Association continued to exert powerful influence over the community's industrial recruiting and immigration. Local news and rumors had either credited or blamed the organization for successfully blocking the entry of several unionized corporations that had considered starting operations in Spartanburg County. The list of companies that the association supposedly had headed off at the pass included Mazda, Ford Motor Company, and Philip Morris. These companies would have brought higher wages, which would have triggered more competition for labor by local textile mills and other long-established corporations, and the arrival of unionized corporations, especially the auto manufacturers, would have brought an unwanted transformation in the community. As one Spartanburg Development Association official, in a rare moment of openness, confessed: "It is our considered view that the Mazda plant would have a long-term chilling effect on Spartanburg's orderly industrial growth. An auto plant, employing over 3,000 card-carrying, hymn-singing members of the UAW would, in our opinion, bring to an abrupt halt future desirable industrial prospects."[17]

The development association's possible clandestine schemes aside, Spartanburg's open, well-publicized, and determined opposition to unions has been an essential facet of the community's economic character and its industrial recruiting strategies for decades. The City of Spartanburg tied subsidies for incoming companies to a no-union pledge.[18] The op-ed pages of the *Spartanburg Herald* often featured essays in which high-profile members of the local business elite promoted their vision for Spartanburg's economic future.[19] Local bosses were not free from pressures either. One employer said that he was not dealing with the union, because, if he did, he "would wind up in a chain gang" for his violation of local labor practices.[20]

The culmination of Spartanburg's internationalization was the community's successful recruitment of the German automotive giant Bayerische Motoren Werke, better known as BMW, in the early 1990s. Landing BMW had been a multination, multistate competition, in which the pursuers pulled out all the stops in their recruitment of the company. An entire recruiting industry grew up around enticing BMW, with chambers of commerce and state-level politicians and public officials investing millions of dollars and thousands of hours of labor to secure the company, which expected to invest about $600 million, provide two thousand to three thousand jobs, and attract a large number of supporting industries and very impressive potential for further growth.[21]

When BMW first decided to open a new factory outside Germany, it began its location hunt with a list of 250 communities around the world. Through the process of elimination BMW eventually decided that its factory should be located in North America, which offered enormously profitable markets for expensive and sporty automobiles. The size of the markets, political stability, opportunity to reduce the effects of potentially dangerous currency fluctuations, and the skill level of the workforce tilted the scale heavily in favor of North America, even when taking into consideration its higher cost of labor. However, even U.S. labor costs were lower than those in Germany, a country known for its generous benefits, large and powerful unions, five-week summer vacations, and high wages. In the early 1990s Eberhard von Kuenheim, BMW's chairman, estimated that production costs for the company's automobiles in the United States would be roughly 30 percent lower than back home.[22]

As the company narrowed its list of potential host communities, Georgia, Nebraska, and both Carolinas made the cut. The rules of the game were familiar, but the stakes were unlike anything that the competitors had ever seen before. The states tempted the Bavarian executives with enormous incentive packages, almost running ahead of BMW itself in trying to guess what the company might need or want next. Any community determined to catch BMW had to be prepared to spend more than $300 million in tax breaks, free land, and a host of other incentives. The cost of the lobbying operation itself proved substantial, as the competing communities were spending millions of dollars in travel, sales pitches, marketing studies, and other recruiting expenses.

As the summer 1992 deadline for the announcement approached, BMW's top choices were Omaha and Spartanburg. Both locations offered substantial tax breaks, free worker training, and other location subsidies worth tens of millions of dollars. Their labor pools were relatively equal in size and skill, both communities' transportation infrastructures suitable for BMW's needs, and their political commitment to business and corporate well-being was unwavering. The jockeying continued up to the deadline. Less than a week before BMW's announcement, the South Carolina Ports Authority sweetened the Spartanburg package by announcing that it planned to spend $5 million to develop the BMW plant site and its adjacent hundred-acre foreign trade zone.[23]

Finally, on June 23, 1992, BMW announced it would be building its new plant in Spartanburg. The reaction was emotional, for a variety of reasons. For tens of thousands of cheering locals, including those who would not benefit directly from the new factory, the decision signaled that Spartanburg had arrived. Whereas previously BMW had trusted foreign labor only to build components that the company's Bavarian workers would assemble into complete vehicles, the enormous factory in Spartanburg would be the quality-conscious company's first facility outside Germany to produce entire automobiles. BMW's location choice meant not only thousands of jobs and millions of dollars in anticipated annual revenue for the community; it also became a powerful symbol of faith in and approval of the new Spartanburg, a community that had now shed the last remnants of its old character and reputation as a low-tech town known largely for its semiskilled labor and coarse textiles.

Just two decades earlier no one would even have imagined that a high-end German automobile company might build a factory in Spartanburg. The rapid internationalization of the community, the global perspective of its leadership, the town's solid ties to the European business community, the quality and quantity of its workers, and the affectionate relations between the community and its industrial inhabitants had made this coup possible. The arrival of BMW not only signaled better times and economic survival for the future. It also offered a validation of the past, a justification for the community's transformation efforts, and an opportunity for its economic leaders to congratulate themselves for their wise and benevolent stewardship of the community.

Quality-conscious BMW's confidence in the ability of Spartanburg's workers to launch new models and experiment with new production methods was a thrilling development for the Spartans. Whereas Japanese auto manufacturers located in the United States were building only models that had first been assembled in Japan and tested with Japanese staff, BMW's factory in Spartanburg was going to produce brand new models, designed and built especially for U.S. consumers. During only the second year of its operations, Spartanburg's BMW factory started exporting and selling Spartanburg-made vehicles to European and Japanese customers. Additionally, just-in-time parts delivery, entrusted to BMW's U.S. and South Carolina subcontractors, marked a clear departure from the experiences of foreign auto manufacturers who had previously built factories in the United States. Bold experimentation with new modes of production formed an essential part of the Spartanburg factory's assignment.[24]

Perhaps most important, BMW's decision was the crowning achievement of the international recruitment operations of both Spartanburg and South Carolina. Landing BMW had required the talent and resources of both the state and the town. Their efforts were based on the old Tukey doctrine of offering fiscal sanity and Spartanburg's winning combination of Yankee hustle and southern gentility. This time, however, the interstate competition had required deal-sweetening subsidies that were beyond the wildest dreams of any industrial recruiter of yore.

During the years of competition the states on BMW's list were engaged in massive lobbying blitzes run by operative shock troops of governors, members of Congress, community leaders, and professional recruiting specialists, usually operating in perfect bipartisan, nonideological harmony.[25] South Carolina governor Carroll A. Campbell, a Republican, spearheaded the two-year recruiting campaign, receiving support from the state's senators Fritz Hollings, a Democrat, and Republican Strom Thurmond. Public officials from Spartanburg to Columbia and Charleston participated. Spartanburg's business elite, true to its well-established modus operandi, contributed as well; its starting lineup included several of Spartanburg's Germans, starting with the retired Hoechst executive Paul Foerster. Roger Milliken lent his personal airplane to the recruiting campaign.[26]

According to Robert M. Ady, president of PHH Fantus, an international business location consulting firm hired by BMW to help it pick the right location, the fast response of Spartanburg and South Carolina to BMW's requests and their "rare flexibility" were essential factors in the location decision.[27] Early estimates placed the state's incentive package at $145 million, including $30 million to buy and prepare the land for the factory, $10 million for road improvement projects around the plant site, subsidized office space in Spartanburg and Greenville, a multimillion-dollar expansion of the Greenville-Spartanburg airport to make it capable of accommodating Boeing 747 jets, and even fifty-five free apartments in Spartanburg and Greenville for BMW's use. Additional breaks on water and sewer costs would save the company $50 million in the factory's first two decades.[28]

That flexibility included the creation of a suitable eleven-hundred-acre lot for the factory. The Spartanburg site was put together from 130 separate pieces of property. Within four weeks Governor Campbell had arranged for the state to purchase the properties. And as soon as the Germans announced that the plant would be built in Spartanburg, the state had began work on a four-lane access road between the factory site and Interstate 85, completing the project well ahead of the initial construction schedule.[29]

Subsidies aside, in the end the most important reason for choosing Spartanburg, Ady declared, was the community's labor force. The community's oldest recruiting tool continued to be its most effective. The technical training program, flexible and carefully tailored to suit BMW's needs, offered an abundant supply of trained labor to feed the factory, even in the case of the factory's substantial expansion.[30] Also, the "harmonious relationships" between companies and their workers that BMW and its consultant, PHH Fantus, found in the region played a substantial role in the location decision, Ady said.[31] Attracted by regionally competitive wages and expectations of job stability, roughly eighty thousand applicants were soon lining up for the fifteen hundred jobs in the new factory.[32]

But the jobs at the BMW plant were not the only jobs that the deal brought to Spartanburg. Some early estimates said that the subcontractors that followed BMW into the region were bringing as many as four thousand new positions and almost $1 billion in investment.[33] In 1998, in response to the market success of the factory's Z3 model and corporate plans to expand the factory's product line, BMW announced the construction of a $600 million expansion to the factory, which increased the size of its workforce to three thousand.[34] Two years later the car maker added another $300 million expansion with five hundred new jobs, pushing the total value of BMW's investment in Spartanburg to the neighborhood of $1.7 billion.[35]

BMW contributed heavily to the economy of Spartanburg and the entire South Carolina Piedmont through wages and indirect tax income, but its direct tax contributions proved to be spotty. Through the end of 2000, BMW had never paid income tax in South Carolina. During its first eight years in Spartanburg, the company contributed $5.1 million in user fees; $35.5 million in county property taxes, of which $30.3 million went to Spartanburg County; and $221.8 million in U.S. import taxes.[36] The state of South Carolina, the biggest contributor to the recruiting subsidies, got nothing.

By the 1990s Spartanburg had effectively modernized and internationalized its economy. The arrival of BMW had capped the town's recruiting efforts with an exclamation mark. Over the years foreign corporations and their international staffs had established themselves as practically inseparable elements of Spartanburg's culture and economy. BMW's continuously expanding factory in western Spartanburg County symbolized the irreversibility of the internationalization for thousands of locals. The mere size of the operation gave it an aura of permanency, almost immediately rooting it deeper into Spartanburg County's soil than many of its older, but vulnerable and visibly struggling, textile interests.

Perhaps the most telling symbol of the maturation of Spartanburg's international economy was the nonchalant attitude that locals displayed toward BMW's nationality. The excitement at the auto manufacturer's location decision was largely focused on its size and economic impact. The romanticism associated with foreign executives and globalization during the earlier decades had given way to a matter-of-fact understanding of the nature of the contemporary global economy. The earlier combination of local excitement at progress and scattered, remote scholarly concerns about the survival of the regional culture and economy had been replaced by more resigned and tacit acceptance of the new economic and cultural characteristics of the region.

The South Carolina Piedmont and Spartanburg offer an almost caricaturized reflection of much of the South's experiences in the global economy. When foreigners began to arrive, Spartanburg already had a long tradition of industrial immigration. It was accustomed to affluent newcomers with noticeable sway in the community's affairs. The town had been less of a colony for external economic interests than a willing participant in selling itself to the highest bidder, who was then carefully incorporated into the community. Now Spartanburg was in the progressive forefront, adding more modern global economic affiliations to its long-time close relationships with northern economic interests.

Gavin Wright has famously described the impact of globalization in the South by pointing out how the contemporary South is "not a colony to any other geographic region, but to placeless global organizations and markets."[37] The observation makes very good sense. Yet the South has also demonstrated remarkable ability to shape and influence the terms of its interaction with the world. The Spartanburg example proves that even in the midst of intense economic transformation, determined political and economic leaders can keep the fundamental characters of their home communities intact. Local southern elites have proved capable of directing globalization's impact upon their communities, making it serve their goals and aspirations. Globalization is not a faceless monolithic force, nor are its economic and cultural effects unavoidable or uncontrollable.

Spartanburg has consciously and successfully recruited foreign corporations. At the same time the town's leadership has effectively defended its industrial character of strict control, fervent antiunionism, and modified paternalism. The town has grown yet maintained its small-town economic character, including carefully controlled wages and a sense of closeness and community. Even more paradoxically, the leadership of the community has simultaneously sought and resisted globalization. Often the same powerful individuals who have fought rigorously against encroaching foreign competition and lowering of trade barriers have played dominant roles in campaigns to recruit foreign corporations. These attitudes have trickled down to the community's workers as well. Families in which one spouse works for Hoechst and the other for Milliken have stood squarely in the middle of the battlefield of globalization, fighting doggedly to both advance and retreat simultaneously. This contradictory, even schizophrenic, attitude has been reflected, fostered, and even partially created by the community's economic and political leadership.

Throughout its history Spartanburg has been an unwavering supporter of business, but its commitment to open capitalism has been more conflicted. The paternalistic traditions of mill village industrialism and boosterism continue to influence its economic culture and value systems, enforcing a noticeably corporatist outlook on the local economy. The community's leadership has sought to maintain a rigorous sense of unity, enforced by old and recurring warnings about external competition and homegrown complacency.[38]

Spartanburg's globalization has not always followed the optimistic celebration of opportunities afforded by an open and competitive society. The capitalism in Spartanburg has not been the idealistic, free-market variation celebrated by Milton Friedman and others. Spartanburg's has been a managed economy, based on planning, executive cohesion, and corporate consensus. The community's leadership has controlled and maintained its best commodity—inexpensive, skilled, and pacified labor—with practices that often correspond to monopolistic or, at least, corporatist principles. Its businesses have fused culturally and often even administratively into a larger economic unit, Spartanburg itself, which treats the community as a large economic project and benevolent fiefdom, with the promise of carefully distributed and appropriate amounts of prosperity and peace for all.

Many economic groups within the community have largely welcomed this corporatist attitude. The unpredictability and creative chaos of competitive capitalism has often been scary to Spartanburg's workers and bosses alike. In the wallets of the community's workforce, Schumpeterian creative destruction has often been more destructive than creative. Still, as demonstrated by the united front of textile workers and bosses during the tariff showdowns, employees have blamed Washington more than their bosses or other local economic and political leaders for their hardships.

In 1971 Daniel R. Fusfeld, a professor of economics at the University of Michigan, described the functioning of a corporate state in a speech to a convention of evolutionary economists:

> The self-selecting elite of the supercorporation dominates the decision-making process, while lesser centers of power in labor unions and the universities are drawn into the system as junior partners by a variety of economic and political mechanisms. . . . The corporate state in this country involves an economic and political compromise between those who hold power and those who do not. As long as the economic system provides an acceptable degree of security, growing material wealth, and opportunity for further increase for the next generation, the average American does not ask who is running things or what goals are being pursued.[39]

His sweeping cynicism aside, the characteristics that Fusfeld assigns to the state and supercorporation, as well as his discussion of the nature of the relationship between the powerful and powerless, can easily be used to describe the situation in Spartanburg. The thinking and attitudes behind the corporatist state, the old government-business contract, enforced by cold war ideology, regulation, and security, never fully left Spartanburg.[40] The words *community* and *business* often seem intertwined in this town. The local economic leadership has replaced the old southern romanticism of "magnolias and moonlight" with the business-Republican romanticism of proper social order, community cohesion, and business progressivism. Spartanburg has been led by what the legal scholar Arthur Selwyn Miller has called a "group-person," namely, a fusion of political and economic powers that "at once transcends the arithmetical sums of its parts, which are the public group of government and the private group of corporations."[41] In Spartanburg the powerful "group-person" is also supported by other important social organizations that have come together to create a powerful alliance for searching for public good and private benefit alike.

Compared with the destinies of dozens of dying textile mill towns throughout the Southern Piedmont, Spartanburg has been a success story. It has faced new challenges head first, expanded its economic playbook, and secured growth and success in the era of industrial transformation and uncertainty. Between 1985 and 1992 Spartanburg, with nearly twenty thousand new jobs, ranked first in job development in South Carolina.[42] The atmosphere of community pride and sense of success are unquestionable, radiating from downtown to suburbia, fancy homes, and even some trailer parks. However, in the working-class neighborhoods the sense of success is perhaps even stronger than the real, quantifiable economic achievements in residents' pocketbooks.

While Spartanburg was far more successful than most other textile communities, comparing Spartanburg's economy with the state's is a more complex matter. In 1977 per-capita income in Spartanburg County was seventh-highest among South Carolina counties. By 1994 its ranking had fallen one spot. The number of poor people in the county has also varied surprisingly little. Between 1979 and 1989 the number of poor in the town of Spartanburg rose by 2.3 percent, from 8,741 to 8,946, while the number of people living below the poverty level in Spartanburg County declined from 27,177 to 26,053. Reflecting national trends, the distribution of income and the representative sizes of different socioeconomic groups have been relatively persistent, except that more cream has gone to the very top economic levels in Spartanburg.[43]

From the perspective of the old working-class neighborhoods and blue-collar hangouts, the change does not look as revolutionary as it does from Interstate 85. The social structure and fundamental economic characteristics of the town have proved to be more resilient and enduring than global economic trends or even the nation's economic policies. The soft humming of the technologically revamped mills and the rhythmic clatter of the tire and car factories have transformed the town's image, but in the streets and neighborhoods, bars, and shopping centers, the change has been limited.

Life in Spartanburg testifies to the strength of the place, persistence of culture, tradition, and established cultural and economic centers. Incoming foreign corporations might have diversified Spartanburg a bit, altering and influencing it with their cultural and economic input, but they lack both the power and the will to change Spartanburg's culture. Observing the shifts in the British postindustrial landscape, Raymond Williams, a British cultural historian and theorist, concluded that "when capital leaves, place remains."[44] Here the capital has arrived and the place remains.

NOTES

Introduction. To the Souths—Both the New and the Latest

1. For an excellent journalistic account on the importance of Interstate 85 to the economic growth of the Southern Piedmont, see Foust and Mallory, "Boom Belt."

2. Milton Friedman, *Free to Choose*, episode 8, "Who Protects the Worker?" (TV series, 1980); Kantner, *World Class*.

3. Woodward, *Origins of the New South*; Carlton, *Mill and Town*.

4. For a good summary of continuity-discontinuity debates in the historiography of the postbellum South, see Beck, "Building the New South," 441–45.

5. For a dated, but nevertheless fascinating, study of South Carolina's Reconstruction-era immigrant recruitment policies, see Moody, "Labor and Immigration Problem."

6. Moody, "Labor and Immigration Problem," 195–98.

7. Ibid., 206.

8. Fink and Reed, *Essays in Southern Labor History*; Fink, Reed, and Hough, *Southern Workers and Their Unions*. For an effective historiographical analysis of the development of new worker-centered labor history, see Brody, "Reconciling."

9. For mill-town relationships in southern textile communities, see Carlton, *Mill and Town*. Fink and Reed, *Race, Class, and Community* also explored the topic in some important essays.

10. For a good study of the colonial South in a heavily global context, see Coclanis, *Shadow of a Dream*. The essays in Stueck and Cobb, *Globalization and the American South*, observe globalization in a more contemporary context. See also the Southern Industrialization Project's collection, edited by Delfino and Gillespie, *Global Perspectives*.

11. See, for example, Stueck and Cobb, *Globalization and the American South*.

Chapter One. A New Game in South Carolina

1. Carlton, *Mill and Town*, 33.

2. *Spartanburg Herald*, June 27, 1945, 4.

3. *Spartanburg Herald*, May 4, 1945, 2; *Spartanburg Herald*, May 8, 1945, 2; *Spartanburg Herald*, May 12, 1945, 2; *Spartanburg Herald*, May 19, 1945, 4; *Spartanburg Herald*, June 20, 1945, 4.

4. *Spartanburg Herald*, May 4, 1945, 2; *Spartanburg Herald*, May 8, 1945, 2; *Spartanburg Herald*, May 12, 1945, 2. For more information about the statewide campaigns of economic reform for post–World War II Carolina, see Calcott, *South Carolina*.

5. U.S. Department of Commerce, *Fifteenth Census of the United States: Manufacturers, 1929*, 3:489; U.S. Department of Commerce, *Sixteenth Census of the United States: Manufacturers, 1939*, 3:943.

6. McGill, *South and the Southerner*, 207.

7. U.S. Department of Commerce, *Fifteenth Census of the United States: Manufacturers, 1929*, 489; U.S. Department of Commerce, *Sixteenth Census of the United States: Manufacturers, 1939*, 3:943.

8. Racine, *Seeing Spartanburg*.

9. The AAA's negative impact on sharecroppers and other tenant farmers is, by now, textbook-level common knowledge. Whayne, *New Plantation South*, is a good recent study of the groups that fell through the cracks of the AAA program, including sharecroppers and other small southern farmers. Pete Daniel, "The New Deal, Southern Agriculture, and Economic Change," in Cobb and Namorato, *New Deal and the South*, 37–61, is a good article-length work on the topic. For true classics see Kirby, *Rural Worlds Lost*; Daniel, *Breaking the Land*; or Fite, *Cotton Fields No More*.

10. Kirby, *Rural Worlds Lost*, 289; Smith, "Redistribution of the Negro Population," 155–73.

11. U.S. Department of Commerce, *Fifteenth Census of the United States: 1930*, vol. 3, part 2, 788, 804; U.S. Department of Commerce, *Sixteenth Census of the United States: 1940*, vol. 3, part 6, 378, 394, 429.

12. Lander, *History of South Carolina*, 73–74; Edgar, *South Carolina in the Modern Age*, 82.

13. Minchin, *What Do We Need a Union For?* 2–10; U.S. Department of Commerce, *U.S. Census of Manufacturers*, 1947, 3:555; U.S. Department of Commerce, *U.S. Census of Manufacturers*, 1954, 3:139–40; U.S. Department of Commerce, *County Business Patterns*, 1956, part 6, 301.

14. For good general histories of Spartanburg town and county, see Writers Program of the Work Project Administration, *History of Spartanburg County*, and Teter, *Textile Town*.

15. For more on southern labor politics and union activities during the Great Depression era, including the tragedy in Honea Path, see, for example, Irons, *Testing the New Deal*; Hodges, *New Deal Labor Policy*; Hall, Korstad, and Leloudis, "Cotton Mill People"; or Simon, *Fabric of Defeat*.

16. Minchin, *What Do We Need a Union For?* 17; Richter, *Labor's Struggles*.

17. Minchin, *What Do We Need a Union For?* 30.

18. A CIO flyer, Operation Dixie: The CIO Organizing Committee Papers, 1946–1953 (microfilm), South Carolina, 1941–53, reel 17, series 2–21, Perkins Library, Duke University.

19. Lucy Mason, southern public relations representative of the CIO, letter to Franz E. Daniel, South Carolina director of Operation Dixie, September 14, 1946, CIO Organizing Committee Papers, 1946–53, South Carolina, 1941–53, reel 19; Charles Auslander, South Carolina state director of TWUA, letter to CIO's Organizing Committee Headquarters in Atlanta, June 25, 1951, CIO Organizing Committee Papers, 1946–1953, South Carolina, 1941–53, reel 16; minutes of joint board meetings, 1946–51, Textile Workers Union of America, Cherokee-Spartanburg Joint Board Records, box 273, Rare Books, Manuscript, and Special Collections Library, Duke University.

20. Operation Dixie: CIO Organizing Committee Papers, 1946–53 (microfilm), South Carolina, 1941–53, reel 17, series 2–21.

21. Minchin, *What Do We Need a Union For?* 19. For currency conversions I use eh.net's Consumer Price Index (CPI) calculator, found at www.measuringworth.com/uscompare.

22. Minchin, *What Do We Need a Union For?* 23. The strategy continued to work effectively in the South Carolina Piedmont for decades. As late as 1964 a large-scale union drive was met with a well-publicized, regional wave of wage increases, reaching even parts of neighboring states (*Spartanburg Herald*, August 26, 1964, 1).

23. For more information on Gaffney-strike see Minchin, *What Do We Need a Union For?* 71–72.

24. Jesse B. Smith to George Baldanzi, assistant director of the CIO Organizing Committee, December 11, 1946, CIO Organizing Committee Papers, 1946–53, South Carolina, 1941–53, reel 16.

25. AFL-CIO Region 5/8, Records, 1940–74, box 2771, folder 8: United Garment Workers of America, 1956–60, Southern Labor History Archives, Georgia State University, Atlanta.

26. After three decades of work by labor unions, the unionization rate in Spartanburg by 1977 was 8.7 percent (AFL-CIO Region 5, Records, South Carolina Labor Council, AFL-CIO, 1976–78, box 1838, folder 22, Southern Labor Archives, Georgia State University, Atlanta).

27. For good, recent discussions of the reasons behind the failures of unionization, especially in the South, see Minchin, *Fighting against the Odds,* and Simon, "Rethinking."

28. International Ladies Garment Workers Union (ILGWU), Southeast Regional Office (SERO), Records, 1945–78, box 3051, folder 16, Southern Labor Archives, Georgia State University, Atlanta.

29. Robert Cohn, letter to Morris P. Glushien, general counsel of ILGWU, August 24, 1962, ILGWU, SERO, Records, 1945–78, box 3051, folder 16, Southern Labor Archives, Georgia State University, Atlanta. .

30. Carey E. Haigler, regional director of American Federation of Hosiery Workers, letter to general president of AFHW, Andrew Janaskie, AFL-CIO Region 5/8, May 2, 1960, Records 1940–74, box 2772, folder 3, Southern Labor Archives, Georgia State University, Atlanta.

31. P. Garvan Incorporated organizing drive, UTWA Southern Region Records, 1948–75, box 1074, folder 23, Southern Labor Archives, Georgia State University, Atlanta.

32. AFL-CIO Region 5/8, Records, 1940–74, box 2772, folder 3: American Federation of Hosiery Workers, 1956–65, Southern Labor History Archives, Georgia State University, Atlanta.

33. While I acknowledge the dangers of regional or cultural typecasting, the unique culture of the historical southern mill worker community is hardly a debatable concept. From early studies to contemporary scholarship, numerous social scientists, artists, labor activists, journalists, business managers, and politicians have noticed and emphasized the clannish, withdrawn, and often suspicious culture that has marked the people of mill villages. For perhaps the earliest scholarly study of the topic, see Thompson, *From the Cotton Field.* J. Kenneth Moreland's classic *Millways of Kent* is an interesting inside look at the social and behavioral norms of the South Carolina Piedmont mill communities, with a good analysis of the tension between workers who accepted paternalism and workers who favored unionization. Joan Hoffman, *Racial Discrimination and Economic Development,* presents a somewhat caricaturized, yet largely accurate, image of instinctive South Carolina cultural conservatism. Potwin's *Cotton Mill People* was a pathbreaking early study in its insightful observance of the peculiar character of southern mill communities. Potwin notices the substantial industrial programs in the South and their thoroughly modernized, anti-Bourbon character; yet she acknowledges the strong traditionalist characteristics of southern textile workers and their determination to create a community as culturally familiar as possible, that is, an agrarian one (see esp. 13–21, 37–39).

34. Cobb, *Industrialization and Southern Society,* 51; Gilman, *Human Relations,* 271–74.

35. Potwin, *Cotton Mill People,* 37–39.

36. Gilman, *Human Relations,* 271–74. For an alternative viewpoint that actually argues that southern workers welcomed the formality of the union contracts and other involvement, see Clark, *Like Night and Day.*

37. Herring, *Passing of the Mill Village,* 3–9; McHugh, *Mill Family,* 101–2.

38. Gilman, *Human Relations,* 278–80.

39. Mitchell, *Rise of the Cotton Mills,* 160.

40. Mill village paternalism is, of course, a thoroughly discussed and analyzed topic in southern historiography. I share the view of Howard Newby, who argues that dominant classes

attempt to obtain stability by getting subordinate classes to identify with the system. One effective tool of identification, Howard Newby argues in *Deferential Worker*, is tradition. Although Newby's research is focused on English workers, his observations translate well to southern textile mills, where bosses learned to use tradition and old cultural patterns and combine them with sense of mutual interest. For recent discussion of paternalism and textile mills, see Wingerd, "Rethinking Paternalism"; David L. Carlton, "Paternalism and Southern Textile Labor: A Historiographical View," in Fink and Reed, Race, Class, and Community, 17–26; Flamming, Creating the Modern South.

41. McHugh, *Mill Family*, 100; Cash, *Mind of the South*, 205.

42. Toby Moore, "Dismantling the South's Cotton Mill Village System," in Scranton, *Second Wave*, 114.

43. Suggs, *My World Is Gone*; Gilman, *Human Relations*, 280; Moore, "Dismantling the South's Cotton Mill Village System," 130.

44. Bartley, *New South*, 21–22.

45. Cohodas, *Strom Thurmond*, 83–84; Bartley, *New South*, 21–22.

46. Cohodas, *Strom Thurmond*, 84–89.

47. Ibid.

48. *Spartanburg Herald*, September 1, 1946, 4.

49. *Spartanburg Herald*, September 4, 1946, 1.

50. For more on Olin D. Johnston and his standing among South Carolina textile workers, see Simon, *Fabric of Defeat*, and Hayes, *South Carolina and the New Deal*.

51. Simon, *Fabric of Defeat*, 167–87.

52. Smith, "Redistribution of Negro Population."

53. Hoffman, "Genesis of the Modern Movement," 352; Eldridge and Thomas, *Population Redistribution and Economic Growth*, 3:90.

54. Hughes, "Cowards from the Colleges!" in *Good Morning Revolution*, 62.

55. Langston Hughes, "Cowards from the Colleges," in *Good Morning Revolution*, 68.

56. Hoffman, "Genesis of the Modern Movement," 363–64.

57. The invigorating effect of wars and, especially, war propaganda on African American political and civil rights activism is today largely beyond historical dispute. For a solid work addressing the topic, see Hemmingway, "Prelude to Change." Although the article focuses on African Americans' political perspective during World War I, its discussions of African American eagerness to serve, migration to find work in war industries, and, especially, the impact of democratic propaganda on black political thought are largely transferable to the World War II era, as further discussed in I. A. Newby, *Black Carolinians*, and more general studies of twentieth-century Palmetto State history, such as Edgar, *South Carolina*. For an effective polemical discussion, from the viewpoint of 1950s racial sociology, see Quint, *Profile in Black and White*.

58. Hoffman, "Genesis of the Modern Movement."

59. Frederickson, "Slowest State."

60. Edgar, *South Carolina*, 516–20; Fredrickson, "Slowest State," 188–97.

61. I. A. Newby, *Black Carolinians*, 274.

62. Ibid., 343.

63. Black, *Southern Governors and Civil Rights*, 29–33.

64. Pruitt, *Things Hidden*, 51.

65. *Spartanburg Herald*, February 2, 1950, 4; *Spartanburg Herald*, June 24, 1951, 4; *Spartanburg Herald*, January 1, 1959, 15.

66. Ibid.

67. Black, *Southern Governors and Civil Rights*, 81.

68. *Spartanburg Herald*, February 2, 1950, 4; *Spartanburg Herald*, June 24, 1950, 4; *Spartanburg Herald*, June 20, 1951, 4; *Spartanburg Herald*, January 1, 1959, 1. See also Martin, "Attitude."

Chapter Two.   Origins of the Latest South

1. Flora, "Dynamic Economy of South Carolina," 1; Edwards, "South Carolina Economy in Perspective," 45.

2. James A. Morris, "South Carolina Economy," 3–4.

3. U.S. Department of Commerce, Bureau of Economic Analysis, *Long-Term Economic Growth, 1860–1970*, 236.

4. *Journal of the House of Representatives of the 2nd Session of the 91st General Assembly of the State of South Carolina, 1956*, 374.

5. U.S. Department of Commerce, *U.S. Census of Manufacturers*, 1947, 3:557; U.S. Department of Commerce, *U.S. Census of Manufacturers*, 1958, 39:9; U.S. Department of Commerce, *U.S. Census of Population*, 1950, 40:49; U.S. Department of Commerce, *U.S. Census of Population*, 1960, 42:157.

6. *Spartanburg Herald-Journal*, January 1, 1960, sec. 2, 3.

7. U.S. Department of Commerce, *U.S. Census of Population*, 1940, vol. 3, part 6, 429; U.S. Department of Commerce, *U.S. Census of Population*, 1960, 42:13.

8. U.S. Department of Commerce, *U.S. Census of Population*, 1940, vol. 3, part 6, 418; U.S. Department of Commerce, *U.S. Census of Population*, 1960, 42:73; Racine, *Seeing Spartanburg*.

9. *Spartanburg Herald-Journal*, January 1, 1960, sec. 2, 3.

10. U.S. Department of Commerce, *U.S. Census of Manufacturers*, 1947, 3:555–57; U.S. Department of Commerce, *U.S. Census of Manufacturers*, 1958, 39:9.

11. U.S. Department of Commerce, *County Business Patterns*, 1951; U.S. Department of Commerce, *County Business Patterns*, 1956, part 6, 301.

12. Ibid.; U.S. Department of Commerce, *U.S. Census of Manufacturers*, 1958, 39:9.

13. U.S. Department of Commerce, *U.S. Census of Manufacturers*, 1947, 3:557; U.S. Department of Commerce, *U.S. Census of Manufacturers*, 1958, 39:9; U.S. Department of Commerce, *U.S. Census of Population*, 1950, 40:49; U.S. Department of Commerce, *U.S. Census of Population*, 1960, 42:157.

14. Although a visible group of (proto-)industrial middle class had played an important role in the region since its industrial origins, its size and influence grew dramatically during the postwar decades. For more discussion about the formation and development of the region's social and economic division, see Ford's "Rednecks and Merchants." The article provides an effective analysis of the development of commercial and social hierarchies in the region. Beck's "Building the New South" provides a valuable discussion of the persistence of the region's socioeconomic structures, even during economic transition. David L. Carlton and Peter A. Coclanis discuss the maturation of southern industry and the role of the Piedmont's middle classes in "Capital Mobilization and Southern Industry." Carlton, *Mill and Town*, continues to be the groundbreaking book about the history of social division in the South Carolina Piedmont.

15. The average age of Spartanburg County's farm owners increased rapidly throughout the postwar era, reaching 52.1 in 1959 (U.S. Department of Commerce, *U.S. Census of Agriculture, 1959*, vol. 1, part 27, 175).

16. Street, *New Revolution*, 78.

17. Ibid., 18.

18. Fite, *Cotton Fields No More*, 211.

19. Kirby, *Rural Worlds Lost*, 123.

20. For southern BAWI-programs, see Cobb, *Selling of the South*, 5–34.

21. *Spartanburg Herald*, May 4, 1945, 2; *Spartanburg Herald*, May 8, 1945, 2; *Spartanburg Herald*, May 12, 1945, 2.

22. U.S. Department of Commerce, *U.S. Census of Agriculture: 1954*, 1:381–401; Department of Commerce, *U.S. Census of Agriculture, 1959*, vol. 1, part 27, 163–75.

23. For a more general discussion of the South's agricultural problems in the twentieth century, see Fite, *Cotton Fields No More*; Daniel, *Breaking the Land*; Kirby, *Rural Worlds Lost*. For a good comparative study about the differing destinies of the rural and nonrural South, see Lyson, *Two Sides of the Sunbelt*.

24. The semiagrarian culture of mill villages and mill workers has gained scholarly attention since the early twentieth century. The historiography is too long and substantial to list here, but a few works demonstrate the transformation of the lives of mill workers, with periodic insights into their lives. Potwin, *Cotton Mill People of the Piedmont*, is a pioneering study of cotton mill workers as a socioeconomic group. Morland, *Millways of Kent*, is an "inside out" sociological study of life and labor in an anonymous southern mill town; Hall et al., *Like a Family*, continues to be the standard-bearer in the field.

25. Ford, *Origins of Southern Radicalism*, 73–74.

26. The literature on the post–World War II changes in the South is, of course, plentiful. From politics to economics and history this topic has produced a plethora of good studies. Bartley's *New South* provides probably the best general summary of the region's transformation. Black and Black, *Politics and Society*, is an insightful book about the South's unique political culture and the changes it experienced during the twentieth century. Tindall, *Disruption of the Solid South*, offers a brief and polemic but eloquent analysis of the forces that destroyed the pre–World War II image of the solid, impenetrable South. Also from Tindall, *Emergence of the New South*, is an early standard in the field, providing a rich discussion of the cultural intangibles and new industrial mind-set affecting the South's postwar economic takeoff (see 687–731). Wright, *Old South, New South*, esp. 198–274, discusses the disappearance of the separate southern labor markets and other structural changes shaping the South's economy since the 1930s.

27. Tindall, *Disruption of the Solid South*, 56.

28. For a good recent study on the movement of textile industries, see English, *Common Thread*.

29. Weinstein and Firestine, *Regional Growth and Decline*, 3, 6–7.

30. U.S. Department of Commerce, *U.S. Census of Population, 1960*, vol. 1, part 42, 149; Tindall, *Disruption of the Solid South*, 55–56.

31. For Sunbelt movement see, for example, Bartley, *New South*; and Weinstein and Firestine, *Regional Growth and Decline*.

32. Tindall, *Disruption of the Solid South*, 55–56.

33. Francis Pickens Miller, "Democratic Party in the South," 63–64.

34. Carlton, "Textile Town Settles In," 96, 213–15.

35. *Columbia State*, March 2, 1992, 7; "How Roger Milliken Runs Textiles' Premiere Performer," 64.

36. *Spartanburg Herald*, February 7, 1961, 7.

37. "How Roger Milliken Runs Textiles' Premiere Performer," 63.

38. *Columbia State*, March 2, 1992, 7.

39. Lizza, "Silent Partner" ; *Columbia State*, March 2, 1992, 7.

40. *Spartanburg Herald*, February 7, 1961, 7.

41. Carlton, "Textile Town Settles In," 214–15.

42. Ibid. For more on modernization of the U.S. and southern textile industry, see Fuller, "Diffusion and Location,".

43. U.S. Department of Commerce, *U.S. Census of Population, 1920*, 225.

44. U.S. Department of Commerce, *City Directories of the United States*; U.S. Census, *Census of Population*, 1930.

45. *Spartanburg Herald*, June 9, 1951, 2; *Spartanburg Journal*, July 26, 1979, A-1. The *Herald* was the morning paper, the *Journal* the afternoon paper. They merged in 1982 under the masthead of the *Herald-Journal*, as the Sunday paper had long been known.

46. *Spartanburg Herald*, June 9, 1951, 2; *Spartanburg Journal*, July 26, 1979, A-1.

47. *Spartanburg Herald*, June 9, 1951, 2.

48. *Spartanburg Herald*, March 29, 1951, 6.

49. An identified magazine clipping, vertical files: Spartanburg County, South Caroliniana Library, University of South Carolina, Columbia.

50. Parris, "South Carolina's Secret Weapon," 42.

51. *Spartanburg Herald*, January 1, 1954, 9.

52. *Spartanburg Herald*, January 27, 1954, 3.

53. Eckes, *Opening America's Market*, 157, 169.

54. Cohn, *Life and Times*, 225–227; *Journal of the Senate of the 2nd Session of the 91st General Assembly of the State of South Carolina*, 1956, 865.

55. *Journal of the House*, 377.

56. *Spartanburg Herald*, April 22, 1956, D8.

57. Street, *New Revolution*, 68, 83.

58. "Objectives of United States Foreign Economic Policy," Council on Foreign Trade Policy, Chronological File, July 1955, box 5, Dwight D. Eisenhower Presidential Library, Abilene, Kans.

59. Ibid.

60. C. Edward Galbreath, CIA economist and consultant to the White House on foreign economic policy, memo to Clarence B. Randall, special consultant and later a chairman of the Council on Foreign Economic Policy, Council on Foreign Trade Policy, Chronological File, May 1955, box 5, Eisenhower Library.

61. "Memorandum to the Secretary of the State," by C. D. Jackson, special assistant to the president in cold war planning and psychological warfare, Council on Foreign Economic Policy, Office of the Chairman, Records 1954–61, Dodge series, subject subseries, box 2, Economic Policy, Eisenhower Library.

62. "Stimulation of Private Foreign Investment," Department of Commerce study, May 11, 1955, Council on Foreign Economic Policy, Policy Papers series, box 3, CFEP 511, Stimulation of Investment, Eisenhower Library; "Concessions for Developing U.S. Private Investments

Abroad," Council on Foreign Economic Policy, Office of the Chairman, Records 1954–61, Dodge series, correspondence subseries, Eisenhower Library.

63. For a good general history of American private enterprise abroad, see Wilkins, *Maturing of Multinational Enterprise.*

64. "Concessions for Developing U.S. Private Investments Abroad"; See also C. Edward Galbreath, "Memorandum for Mr. Randall," January 10, 1958, Chronological File, Foreign Economic Policy, box 3, Eisenhower Library.

65. Hoover and Ratchford, *Economic Resources,* 434.

66. *Spartanburg Herald,* January 1, 1954, 9; *Spartanburg Herald,* February 5, 1954, 16.

67. For a persuasive and concise, if somewhat dated, critique of the classic view of southerners as avid internationalists, see DeConde, "South and Isolationism."

68. DeConde, "South and Isolationism," 339.

69. Herbert V. Prochnow, deputy under secretary for economic affairs, memo to Dr. Gabriel Hauge, assistant to the president in economic affairs, March 8, 1956, Central Files, Official File 149–B-2, box 801, Textiles, Eisenhower Library; Dwight D. Eisenhower, Papers as President, Cabinet series, box 8, Eisenhower Library.

70. Edgar, *South Carolina in the Modern Age,* 91–92; "U.S.-Japanese Exchange on Export of Cotton Goods to the U.S.," press release, Central Files, Official File 149–B-2, box 802, Textiles, Eisenhower Library.

71. Cohn, *Life and Times,* 225–26; Lander, *History of South Carolina,* 213.

72. For a good summary of the U.S.-Japanese post–World War II relations, including trade, see Schaller, *Altered States.*

73. Lander, *History of South Carolina,* 224.

74. U.S. Department of Commerce, *U.S. Census of Manufacturers,* 1947, 3:557; U.S. Department of Commerce, *U.S. Census of Manufacturers,* 1958, 39:9.

75. *Spartanburg Herald,* February 12, 1958, 1.

76. *Spartanburg Herald,* February 5, 1954, 16; *Spartanburg Herald,* February 5, 1955, 33.

77. *Spartanburg Herald-Journal,* January 9, 1960, 5.

78. Draft of textile industry situational report by A. Henry Thurston, secretary of Interagency Textile Commission, to Senate Interstate and Foreign Commerce Committees, December 16, 1959, CFEP, Office of the Chairman, records 1954–61, Randall series, subject subseries, box 6, Interagency Textile Committee, Eisenhower Library.

79. Carlton, "Textile Town Settles In," 216; *Spartanburg Herald-Journal,* February 6, 1955, 33.

80. *Spartanburg Herald,* May 4, 1955, 2.

81. *Spartanburg Herald-Journal,* January 22, 1956, A8; *Spartanburg Herald-Journal,* February 9, 1957, 15.

82. Kohler's antiunion rants attracted the attention and concern of South Carolina and Spartanburg labor activists, prompting them to discuss the fiery rhetoric of the town's new industrial migrant. See South Carolina Federation of Labor president Earle R. Britton, letter to J. W. Harrison, president of Spartanburg Central Labor Union, January 31, 1956, AFL-CIO Region 5/8, Records, 1940–74, box 2749, folder 6, Southern Labor History Archives, Georgia State University, Atlanta.

83. *Spartanburg Herald-Journal,* January 22, 1956, A8.

84. *Spartanburg Herald-Journal,* February 9, 1957, 52.

85. U.S. Department of Commerce, *U.S. Census of Manufacturers,* 1947, 3:555–57; *U.S. Census of Manufacturers,* 1958, 39:9.

86. *Spartanburg Herald*, February 12, 1960, 1C.

87. *Spartanburg Herald*, January 20, 1956, 1, 28.

88. *Spartanburg Herald*, January 27, 1954, 1; *Spartanburg Herald*, January 29, 1954, 13.

89. Ibid.; *Spartanburg Herald*, February 15, 1958, 15.

90. Carlton, "Textile Town Settles In," 217–218; *Spartanburg Herald-Journal*, January 9, 1960, 5; Dr. G. B. Hodge, interview by author, September 24, 2002, Spartanburg, S.C.; Dr. Paul Foerster, retired Hoechst executive, interview by author, September 24, 2002, Spartanburg, S.C.; Falk and Lyson, *High Tech, Low Tech*, 84–85.

91. *Spartanburg Herald*, February 17, 1960, 5A; Hodge interview.

92. Hammer, Greene, Siler Associates, "Economy of Spartanburg County," 164, South Caroliniana Library.

Chapter Three. The Roots of International Recruiting

1. "European Business People Like Carolina," 62.

2. Parris, "South Carolina's Secret Weapon," 41.

3. Ibid.

4. Vogl, "Spartanburg Example," 26; Tunley, "In Spartanburg," 166.

5. Vogl, "Spartanburg Example," 26.

6. Greater Spartanburg Area Chamber of Commerce, "Spartanburg County International Industry List, 1997," Greater Spartanburg Area Chamber of Commerce Papers, Greater Spartanburg Area Chamber of Commerce, Spartanburg, S.C.

7. Trip Reports, 1944–72, Luther Hartwell Hodges Papers, Southern Historical Collections, University of North Carolina at Chapel Hill; Kincaid, "American Governors in International Affairs," 102; Casey, *Beyond the Numbers*, 133.

8. For a celebratory but nevertheless informative history of the Research Triangle Park, see Link's two-volume history of the RTP, *Generosity of Spirit*, and *From Seed to Harvest*.

9. Speech: Governor Ernest F. Hollings to the General Assembly of South Carolina, January 21, 1959; speech draft: Statement of the Honorable Ernest F. Hollings, Governor of South Carolina, before the subcommittee on Constitutional Rights Legislation of the Judiciary Committee of the United States House of Representatives, Washington, D.C., April 14, 1959, Governor (1959–63: Hollings), General File, 1958–62, South Carolina Department of Archives and History, Columbia (hereafter South Carolina archives); Cobb, *Industrialization and Southern Society*, 114.

10. Governor (1959–1963: Hollings), General File, 1958–62,South Carolina archives.

11. *Spartanburg Herald-Journal*, February 13, 1960, 3B; speech: Governor Ernest F. Hollings to the General Assembly of South Carolina, January 11, 1961; speech draft: Proposed Remarks, European Tour, Governor (1959–63: Hollings), General File, 1958–62,South Carolina archives.

12. Speech draft: Proposed Remarks, European Tour, Governor (1959–1963: Hollings), General File, 1958–62,South Carolina archives.

13. *Spartanburg Herald*, January 12, 1960, 1; address by Governor Ernest F. Hollings for Sixty-fifth Congress of American Industry, December 8, 1960, Governor (1959–63: Hollings), General File, 1958–62,South Carolina archives; statement of the Honorable Ernest F. Hollings, governor of South Carolina, before the subcommittee on Constitutional Rights

Legislation of the Judiciary Committee of the United States House of Representatives, Washington, D.C., April 14, 1959, Governor (1959–1963: Hollings), General File, 1958–62, South Carolina archives.

14. History of the South Carolina Development Board, Development Board: General Correspondence, 1978, Governor's Office: James B. Edwards (1975–79), South Carolina archives.

15. Cobb, *Selling of the South*, 166–70; Shaw, "Special Education for Industrial Expansion," 2.

16. Byrnes, *All in One Lifetime*, 411.

17. South Carolina State Development Board Files, South Carolina archives.

18. See, for example, Paterson, "Why Industry Moves to the Southland," 1–4; Tomb, "Should Industry Move South?"; Kennedy, "New England and the South," 32–36.

19. Editorial, *University of South Carolina Business and Economic Review*, January 1, 1954, 1–3.

20. Research Reports, 1962–79, State Development Board Files, South Carolina archives.

21. "South Carolina's New Plant Boom," 126; "South Carolina's Upper Piedmont."

22. Hammer, Greene, Siler Associates, "Economy of Spartanburg County," 164.

23. *Spartanburg Herald*, February 15, 1964, C1.

24. Ibid.; *Spartanburg Herald*, March 4, 1972, B6, D10.

25. "Business and Industrial Review," *Spartanburg Herald-Journal*, 1955–66. Published annually as January or February supplements to the *Herald-Journal*.

26. *Spartanburg Herald*, February 12, 1960, 1C.

27. *Spartanburg Herald-Journal*, February 18, 1960, 2B; *Spartanburg Herald*, July 31, 1963, 9; *Spartanburg Herald*, February 15, 1964, B1; *Spartanburg Herald*, February 12, 1966, C1, C8; Carlton, "Textile Town Settles In," 226; U.S. Department of Commerce, *Censuses of Manufacturers*, 1954–66; Flora, "Spartanburg County,", 36–37.

28. *Spartanburg Herald*, September 15, 1958, 30; *Spartanburg Herald*, February 13, 1965, 5C, 8B; *Spartanburg Herald-Journal*, February 12, 1966, C8.

29. Dr. Paul E. Foerster, interview by author, January 30, 1998, Spartanburg, S.C.; *London Independent*, May 9, 1993; *Sunday-Times* of London, November 1, 1970; a newspaper clipping, Vertical Files: Spartanburg County, South Caroliniana Library, University of South Carolina, Columbia.

30. Tunley, "In Spartanburg," 167; Foerster interview.

31. "New Rich South"; I. A. Newby, *Black Carolinians*, 342–44; Black, *Southern Governors and Civil Rights*, 29–33.

32. Dyer and Sicilia, *Labors of a Modern Hercules*, 354–55.

33. Foerster interview; Vogl, "Spartanburg Example," 26.

34. *Richard E. Tukey*, promotional biography-video; "European Business People Like Carolina," 62.

35. *Richard E. Tukey*, video; Foerster interview.

36. *Spartanburg Herald-Journal*, October 23, 1966, 1.

37. *Spartanburg Herald-Journal*, February 21, 1970; Greater Spartanburg Area Chamber of Commerce, "Spartanburg County International Industry List, 1997."

38. "Investing in the U.S.," 101–2; *Spartanburg Herald*, October 17, 1980, B1; *Spartanburg Herald-Journal*, November 18, 1982, C13. For a groundbreaking study of southern industrial recruiting strategies, see Cobb, *Selling of the South*. For more on the industrial shift from

the North to the South and the West, see, for example, Weinstein, Gross, and Rees, *Regional Growth and Decline.*

39. Parris, "South Carolina's Secret Weapon," 42.

40. Foerster interview; Greater Spartanburg Area Chamber of Commerce of, "Points of Interest"; Greater Spartanburg Area Chamber of Commerce, "Spartanburg . . . the South's International Community."

41. Dr. G. B. Hodge, long-term chamber of commerce member and civic leader, interview by author, September 24, 2002, Spartanburg, S.C.

42. Jim Adler, letter to CIO, Political Action Committee (PAC), September 27, 1977, States: South Carolina, box 1883, Southern Labor Archives, Georgia State University, Atlanta.

43. *Spartanburg Herald-Journal,* October 23, 1966, 1; *Richard E. Tukey,* video; untitled magazine clipping, Vertical Files: Spartanburg, South Caroliniana Library.

44. Tunley, "In Spartanburg," 167.

45. Foerster interview; Carlton, "Textile Town Settles In," 218.

46. *Spartanburg Herald-Journal,* February 21, 1970, C2; *Spartanburg Herald-Journal,* March 3, 1973, C3, D5; *Spartanburg Herald-Journal,* October 3, 1976, C1; *Spartanburg Herald-Journal,* March 5, 1977, E1.

47. Philip A. "Pat" Tukey, son of Dick Tukey, interview by author, January 30, 1998, Spartanburg, S.C.; *Spartanburg Journal,* July 26, 1979, A1.

48. The records are silent as to how West, who died in 2004, came to take the trip.

49. Parris, "South Carolina's Secret Weapon," 40.

50. Despite the publication of several thorough, occasionally excellent, and informative monographs about the formation and motives of U.S. foreign economic policy during the early cold war, the field could use another larger, chronologically expansive study. Kaufman, *Trade and Aid,* continues to be the most informative, fundamentally sound (if overtly critical) account of Eisenhower's economic policy. Kunz, *Butter and Guns,* is a more optimistic yet occasionally simplistic look at the topic, arguing that the military-industrial complex and the nation's other economic policies were hugely successful and responsible for its rapid economic growth. Although it does not directly address postwar foreign economic policy, Fordham, *Building the Cold War Consensus,* gives a good look at the mind-set surrounding American political and economic thinking during this period. Audretsch and Claudon, *Internationalization of U.S. Markets,* is a refreshing and polemical collection of essays on the topic. Norton, *Quest for Economic Stability,* is an effective yet concise handbook into the policies and mind-sets that governed the U.S. economy during the cold war.

51. "Commission on Foreign Economic Policy: Report to the President and the Congress," White House Office, National Security Council Staff: Papers, 1948–61, OCB Central File Series, box 58, OCB 091.3, October 1953–December 1954, Dwight D. Eisenhower Presidential Library, Abilene, Kans.

52. Kaufman, *Trade and Aid,* 176.

53. "Objectives of United States Foreign Economic Policy," Council on Foreign Trade Policy, Chronological File, July 1955, box 5, Eisenhower Library; C. Edward Galbreath, a CIA economist and consultant to the White House in matters of foreign economic policy, memo to Clarence B. Randall, special consultant and later a chairman of the Council on Foreign Economic Policy, Council on Foreign Trade Policy, Chronological File, May 1955, box 5, Eisenhower Library.

54. Galbreath to Randall, Council on Foreign Trade Policy, Chronological File, January 1958, box 3; Dwight D. Eisenhower: Papers as President (hereafter, Eisenhower presidential papers), Administration Series, box 3, Anderson, Robert B., 1960–61, Eisenhower Library.

55. Kaufman, *Trade and Aid*, 179.

56. Eisenhower presidential papers, Administration Series, box 3, Anderson, Robert B., 1960–61, Eisenhower Library.

57. Senate Finance Committee statement, quoted in Lovett, Eckes, and Brinkman, *U.S. Trade Policy*, 85.

58. Galbreath to Randall, memorandum: "The Effects of Nationalism on Foreign Economic Policy," Council on Foreign Trade Policy, Chronological File, January 10, 1958, box 3, Eisenhower Library.

59. For the groundbreaking book-length discussion of the free trade versus protectionism debates in Congress, see Pastor, *Congress*. Pastor argues that during the first three post–World War II decades, Congress remained solidly in the free-trade camp.

60. "Narrative History of the Kennedy Round Crisis," National Security Council History, April–June 1967, NSC Histories, Lyndon B. Johnson Presidential Library, Austin, Tex.

61. Alfred E. Eckes Jr., "U.S. Trade History," in Lovett, Eckes, and Brinkman, *U.S. Trade Policy*, 83.

62. Ibid., 81–83; Malmgren, "Coming Trade Wars?" 121.

63. "Congress Opens a Door," 102.

64. "How Companies Are Wooing Investors," 154–55; "Trying to Lure Foreign Investors," 94; "Foreigners Are Coming." For a good general study on history of foreign investment in the United States, see Wilkins, *History of Foreign Investments*.

65. "Congress Opens a Door," 102; "Going International in Reverse," 34; "How Companies Are Wooing Investors," 155.

66. U.S. Council of the International Chamber of Commerce, "U.S. Direct Investments and the Balance of Payments," October 28, 1966, WHCF, FO 4 (January 23, 1965–), Johnson Library.

67. Stanley, "Stimulating State Economic Growth," 3.

68. "South Carolina Mission," 22.

69. *Spartanburg Herald-Journal*, August 5, 1979, A4.

70. Undated newspaper clipping, *Columbia State*, Vertical Files: International Relations, South Caroliniana Library.

71. South Carolina State Development Board Files, South Carolina archives.

72. Peppas, "Comparative Study," 124–25.

73. *Spartanburg Herald-Journal*, February 12, 1966, C5.

74. *Spartanburg Herald*, February 5, 1955, 33; *Spartanburg Herald*, February 1958, 30; *Spartanburg Herald*, January 9, 1960, 5; *Spartanburg Herald*, February 13, 1960, A1, F5.

75. Hammer, Greene, Siler Associates, "Economy of Spartanburg County," 164–65.

Chapter Four. The Maturing of Foreign Investment in Spartanburg

1. John Kenneth Galbraith, letter to the president, February 4, 1965, White House Central Files (hereafter WHCF), FO4-1 (August 1, 1964–March 2, 1965); "President's Proclamation of Free Trade Week of 1966," April 30, 1966, WHCF-SP, 1968, TA; "President's Trade Message to Congress," final draft, May 28, 1968, WHCF-SP, 1968, TA; "President's Proclamation of Free

Trade Week of 1968," March 27, 1968, WHCF-SP, 1968, TA; memorandum from president, WHCF-FO 4–3, box 40, Lyndon B. Johnson Presidential Library, Austin, Tex.

2. Alfred E. Eckes Jr., "U.S Trade History," in Lovett, Eckes, and Brinkman, *U.S. Trade Policy*, 85; U.S. Department of Commerce, *Foreign Direct Investment in the United States: Report*, vol. 5, G-27.

3. Malmgren, "Coming Trade Wars?"

4. Spero, *Politics of International Economic Relations*, 53–55.

5. For more literature about the Bretton Woods agreement and the impact of its demise, see Kenen, *Managing the World Economy*, and McCormack, *Bretton Woods Legacy*.

6. Until the early 1970s microeconomic explanations largely dominated the academic discussion of the slowly growing foreign direct investment in the United States. Perhaps the most popular explanation for foreign direct investment (FDI) in the late 1960s was the microeconomic monopolistic theory, promoted by Charles Kindleberger in his 1969 book, *American Business Abroad*. According to Kindleberger, foreign direct investment resulted from market imperfections, where a foreign company was able to compete despite the domination of local companies because of its superior product and production methods. The theory had supporters throughout the 1970s, including Kindleberger's student Stephen Hymer, author of *The International Operations of National Firms*. FDI trends during the 1960s, including Spartanburg's experience with the textile machinery manufacturers, lends validity to the argument, but events of the 1970s proved this theory to be too limited.

As the scope of multinationalization grew, it became obvious that the growth and investment motives would require a more macroeconomic explanation. Proponents of the internationalization theory, led by Stephen P. Magee, believed that in the new industrial society, information is the key factor in decisions to locate new plants abroad. When information is better handled within a company than through licensing or other arrangements, companies often choose to expand by becoming multinational. See Stephen P. Magee, "Information and Multinational Corporation: An Appropriability Theory of Direct Foreign Investment," in Bhagwati, *New International Economic Order*, 317–40.

The eclectic theory, devised by John Dunning in the 1980s, pulls the arguments together, emphasizing immigrating corporations' productive edge, practicality of information control, and direct financial profit from exploiting assets internationally rather than only domestically. The broad nature of the argument has given it longevity (Dunning, "Eclectic Paradigm"; Dunning, "Reappraising the Eclectic Paradigm," 461–89).

7. In 1960 the combined GNP of Canada, West Germany, the Netherlands, Japan, Switzerland, and United Kingdom totaled $452 billion (in 1972 dollars). By 1973 it had grown to $1.032 billion, or 77 percent of the U.S. budget of $1.346 billion (U.S. Department of Commerce, *Foreign Direct Investment in the United States: Report*, G-1-6, G-23).

8. "Buying a Slice of America," 90; "Foreigners Are Coming," 25–26.

9. U.S. Department of Commerce, *Foreign Direct Investment in the United States: Report*, G-25.

10. Casey, *Beyond the Numbers*, 55; "U.S. Market," 43–53; "Why Foreign Companies Are Betting," 50. The gap in labor costs between the United States and the rest of the industrialized world closed rapidly. In 1965 German labor unit costs were 55 percent of the U.S. costs, while Japanese costs averaged 57 percent of U.S. labor expenses. By 1974 German labor unit cost 99 percent of U.S. costs, and the Japanese costs had climbed to 91 percent (U.S. Department of Commerce, *Foreign Direct Investment in the United States: Report*, G-232).

11. Between 1971 and 1973 the U.S. dollar fell 35 percent against the mark, 35 percent against the Swiss franc, 28 percent against the guilder, 27 percent against the French franc, and 26 percent against the yen (Sagarin, *Foreign Investment in the United States*, 9).

12. "Foreigners Are Coming," 28.

13. "New Immigration," 29.

14. Rachel McCulloch, "Japanese Investment in the United States," in Audretsch and Claudon, *Internationalization of U.S. Markets*, 178.

15. Pastor, *Congress*, 222.

16. Malmgren, "Managing Foreign Economic Policy," 43. Federal policy on foreign direct investment in the United States was confused and poorly organized, which was true of most of the U.S. foreign economic policy. For more discussion see Cohen, *Making of United States International Economic Policy*, esp. 137–88.

17. Eisinger, *Rise of the Entrepreneurial State*, 68.

18. Culver, "Foreign Direct Investment," 159.

19. "New Immigration," 28.

20. "Challenge in Reverse."

21. U.S. Department of Commerce, *Foreign Direct Investment in the United States: Report*; Rose, "Misguided Furor," 172–73. Even before the mid-1970s, the federal government had protected some U.S. industries and resources, such as mining and interstate transportation, from foreign ownership. Additionally, many states had laws limiting the size of foreign land-ownership within their borders. Also the Buy American Act of 1970 required that the content of defense products had to be at least 50 percent American (Gordon and Lees, *Foreign Multinational Investment*, 4–6, 25).

22. Congressional Research Service, "Foreign Investments," 2.

23. "Foreigners Are Coming," 28; MacEvan and Tabb, *Instability and Change*, 28.

24. "Welcome, Y'all," 114. See also Rose, "Misguided Furor," 172.

25. For gubernatorial attention and interest in foreign direct recruitment, read Kincaid, "American Governors in International Affairs." Watson, *New Civil War*, is a good participant's account of the new, government-led industrial recruitment. Also Culver, "Foreign Direct Investment," notes the widely differing attitudes of the federal and state governments toward international recruitment (163). The need for improved language education for U.S. businessmen had been widely discussed since the 1960s. The Higher Education Act of 1965 recognized the need to encourage this group to learn foreign languages (Higher Education Act, Title VI, § 611, Pub. L. No. 89–329, 79 Stat. 1219 [1965]). Still, more specific measures, such as substantially expanded teaching programs, did not emerge until the late 1970s (Voght and Schaub, *Foreign Languages and International Business*, 2–4).

26. Glickman and Woodward, *New Competitors*, 17; "Welcome, Y'All," 114; Rose, "Misguided Furor," 172.

27. "Welcome, Y'All," 114; *Atlanta Journal and Constitution*, April 11, 1971, 8–C; *Atlanta Constitution*, March 5, 1975, 7–C; *Atlanta Journal*, April 23, 1969, 15D.

28. *Wall Street Journal*, February 26, 1975, 38.

29. *Atlanta Constitution*, May 2, 1974, 20–D; *Atlanta Constitution*, November 28, 1974, 6–F; *Wall Street Journal*, November 11, 1976, 1; Meade, "Foreign Investment," 9.

30. Glickman and Woodward, *New Competitors*, 233.

31. The literature on the Sunbelt movement is plentiful. For convincing sociological, economic, and historical summaries relevant to international industrial immigration—in

addition to those noted earlier in this book—see, for example, Miller and Pozzetta, *Shades of the Sunbelt*; Mohl, *Searching for the Sunbelt*; and Newman, *Growth in the American South*.

32. "Investing in the U.S.," 101–2.

33. U.S. Department of Commerce, *Foreign Direct Investment in the United States: Operations*, 66.

34. "Foreigners Are Coming," 26; "Investing in the U.S.," 101–2.

35. "Investing in the U.S.," 101–2.

36. "Remarks by Caleb C. Whitaker Regarding South Carolina's Foreign Investment Program, Scida Meeting, Hilton Head Island, May 1979," Vertical Files: International Relations, South Caroliniana Library, University of South Carolina, Columbia.

37. Cobb, *Selling of the South*, 190–92; *Wall Street Journal*, November 5, 1973, 6.

38. Neil Reid, "Japanese Direct Investment in the United States Manufacturing Sector," in Jonathon Morris, *Japan and the Global Economy*, 61–88.

39. Daniels, "Recent Foreign Direct Manufacturing Investment," 125–32; Casey, *Beyond the Numbers*, 40; Glickman and Woodward, *New Competitors*, 195.

40. *Spartanburg Herald-Journal*, April 23, 1989, B9.

41. While this observation is, by its very nature, subjective, some scholars of the South Carolina Piedmont, such as the writers of the WPA's classic history of Spartanburg County, have also noted the similarity of its culture and the German culture and work ethic (Writers Program of the Work Projects Administration, *History of Spartanburg County*, 11–16).

42. Davidson, "Location."

43. *Columbia Record*, May 19, 1981, 6–C. See also Arpan and Ricks, *Directory of Foreign Manufacturers*.

44. "Michelin Goes American," 26–28.

45. U.S. Department of Commerce, *Foreign Direct Investment in the United States, Report*, A-231–232.

46. *Wall Street Journal*, November 5, 1973, 6.

47. *Columbia Record*, August 23, 1977, 2; South Carolina State Development Board, "Industrial Growth from New and Expanded Plants in South Carolina, 1965–1974," in Capital Investment and New Jobs, Governor: James B. Edwards (1975–1979), Development Board, 1978, box 2: Information Files, South Carolina Department of Archives and History, Columbia.

48. *Columbia Record*, November 26, 1981, C1.

49. Greater Spartanburg Area Chamber of Commerce, "Spartanburg County International Industry List, 1997."

50. *Sunday Times* of London, November 1, 1970; Tunley, "In Spartanburg," 165–68; Vogl, "Spartanburg Example,"; "European Business People Like Carolina," 62; "Oompah in the Bible Belt," 50; "Southern Curiosity," 26.

51. Ibid.

52. Peppas, "Comparative Study," 127.

53. For a good discussion about the rapid formation of a regional American identity among industrial immigrants, see Garreau, *Nine Nations of North America*, 12, 129–31.

54. *Spartanburg Herald-Journal*, March 6, 1976, F4; "Southern Hospitality," *Trends*, Winter 1975, 17.

55. "Southern Hospitality"; Dr. Paul Foerster, interview by author, January 30, 1998, Spartanburg, S.C.

56. For an outstanding look at Spartanburg's culture, history, and textile industry, see Teter, *Textile Town*.

57. "Southern Hospitality," 17; Foerster interview.

58. *Columbia Record*, August 23, 1977, A1.

59. U.S. Department of Commerce, *U.S. Census of Population, 1970*, vol. 1, part 42, 42–260.

60. *Information UBS* (Unione di Banche Swizzere), August 17, 1972, 7.

61. Undated newspaper clipping about Franz Kastner's deli, Vertical Files: Spartanburg County, South Caroliniana Library; U.S. Department of Commerce, *U.S. Census of Population, 1960*, 42–149; U.S. Department of Commerce, *U.S. Census of Population, 1970*, vol. 1, part 42,, 42–260.

62. An undated newspaper clipping, *Chicago Tribune*, Vertical Files, Headquarters Library, Spartanburg County Public Libraries, Spartanburg, S.C.

63. *Spartanburg Herald*, March 13, 1971; a newspaper clipping found Vertical Files: Hoechst, Headquarters Library.

64. Undated newspaper clipping, Vertical Files: Spartanburg County; undated newspaper clipping, *Columbia State*, Vertical Files: International Relations, box 2, South Caroliniana Library.

65. *Independent* (London), May 9, 1993, 16; "Southern Curiosity," 26.

66. *Columbia Record*, November 26, 1981, C-1.

67. *USA Today*, November 30, 1995, A11.

68. *Wall Street Journal*, January 28, 1971, 4; *Wall Street Journal*, April 13, 1; "Wary," 66.

69. "Investing in the U.S.," 101.

70. *Spartanburg Herald-Journal*, March 6, 1976, E16; *Spartanburg Herald-Journal*, March 5, 1977, E4.

Chapter Five.   Change and Continuity in Spartanburg

1. *Spartanburg Journal*, July 26, 1979, A1, A4.

2. *Spartanburg Herald-Journal*, March 17, 1995, A10.

3. Ibid.

4. The historiography of the U.S. transformation from Keynesian economics to monetarism is yet to be conclusively written, but for some early works in the field, see Halistones, *Viewpoints in Supply-Side Economics*, or Biven, *Who Killed John Maynard Keynes?* Biven gives a good brief account of Volcker's impact; see pp. 67–77. Don Patinkin's autobiographical memories of the University of Chicago's economics department after World War II, *Essays on and in the Chicago Tradition*, provides a good introduction to the Chicago school for readers with moderate economic training. George Maceshich, *Monetarism*, describes how monetarism replaced Keynesian thinking as the leading policy force during the late 1970s.

5. *1987 Survey of Foreign-Based Companies with U.S. Headquarters in South Carolina*, an analysis produced by the KMPG accounting firm for state development authorities, 10, Governor: Carroll A. Campbell Jr. (1987–95), Economic Development Correspondence, International Files, 1987–89, South Carolina Department of Archives and History, Columbia (hereafter South Carolina archives). See also Richard E. Caves, "Exchange-Rate Movements and Foreign Direct Investment in the United States," in Audretsch and Claudon, *Internationalization of U.S. Markets*, 199–225.

6. Gordon and Lees, *Foreign Multinational Investment*, 32.

7. KMPG, *1987 Survey of Foreign-Based Companies*, 6–10.

8. U.S. Department of Commerce, *Foreign Direct Investment in United States: Operations*, 66, 73, 136, 139; U.S. Department of Commerce, *Foreign Direct Investment in the United States: 1987 Benchmark Survey*, 101; Riger, "Flow of Funds," 9–10.

9. U.S. Department of Commerce, *Foreign Direct Investment in the United States: 1987 Benchmark Survey*, 101.

10. U.S. Department of Commerce, *Foreign Direct Investments in United States: Operations*, 66, 73, 136, 139.

11. U.S. Department of Commerce, *Foreign Direct Investment in the United States: 1987 Benchmark Survey*, 101.

12. Peppas, "Comparative Study," 128.

13. "Jobs from Abroad," *Columbia State*, 1980 newspaper clipping, Vertical Files: Spartanburg County, South Caroliniana Library, University of South Carolina, Columbia; *Columbia Record*, July 25, 1979, 11-B.

14. Governor James B. Edwards, letter to François Michelin, October 20, 1975, Governor: James B. Edwards (1975–79), Bicentennial Committee and Development Files: Germany Trip; Toyoo Tate of Mitsubishi Motor Corporation, letter to Governor Richard Riley, December 24, 1984, Governor: Richard Riley (1979–87), Economic Development Files, 1979–86; other industrial relations correspondence, Governor Riley, Economic Development Files, South Carolina archives.

15. *Spartanburg Herald-Journal*, August 5, 1979, A-4.

16. "Recruiting Industry Abroad," 31–32.

17. Carl-Horst Brune, director of European Business Development, letter to Jim Kuhlman of South Carolina State Development Board, March 21, 1988, Governor: Carroll A. Campbell, Jr. (1987–95), Economic Development Correspondence, International Files, 1987–89, South Carolina archives.

18. U.S. Department of Commerce, *Foreign Direct Investments in United States: Operations*, 66, 73, 136, 139.

19. *Atlanta Constitution*, March 4, 1973, E-1; *Atlanta Constitution*, September 18, 1973, A-4.

20. Georgia Department of Commerce, *Foreign Investment in the State of Georgia*, 1–3.

21. Quoted in Watson, *New Civil War*, 6.

22. Schubart, "State by State," 3, 19.

23. Earl H. Fry, "States in the International Economy: An American Overview," in Brown and Fry, *States and Provinces*, 27.

24. Watson, *New Civil War*, 9.

25. For South Carolina–based companies the state's tax codes were not at all attractive, but for corporations with substantial interstate or international operations, South Carolina's no situs law—sizable exemptions for goods assembled in South Carolina for out-of-state markets—made the state an attractive location (Harrison, *Industrial Tax Analysis*). A copy of Harrison's report may be found in the South Carolina archives.

26. Governor Ernest F. Hollings, address before the New York Municipal Forum, May 21, 1959, Governor (1959–63: Hollings), General File, 1958–62; Governor Richard Riley, Economic Development Files, 1979–86; Governor Carroll A. Campbell, Economic Development Correspondence, International Files, 1987–89, South Carolina archives; *Spartanburg Herald*, January 20, 1971, 1.

27. For a discussion of early subsidies, see Cobb, *Selling of the South*, esp. 28–63.

28. Watson, *New Civil War*, 19–31; Fry, "States in the International Economy," 33.

29. National Association of State Development Agencies, *Directory of Incentives*, 553–57.

30. *Wall Street Journal*, May 5, 1978; "Carolina Trade Zone," an information brochure, Vertical Files: International Relations, South Caroliniana Library.

31. For South Carolina industrial location studies reflecting the values and factors of the day, see Flora, "Industrial Location in South Carolina," 60–67; Whitehurst, "Industrialization," 68–73; *Spartanburg Herald*, February 18, 1961, 3E.

32. In the early and mid 1960s Spartanburg-Greenville area workers in skilled and unskilled trades alike earned 10 to 60 percent less than average in the South. For the wage rates see Pender and Clark, "Wage Rates and Fringe Benefits," 19–34.

33. Pender and Clark, "Wage Rates and Fringe Benefits," 3.

34. U.S. Department of Commerce, *Local Area Personal Income*, 538, 545.

35. Ibid., 538.

36. Greater Spartanburg Area Chamber of Commerce, "Spartanburg County International Industry List, 1997."

37. Teter, *Textile Town*, 231, 251–52, 257–58.

38. Aho and Aronson, *Trade Talks*, 67.

39. *Spartanburg Herald*, August 19, 1986, A6.

40. Nivola, *Regulating Unfair Trade*, 75.

41. Brandis, *Making of Textile Trade Policy*, 67.

42. Rowan and Barr, *Employee Relations Trends*, 22.

43. Nivola, *Regulating Unfair Trade*, 73–75.

44. Ibid., 75–76.

45. *Spartanburg Herald-Journal*, December 4, 1971, A4; Lizza, "Silent Partner," 22–25.

46. *Spartanburg Herald-Journal* clipping from 1986, Vertical Files: Roger Milliken, Sandor Teszler Library Archives, Wofford College, Spartanburg.

47. *Spartanburg Herald*, August 6, 1962; *Spartanburg Herald*, August 8, 1962. Newspaper clippings in Vertical Files: Roger Milliken, Teszler Library Archives.

48. *Spartanburg Herald-Journal*, October 10, 1990, B5; *Columbia State*, October 5, 1994, B8; *Spartanburg Herald-Journal*, August 8, 1995, A1; *New York Times*, October 26, 1985, 8.

49. "Roger Milliken Speaks Out on Crafted with Pride in U.S.A."; *Spartanburg Herald-Journal*, May 19, 1985, A1; *Columbia State*, November 10, 1985, D1.

50. "Roger Milliken Speaks Out"; *Spartanburg Herald-Journal*, July 9, 1985; newspaper clippings from Vertical Files: Roger Milliken, Teszler Library Archives.

51. *Spartanburg Herald-Journal*, October 19, 1986, E4.

52. *Wall Street Journal*, September 17, 1985, 24.

53. *Spartanburg Herald-Journal*, April 6, 1986, 4A; Spartanburg *Herald-Journal*, September 19, 1990, B1; undated newspaper clippings, Vertical Files: Roger Milliken, Teszler Library Archives; Betsy Wakefield Teter, "Textile Town in Transition, 1975–2000," in Teter, *Textile Town*, 268–69.

54. *Spartanburg Herald-Journal*, August 7, 1986, 1.

55. In 1977 the total value added of the U.S. textile industry was $13.296 billion ($45.485 billion in 2007 dollars). By 1987 the total value added had reached $24.074 billion ($43.940 billion in 2007 dollars). Approximately 916,000 people were employed in the textile industry in the United States in 1977; by 1987 that number had dropped to 740,000 (U.S.

Department of Commerce, Bureau of Economic Analysis, "1947–97 NAICS [North American Industry Classification System]-based GDP-by-Industry Data"; Gross-Domestic-Product-by-Industry Accounts, 1947–2007, database, http://www.bea.gov/industry/gpotables/gpo_list .cfm?anon=76097&registered=0 [accessed August 28, 2008]).

56. For an effective account on the rise of antiprotectionist sentiments and political activity, see Destler and Odell, *Anti-Protection*. For discussion of textiles, see esp. 16–17, 59.

57. *Spartanburg Herald-Journal*, August 7, 1986, A1, A12; *Southern Textile News*, August 11, 1986, 1.

58. Mintz, *U.S. Import Quotas*, 47–48.

59. Cline, *Future of World Trade*, 2.

60. *Spartanburg Herald-Journal*, August 7, 1986, A1, A12; *Spartanburg Herald-Journal*, August 19, 1986, A4; *Spartanburg Herald-Journal*, September 17, 1987, A1; *Spartanburg Herald-Journal*, March 3, 1988, A1; *Columbia State*, October 10, 1990, 2C; *Spartanburg Herald-Journal*, May 17, 1995, A1.

61. *Spartanburg Herald*, May 4, 1945, 2; *Spartanburg Herald*, May 8, 1945, 2; *Spartanburg Herald*, May 12, 1945, 2; *Spartanburg Herald*, May 19, 1945, 4; *Spartanburg Herald*, June 20, 1945, 4; *Spartanburg Herald*, June 27, 1945, 4.

62. For a good discussion about the emergence and perception of the southern "mill problem," see Carlton, *Mill and Town*, esp. 129–65; Aho and Aronson, *Trade Talks*, 67; *Spartanburg Herald*, February 5, 1958, 4.

63. *Spartanburg Herald*, February 5, 1958, 4.

64. *Spartanburg Herald*, September 15, 1962, B1.

65. *Spartanburg Herald-Journal*, February 9, 1957, 52; *Spartanburg Herald*, September 26, 1959, 4; *Spartanburg Herald-Journal*, February 13, 1960, 4E; *Spartanburg Herald*, January 5, 1966, 14; *Spartanburg Herald-Journal*, February 12, 1966, C1; *Spartanburg Herald-Journal*, February 11, 1967, C1; *Spartanburg Herald-Journal*, February 15, 1969, H11.

66. *Spartanburg Herald-Journal*, February 13, 1960, 4E.

67. *Spartanburg Herald-Journal*, January 31, 1954, 30; *Spartanburg Herald-Journal*, April 22, 1956, A3; *Spartanburg Herald-Journal*, February 15, 1958, 15; *Spartanburg Herald*, September 18, 1959, 1; *Spartanburg Herald-Journal*, February 18, 1961, 6E–7E; *Spartanburg Herald*, October 26, 1966, 11; *Spartanburg Herald*, October 26, 1967, 31; *Spartanburg Herald*, March 11, 1978, D3.

68. Greater Spartanburg Area Chamber of Commerce, "Major Accomplishments."

69. *Spartanburg Herald-Journal*, February 13, 1960, 4E.

70. *Spartanburg Herald*, April 22, 1956, A3.

71. Ibid., *Spartanburg Herald-Journal*, February 9, 1957, 18; *Spartanburg Herald*, February 11, 1967, C2.

72. *Spartanburg Herald*, January 5, 1966, 14; *Spartanburg Herald*, February 2, 1967, 4.

73. *Spartanburg Herald*, February 2, 1967, 4.

74. *Spartanburg Herald*, February 1, 1967, 1; *Spartanburg Herald-Journal*, March 3, 1973, C9; *Spartanburg Herald-Journal*, March 5, 1977, D3; *Spartanburg Herald-Journal*, March 11, 1978, D3.

75. For a concise summary of urban development in the post–World War II American South, including a discussion of downtown-revival movements, see Randall M. Miller, "The Development of Modern Urban South: An Historical Overview" in Miller and Pozzetta, *Shades of the Sunbelt*, 1–20, esp. 7–9.

Conclusion. Persistence of Place

1. *Spartanburg Herald*, January 31, 1954, 8; *Spartanburg Herald*, January 27, 1959, 4; Hammer, Greene, Siler Associates, "Economy of Spartanburg County," i–xii.

2. *Spartanburg Herald*, June 27, 1945, 4; *Spartanburg Herald*, February 1, 1958, 4.

3. U.S. Department of Commerce, *U.S. Census of Population, 1970*, vol. 1, pt. 42, 1.

4. Saporito and Solo, "Why Foreigners Flock," 48.

5. Lonsdale and Browning, "Rural-Urban Locational Preferences," 260.

6. Kelly, *Great Limbaugh Con*, 147; U.S. Department of Labor, *Employment and Earnings, 1979*, 115–19; U.S. Department of Labor, *Employment and Earnings, 1989*, 146–50.

7. Newman, *Growth in the American South*, 152, 178.

8. U.S. Department of Commerce, *County Business Patterns, 1966*, 60; U.S. Department of Commerce, *County Business Patterns, 1990*, 114–15.

9. U.S. Department of Commerce, *County Business Patterns, 1972*, 75; U.S. Department of Commerce, *County Business Patterns, 1990*, 114–15.

10. Hite, Boburg, and Steirer, "Stormy Weather," 7. Report also available at http://www.strom.clemson.edu/teams/ced/econA/StormyWeather.pdf (accessed January 29, 2007).

11. For more about the rise of labor-management committees during the 1970s, see Siegel and Weinberg, *Labor-Management Cooperation*, 75–97.

12. Dr. Paul Foerster, interview by author, September 24, 2002, Spartanburg, S.C.; *Spartanburg Herald-Journal*, April 28, 1989, A1.

13. "Michelin Goes American," *Economist*, July 26, 1976, 56.

14. *Spartanburg Herald-Journal*, March 6, 1976, E16.

15. *Spartanburg Herald-Journal*, March 5, 1977, E4.

16. Ibid.

17. Falk and Lyson, *High Tech, Low Tech*, 84–85; Carlton, "Textile Town Settles In," 227–28; Dr. Donald Romine, professor of political science at University of South Carolina at Spartanburg, interview by author, March 15, 2002, Spartanburg, S.C. For further discussion of the industrial recruitment and wage controls, see James C. Cobb, "The Sunbelt South: Industrialization in Regional, National, and International Perspective," in Mohl, *Searching for the Sunbelt*, 25–46.

18. Carlton, "Textile Town Settles In," 218.

19. *Spartanburg Herald*, January 20, 1956, 1, 28; *Spartanburg Herald*, September 26, 1959, 4; *Spartanburg Herald*, October 13, 1960, 9; *Spartanburg Herald*, February 9, 1966, 1; *Spartanburg Herald*, February 15, 1969, H11.

20. Carlton, "Textile Town Settles In," 218.

21. *Spartanburg Herald-Journal*, April 3, 1992, 1; Roberts, "New South Sees Future," 1–5A.

22. *(London) Independent*, May 9, 1993, 14; *New York Times*, May 26, 1992, D1, D3; "BMW's American Affair," *Economist*, June 27, 1992, 80.

23. *Spartanburg Herald-Journal*, April 3, 1992, A4; *Atlanta Journal-Constitution*, June 18, 1992, D10.

24. "BMW's American Affair," 80; Mahler, "Proud to Call Carolina Home"; Roberts, "New South Sees Future," 1–5A; *Charlotte Observer*, September 11, 2000, 12D.

25. *Spartanburg Herald-Journal*, April 3, 1992, 1, 4; *New York Times*, June 23, 1992, D6; *Wall Street Journal*, July 6, 1992

26. Foerster interview; *Spartanburg Herald-Journal*, April 3, 1992, 1, 4.

27. *Wall Street Journal,* July 6, 1992, A10.

28. *New York Times,* June 23, 1992, D6.

29. Richard S. Stickleburger, "BMW: On the Investment Highway in the USA," *Deutschland: Zeitschrift für Politik, Kultur, Wirtschaft und Wissenschaft* (an undated magazine clipping in the Greater Spartanburg Area Chamber of Commerce Papers).

30. *Wall Street Journal,* July 6, A10; *(London) Independent,* May 9, 1993, 14; *New York Times,* June 23, 1992, D-6.

31. *Wall Street Journal,* July 6, 1992, A10.

32. Mallory, "Wheels of Fortune."

33. *Spartanburg Herald-Journal,* April 3, 1992, 1, 4.

34. *Ward's Auto World* 34, no. 6 (June 1998), 24.

35. *Columbia State,* June 28, 2000, B8.

36. *Spartanburg Herald-Journal,* May 11, 2001, A11.

37. Wright, *Old South, New South,* 273.

38. *Spartanburg Herald-Journal,* January 9, 1960, 5.

39. Daniel J. Fusfeld, "The Rise of Corporate State in America," in Samuels, *Economy as a System,* 139–40.

40. The corporate state and its manifestations in post–World War II America are insightfully described in John Kenneth Galbraith's classic *The New Industrial State.*

41. Arthur Selwyn Miller, "Legal Foundations of the Corporate State," in Samuels, *Economy as a System,* 291.

42. *USA Today,* November 30, 1995, A11.

43. South Carolina State Budget and Control Board, *South Carolina Statistical Abstract,* 1977, 57; *South Carolina Statistical Abstract,* 1992, 258, 279, 307; *South Carolina Statistical Abstract,* 1996, 314.

44. Raymond Williams, "Decentralization and the Politics of Place," in Gale, *Resources of Hope,* 242.

BIBLIOGRAPHY

Archives

Dwight D. Eisenhower Presidential Library, Abilene, Kans.

Gerald Ford Presidential Library, Ann Arbor, Mich.

Government Document Department, Robert Woodruff Library, Emory University, Atlanta.

Greater Spartanburg Chamber of Commerce Papers, Greater Spartanburg Chamber of Commerce, Spartanburg, S.C.

Lyndon B. Johnson Presidential Library, Austin, Tex.

National Archives and Records Administration, Southeast Region Facility, Morrow, Ga.

Perkins Library, Special Collections, Duke University, Durham, N.C.

Sandor Tezler Library Archives, Wofford College, Spartanburg, S.C.

South Caroliniana Library, University of South Carolina, Columbia.

South Carolina Department of Archives and History, Columbia.

Southern Historical Collections, University of North Carolina at Chapel Hill.

Southern Labor History Archives, Georgia State University, Atlanta.

Spartanburg County Headquarters Library, Local History Collections, Spartanburg, S.C.

University of Georgia Library, Special Collections, Athens.

Richard B. Russell Library, University of Georgia, Athens.

Dissertations, Studies, Government Publications, and General Published Works

Aho, C. Michael, and Jonathan David Aronson. *Trade Talks: America Better Listen!* Washington, D.C.: Council on Foreign Relations, 1985.

Anderson, Cynthia D., Michael D. Schulman, and Phillip J. Wood. "Globalization and Uncertainty: The Restructuring of Southern Textiles." *Social Problems* 48, no. 4 (November 2001): 478–98.

Arpan, Jeffrey S., and David Ricks. *Directory of Foreign Manufacturers in the United States.* Atlanta: Georgia State University Publishing Services Division, 1975.

Audretsch, David B., and Michael P. Claudon, eds. *The Internationalization of U.S. Markets.* New York: New York University Press, 1989.

Ayers, H. Brandt, and Thomas H. Naylor, eds. *You Can't Eat Magnolias.* New York: McGraw-Hill, 1972.

Bartley, Numan V. *The New South: 1945–1980.* Baton Rouge: Louisiana State University Press, 1995.

Beck, John J. "Building the New South: A Revolution from above in a Piedmont County." *Journal of Southern History* 53, no. 3 (August 1987): 441–70.

Bhagwati, Jagdish, ed. *The New International Economic Order*. Cambridge, Mass.: MIT Press, 1976.

Biven, W. Carl. *Who Killed John Maynard Keynes? Conflicts in the Evolution of Economic Policy*. Homewood, Ill.: Dow Jones–Irwin, 1989.

Black, Earl. *Southern Governors and Civil Rights: Racial Segregation as a Campaign Issue in the Second Reconstruction*. Cambridge, Mass.: Harvard University Press, 1976.

Black, Earl, and Merle Black. *Politics and Society in the South*. Cambridge, Mass.: Harvard University Press, 1987.

"BMW's American Affair." *Economist*, June 27, 1992, 80.

Brandis, R. Buford. *The Making of Textile Trade Policy, 1935–1981*. Washington, D.C.: American Textile Manufacturers Institute, 1982.

Brattain, Michelle. *The Politics of Whiteness: Race, Workers, and Culture in the Modern South*. Princeton, N.J.: Princeton University Press, 2001.

Brody, David. "Reconciling the Old Labor History and the New." *Pacific History Review* 62, no. 1 (February 1999): 1–18.

Brown, Douglas M., and Earl H. Fry. *States and Provinces in International Economy*. Berkeley: University of California Institute of Governmental Studies Press, 1993.

Burns, Arthur F. "World Competition and the American Economy." *Political Science Quarterly* 76, no. 3, (September 1961): 321–31.

"Buying a Slice of America." *Economist*, October 9, 1971, 90.

Byrnes, James F. *All in One Lifetime*. New York: Harper, 1958.

Calcott, W. H., ed. *South Carolina: Economic and Social Conditions in 1944*. Columbia: University of South Carolina Press, 1945.

Carlton, David L. *Mill and Town in South Carolina, 1880–1920*. Baton Rouge: Louisiana State University Press, 1982.

———. "Textile Town Settles In: 1950–1974." In *Textile Town: Spartanburg, South Carolina*. Edited by Betsy Wakefield Teter, 209–62. Spartanburg, S.C.: Hub City Writers' Project, 2002.

Carlton, David L., and Peter A. Coclanis. "Capital Mobilization and Southern Industry, 1880–1945: The Case of the Carolina Piedmont." *Journal of Economic History* 49 (March 1989): 73–94.

Casey, William L., Jr. *Beyond the Numbers: Foreign Direct Investment in the United States*. Greenwich, Conn.: Jai Press, 1998.

Cash, Wilbur. *Mind of the South*. New York: Knopf, 1941.

"Challenge in Reverse." *Economist*, October 25, 1980. 1–14.

Choate, Jean. *Disputed Ground: Farm Groups That Opposed the New Deal Agricultural Program*. Jefferson, N.C.: McFarland, 2002.

Clark, Daniel J. *Like Night and Day: Unionization in a Southern Mill Town*. Chapel Hill: University of North Carolina Press, 1997.

Cline, William R. *The Future of World Trade in Textiles and Apparel.* Washington, D.C.: Institute for International Economics, 1987.

Cobb, James C. *Industrialization and Southern Society, 1877–1984.* Lexington: University of Kentucky Press, 1984.

———. *The Selling of the South: The Southern Crusade for Industrial Development, 1930–1980.* Baton Rouge: Louisiana State University Press, 1982.

Cobb, James C., and Michael V. Namorato, eds. *The New Deal and the South.* Jackson: University of Mississippi Press, 1984.

Coclanis, Peter. *The Shadow of a Dream: Economic Life and Death in the South Carolina Low Country, 1670–1920.* New York: Oxford University Press, 1989.

Cohen, Stephen D. *The Making of United States International Economic Policy.* 5th ed. Westport, Conn.: Praeger, 2000.

Cohn, David. *Life and Times of King Cotton.* New York: Oxford University Press, 1956.

Cohodas, Nadine. *Strom Thurmond and the Politics of Southern Change.* New York: Simon and Schuster, 1993.

"Congress Opens a Door to Overseas Investors." *Business Week,* October 29, 1966, 102–4.

Congressional Research Service. "Foreign Investments: How Much Are They Worth?" CRS Report no. 91-865 E, December 9, 1991.

Culver, John C. "Foreign Direct Investment in the United States." *Foreign Policy* 16 (Fall 1974): 157–64.

Daniel, Pete. *Breaking the Land: The Transformation of Rice, Tobacco, and Cotton Cultures since 1880.* Urbana: University of Illinois Press, 1985.

Daniels, John. "Recent Foreign Direct Manufacturing Investment in the United States." *Journal of International Business Studies* 1 (Spring 1970): 125–32.

Davidson, W. H. "The Location of Foreign Direct Investment Activity: Country Characteristics and Experience Effects." *Journal of International Business Studies* 11 (1980): 9–22.

DeConde, Alexander. "The South and Isolationism." *Journal of Southern History* 24, no. 3 (August 1958), 332–46.

Delfino, Susanna, and Michele Gillespie, eds. *Global Perspectives on Industrial Transformation in the American South.* Columbia: University of Missouri Press, 2005.

Destler, I. M., and John S. Odell. *Anti-Protection: Changing Forces in United States Trade Politics.* Washington, D.C.: Institute for International Economics, 1987.

Dunning, John. "The Eclectic Paradigm of the International Production: A Reinstatement and Some Possible Extensions." *Journal of International Business Studies* 19 (1988): 1–31.

———. "Reappraising the Eclectic Paradigm in an Age of Alliance Capitalism." *Journal of International Business Studies* 26 (1995): 461–89.

Dyer, Davis, and David B. Sicilia. *Labors of a Modern Hercules: The Evolution of a Chemical Company.* Boston: Harvard Business School Press, 1990.

Eckes, Alfred E., Jr. *Opening America's Market: U.S. Foreign Grade Policy since 1776.* Chapel Hill: University of North Carolina Press, 1995.

Edgar, Walter. *South Carolina: A History.* Columbia: University of South Carolina Press, 1998.

———. *South Carolina in the Modern Age.* Columbia: University of South Carolina Press, 1992.

Edwards, Charles E. "The South Carolina Economy in Perspective." *University of South Carolina Bureau of Business and Economic Research: Essays in Economics,* no. 15, June 1967.

Egerton, John. *The Americanization of Dixie, the Southernization of America.* New York: Harper's Magazine Press, 1974.

Eisinger, Peter K. *The Rise of the Entrepreneurial State: State and Local Economic Development Policy in the United States.* Madison: University of Wisconsin Press, 1988.

Eldridge, Hope T., and Dorothy S. Thomas. *Population Redistribution and Economic Growth.* Vol. 3. Philadelphia: American Philosophical Society, 1964.

English, Beth. *A Common Thread: Labor, Politics, and Capital Mobility in the Textile Industry.* Athens: University of Georgia Press, 2006.

"European Business People Like Carolina—and It's Mutual." *U.S. News and World Report,* June 26, 1972, 62–63.

Falk, William W., and Thomas A. Lyson. *High Tech, Low Tech, No Tech: Recent Industrial and Occupational Change in the South.* Albany: State University of New York Press, 1988.

Fink, Gary M., and Merle E. Reed, eds. *Essays in Southern Labor History: Selected Papers.* Westport, Conn.: Greenwood, 1976.

———. *Race, Class, and Community in Southern Labor History.* Tuscaloosa: University of Alabama Press, 1994.

Fink, Gary M., Merle E. Reed, and Leslie S. Hough, eds. *Southern Workers and Their Unions, 1880–1975.* Westport, Conn.: Greenwood, 1981.

Fite, Gilbert. *Cotton Fields No More.* Lexington: University Press of Kentucky, 1984.

Flamming, Douglas. *Creating the Modern South: Millhands and Managers in Dalton, Georgia, 1884–1984.* Athens: University of Georgia Press, 1984.

Flora, A. C., Jr. "The Dynamic Economy of South Carolina since 1958." *University of South Carolina Business and Economic Review* 8, no. 2 (November 1961): 1–3.

———. "Education and Economic Progress in South Carolina." *University of South Carolina Business and Economic Review* 7, no. 4 (January 1966): 11.

———. "Industrial Location in South Carolina." *University of South Carolina Bureau of Business and Economic Research: Essays in Economics,* no. 13 (August 1965): 60–73.

———. "Spartanburg County: An Economic Profile." A study prepared for the Spartanburg County Planning and Development Commission, 1966.

Ford, Lacy K. *Origins of Southern Radicalism: The South Carolina Upcountry, 1800–1860.* New York: Oxford University Press, 1988.

————. "Rednecks and Merchants: Economic Development and Social Tensions in the South Carolina Upcountry, 1865–1900." *Journal of American History* 71 (September 1984): 294–318.

Fordham, Benjamin O. *Building the Cold War Consensus: The Political Economy of U.S. National Security Policy, 1949–1951.* Ann Arbor: University of Michigan Press, 1998.

"The Foreigners Are Coming: Should We Cheer or Should We Blench?" *Forbes,* July 15, 1973, 25–31.

Foust, Dean, and Maria Mallory. "The Boom Belt: There's No Speed Limit on Growth along the South's I-85." *Business Week,* September 23, 1993, 98–104.

Frederickson, Kari. "'The Slowest State' and 'Most Backward Community': Racial Violence in South Carolina and Federal Civil Rights Legislation, 1946–1948." *South Carolina Historical Magazine* 98, no. 2 (April 1997): 177–202.

Fuller, Irvin. "The Diffusion and Location of Technological Change in American Cotton Textile Industry, 1890–1970." *Technology and Culture* 15, No. 4 (October 1974): 569–93.

Galbraith, John Kenneth. *The New Industrial State.* New York: Houghton Mifflin, 1967.

Gale, Robin, ed. *Resources of Hope: Culture, Democracy, Socialism.* London: Verso, 1989.

Garreau, Joel. *The Nine Nations of North America.* Boston: Houghton Mifflin, 1981.

Georgia Department of Commerce. *Foreign Investment in the State of Georgia: Summary by County.* December 1978.

Gilman, Glenn. *Human Relations in the Industrial Southeast: A Study of the Textile Industry.* Chapel Hill: University of North Carolina Press, 1956.

Glickman, Norman J., and Douglas P. Woodward. *The New Competitors: How Foreign Investors Are Changing the U.S. Economy.* New York: Basic Books, 1989.

"Going International in Reverse." *Business Week,* August 10, 1963, 34.

Gordon, Sara L., and Francis A. Lees. *Foreign Multinational Investment in the United States: Struggle for Industrial Supremacy.* New York: Quorum, 1986.

Greater Spartanburg Area Chamber of Commerce. "Major Accomplishments." Marketing brochure, 1980s. In the personal files of Dr. G. B. Hodge.

————. "Points of Interest: History and Economics of the South Carolina Piedmont Region." Advertising brochure, 1966. Vertical Files: Spartanburg County, South Caroliniana Library, University of South Carolina, Columbia.

————. "Spartanburg County International Industry List, 1997." Greater Spartanburg Chamber of Commerce, Spartanburg, S.C.

————. "Spartanburg . . . the South's International Community." Information and advertising brochure, 1970s. In the personal files of Dr. G. B. Hodge.

Griffith, Barbara S. *The Crisis of American Labor: Operation Dixie and the Defeat of CIO.* Philadelphia: Temple University Press, 1988.

Halistones, Thomas J., ed. *Viewpoints in Supply-Side Economics.* Richmond, Va.: Dame, 1982.

Hall, Jacquelyn Dowd, Robert Korstad, and James Leloudis. "Cotton Mill People: Work, Community, and Protest in the Textile South, 1880–1940." *American Historical Review* 91, no. 2 (April 1986): 245–86.

Hall, Jacqueline Dowd, James Leloudis, Robert Korstad, Mary Murphy, Lu Ann Jones, and Christopher B. Daly. *Like a Family: The Making of a Southern Cotton Mill World.* Chapel Hill: University of North Carolina Press, 1987.

Hammer, Greene, Siler Associates. "The Economy of Spartanburg County, South Carolina: An Economic Study." A report prepared for the Spartanburg County Planning and Development Commission and the South Carolina Appalachian Regional Planning and Development Commission, June 1971.

Harrison, Durham T., Jr. *Industrial Tax Analysis: Hypothetical Manufacturing Plant.* Columbia, S.C.: State Development Board, Research Division, 1970.

Hayes, Jack Irby, Jr. *South Carolina and the New Deal.* Columbia: University of South Carolina Press, 2001.

Hemmingway, Theodore. "Prelude to Change: Black Carolinians in the War Years, 1914–1920." *Journal of Negro History* 65, no. 3 (Summer 1980): 212–27.

Herring, Harriet L. *Passing of the Mill Village: Revolution in a Southern Institution.* Chapel Hill: University of North Carolina Press, 1949.

Hite, James C., Karin Boburg, and Ada Louise Steirer. "Stormy Weather: The Anderson County Economy in the Late Twentieth Century." A Report to Anderson County Council. Strom Thurmond Institute of Government and Public Affairs, Clemson, S.C., July 20, 1995.

Hodges, James A. *New Deal Labor Policy and the Southern Cotton Textile Industry, 1933–1941.* Knoxville: University of Tennessee Press, 1986.

Hoffman, Edwin D. "The Genesis of the Modern Movement for Equal Rights in South Carolina, 1930–1939." *Journal of Negro History* 44, no. 4 (October 1959): 346–69.

Hoffman, Joan. *Racial Discrimination and Economic Development.* Lexington, Mass.: Lexington Books, 1975.

Hoover, Calvin B., and B. U. Ratchford. *Economic Resources and Policies of the South.* New York: Macmillan, 1951.

"How Companies Are Wooing Investors Abroad." *Business Week,* May 14, 1966, 154–55.

"How Roger Milliken Runs Textiles' Premiere Performer." *Business Week,* January 19, 1981, 62–73.

Hughes, Langston. *Good Morning, Revolution: Uncollected Social Protest Writings by Langston Hughes.* Edited by Faith Berry. New York: Lawrence Hill, 1973.

Hymer, Stephen. *The International Operations of National Firms: A Study of Foreign Direct Investment.* Cambridge, Mass.: MIT Press, 1976.

Information UBS (Unione di Banche Swizzere), August 17, 1972. Vertical Files: Spartanburg County Headquarters Library, Spartanburg, S.C.

"Investing in the U.S.: Let's Go Where the Union's Aren't." *Economist,* June 4, 1977, 101–2.

Irons, Janet. *Testing the New Deal: The General Strike of 1934 in the American South.* Urbana: University of Illinois Press, 2000.

Journal of the House of Representatives of the 2nd Session of the 91st General Assembly of the State of South Carolina, 1956.

Journal of the Senate of the 2nd Session of the 91st General Assembly of the State of South Carolina, 1956.

Kantner, Rosabeth Moss. *World Class: Thriving Locally in the Global Economy.* New York: Simon and Schuster, 1995.

Kaufman, Burton I. *Trade and Aid: Eisenhower's Foreign Economic Policy, 1953–1961.* Baltimore: Johns Hopkins University Press, 1982.

Kelly, Charles M. *The Great Limbaugh Con and Other Right-Wing Assaults on Common Sense.* Santa Barbara, Calif.: Fithian, 1994.

Kenen, Peter B., ed. *Managing the World Economy: Fifty Years after Bretton Woods.* Washington, D.C.: Institute for International Economics, 1994.

Kennedy, John F. "New England and the South." *Atlantic Monthly,* January 1954, 32–36.

Kiker, B. F. "Human Capital Formation through Investing in Education." *University of South Carolina Business and Economic Review* 13, no. 4 (January 1967): 3–9.

Kincaid, John. "The American Governors in International Affairs." *Publius* 14, no. 14 (1984): 95–114.

Kindleberger, Charles. *American Business Abroad: Six Lectures on Direct Investment.* New Haven, Conn.: Yale University Press, 1969.

Kirby, John Temple. *Rural Worlds Lost: The American South, 1920–1960.* Baton Rouge: Louisiana State University Press, 1987.

Kunz, Diana B. *Butter and Guns: America's Cold War Economic Diplomacy.* New York: Free Press, 1997.

Lander, Ernest McPherson, Jr. *A History of South Carolina, 1865–1960.* Chapel Hill: University of North Carolina Press, 1960.

Lester, Richard A. *Labor and Industrial Relations: A General Analysis.* New York: Macmillan, 1951.

Liner, E. Blaine, and Lawrence K. Lynch, eds. *The Economics of Southern Growth.* Durham, N.C.: Southern Growth Policies Board, 1977.

Link, Albert N. *From Seed to Harvest: The Growth of the Research Triangle Park.* Research Triangle Park, N.C.: Research Triangle Park Foundation, 2002.

———. *A Generosity of Spirit: The Early History of the Research Triangle Park.* Research Triangle Park, N.C.: Research Triangle Park Foundation, 1995.

Lizza, Ryan. "Silent Partner: The Man behind the Anti-Free Trade Revolt." *New Republic,* January 10, 2000, 22–25.

Lonsdale, Richard E., and Clyde E Browning. "Rural-Urban Locational Preferences of Southern Manufacturers." *Annals of the Association of American Geographers* 61 (June 1971): 255–68.

Lovett, William, Alfred E. Eckes Jr., and Richard Brinkman. *U.S. Trade Policy: History, Theory, and the WTO*. Armonk, N.Y.: Sharpe, 1999.

Lyson, Thomas A. *Two Sides of the Sunbelt: The Growing Divergence between the Rural and Urban South*. New York: Praeger, 1983.

Maceshich, George. *Monetarism: Theory and Policy*. New York: Praeger, 1983.

MacEvan, Arthur, and William K. Tabb, eds. *Instability and Change in the World Economy*. New York: Monthly Review Press, 1989.

Mahler, Daniel. "Proud to Call Carolina Home." *German American Trade: Magazine of the German-American Chamber of Commerce* 7, nos. 7–8 (July–August 1996): 11.

Mallory, Maria. "Wheels of Fortune." *U.S. News and World Report*, March 4, 1996, 49–50.

Malmgren, Harald B. "Coming Trade Wars? Neo-Merchantilism and Foreign Policy." *Foreign Policy* 1 (Winter 1970–71): 116–22.

———. "Managing Foreign Economic Policy." *Foreign Policy* 6 (Spring 1972): 42–68.

Martin, Dora. "The Attitude of the Spartanburg, South Carolina Press toward the Supreme Court 1954 Decision." MA Thesis, University of South Carolina, 1959.

McCormack, Richard T. *The Bretton Woods Legacy: Its Continued Relevance*. Washington, D.C.: U.S. Department of State, Bureau of Public Affairs, Office of Public Communication, Editorial Division, 1984.

McGill, Ralph. *The South and the Southerner*. Athens: University of Georgia Press, 1992.

McHugh, Cathy L. *Mill Family: The Labor System in the Southern Cotton Textile Industry, 1880–1915*. New York: Oxford University Press, 1988.

Meade, Douglas. "Foreign Investment in the United States." *Inforum*, July 1997, 1–16.

"Michelin Goes American." *Economist*, July 26, 1976, 26–28, 56.

Miller, Francis Pickens. "The Democratic Party in the South: Signs of Restiveness." *Christianity and Crisis* 21 (May 1, 1961): 63–64.

Miller, Randall M., and George E. Pozzetta, eds. *Shades of the Sunbelt: Essays on Ethnicity, Race, and the Urban South*. Westport, Conn.: Greenwood, 1988.

Minchin, Timothy J. *Fighting against the Odds: A History of Southern Labor since World War II*. Gainesville: University Press of Florida, 2005.

———. *What Do We Need a Union For? The TWUA in the South, 1945–1955*. Chapel Hill: University of North Carolina Press, 1997.

Mintz, Ilse. *U.S. Import Quotas: Costs and Consequences*. Washington, D.C.: American Enterprise Institute for Public Policy Research, 1973.

Mitchell, Broadus. *The Rise of the Cotton Mills in the South*. Baltimore: Johns Hopkins University Press, 1921.

Mohl, Raymond A. *Searching for the Sunbelt: Historical Perspectives on a Region*. Knoxville: University of Tennessee Press, 1990.

Moody, R. H. "The Labor and Immigration Problem of South Carolina during Reconstruction." *Mississippi Valley Historical Review* 18, no. 2 (September 1931): 195–212.

Moreland, J. Kenneth. *Millways of Kent*. Chapel Hill: University of North Carolina Press, 1958.

Morris, James A. "The South Carolina Economy: Trends and Prospects." *University of South Carolina Business and Economic Review* 7, no. 7 (April 1961): 1–3.

Morris, Jonathon, ed. *Japan and the Global Economy: Issues and Trends in the 1990s*. London: Routledge, 1991.

National Association of State Development Agencies. *Directory of Incentives for Business Investment and Development in the United States*. Washington, D.C.: Urban Institute Press, 1983.

"The New Immigration." *Forbes*, November 1, 1975, 28–29.

"The New Rich South: Frontier of Growth." *Business Week*, September 2, 1972, 30–37.

Newby, Howard. *The Deferential Worker*. London: Allen Lane, 1977.

Newby, I. A. *Black Carolinians: A History of Blacks in South Carolina from 1895 to 1968*. Columbia: University Press of South Carolina, 1973.

Newman, Robert J. *Growth in the American South: Changing Regional Employment and Wage Patterns in the 1960s and 1970s*. New York: New York University Press, 1984.

Nivola, Pietro S. *Regulating Unfair Trade*. Washington, D.C.: Brookings Institution Press, 1993.

Norton, Hugh S. *The Quest for Economic Stability: From Roosevelt to Bush*. 2nd ed. Columbia: University Press of South Carolina, 1997.

"Of These Four Things . . ." *Forbes*, February 1965, 5, 58.

"Oompah in the Bible Belt." *Time*, July 25, 1977, 50.

Parris, Lou. "South Carolina's Secret Weapon," *South Carolina Business Journal*, February 29, 1988, 40–44.

Pastor, Robert A. *Congress and the Politics of U.S. Foreign Economic Policy, 1929–1976*. Berkeley: University of California Press, 1980.

Paterson, Robert W. "Why Industry Moves to the Southland." *University of South Carolina Business and Economic Review* 1, no. 4 (April 1954): 1–4.

Patinkin, Don. *Essays on and in the Chicago Tradition*. Durham: Duke University Press, 1981.

Pender, David R., and Ronald O. Clark. "Wage Rates and Fringe Benefits in the Manufacturing Industries of South Carolina." *University of South Carolina Bureau of Business and Economic Research: Essays in Economics*, no. 9 (February 1964): 1–183.

Peppas, Spero. "A Comparative Study of Promotional Activities to Attract Foreign Investment: An Application of Marketing Theory to the Efforts of Southeastern States." PhD dissertation, Georgia State University, 1979.

Potwin, Marjorie A. *Cotton Mill People of the Piedmont: A Study in Social Change*. New York: Columbia University Press, 1927.

Pruitt, Dwain. *Things Hidden: An Introduction to the History of Blacks in Spartanburg*. Spartanburg, S.C.: City of Spartanburg Community Relations Office, 1995.

Quick, Dennis. "South Carolina Learns Advanced Technical Skills Training Gives State Its Competitive Edge." *Economic Developments*, Fourth Quarter 1994, 4–5.

Quint, Howard H. *Profile in Black and White: A Frank Portrait of South Carolina.* Washington, D.C.: Public Affairs Press, 1958.

Racine, Philip N. *Seeing Spartanburg: A History in Images.* Spartanburg, S.C.: Hub City Writers Group, 1999.

"Recruiting Industry Abroad." *South Magazine* 5, no. 4 (April 1978):31–32.

Richard E. Tukey. A promotional biographical video, Spartanburg Chamber of Commerce, Spartanburg, S.C.

Richter, Irving. *Labor's Struggles, 1945–1950: A Participant's View.* New York: Cambridge University Press, 1994.

Riger, Rebecca. "Flow of Funds: Foreign Investment in the U.S. Breaks All Records." *Barrons*, August 14, 1978: 9–10.

Roberts, William. "New South Sees Future and It's in Global Trade: Soaring Exports, Foreign Investment Transforming S. Carolina, Neighbors." *Journal of Commerce*, October 31, 1996, 1A–5A.

"Roger Milliken Speaks Out on Crafted With Pride in U.S.A." *Textile World*, January 1985, 35–38.

Rose, Sanford. "The Misguided Furor about Investments from Abroad." *Fortune*, May 1975, 170–75.

Rowan, Richard L., and Robert E. Barr. *Employee Relations Trends and Practices in the Textile Industry.* Philadelphia: Wharton School Industrial Research Unit, 1987.

Sagarin, Bruce. *Foreign Investment in the United States.* New York: Praeger, 1980.

Sale, Kirkpatrick. *Power Shift: The Rise of the Southern Rim and Its Challenge to the Eastern Establishment.* New York: Random House, 1975.

Samuels, Warren J., ed. *The Economy as a System of Power.* Vol. 1, *Corporate Systems.* New Brunswick, N.J.: Transaction, 1989.

Saporito, Bill, and Sally Solo. "Why Foreigners Flock to South Carolina." *Fortune*, November 2, 1992, 48.

Schaller, Michael. *Altered States: The United States and Japan since the Occupation.* New York: Oxford University Press, 1997.

Schubart, Ellen. "State by State, 30 Governors Talk Only of Safe Issues." *City and State*, May 7, 1990, 3–19.

Schulman, Bruce J. *From Cotton Belt to Sunbelt: Federal Policy, Economic Development, and the Transformation of the South, 1938–1980.* New York: Oxford University Press, 1991.

Schulman, Read. *From Rust Belt to Sunbelt.*

Scranton, Philip, ed. *The Second Wave: Southern Industrialization from the 1940s to the 1970s.* Athens: University of Georgia Press, 2001.

Servain-Schreiber, Jean-Jacques. *Le Défi Américain.* Paris: Denoël, 1967.

Shaw, Steven J. "Special Education for Industrial Expansion." *University of South Carolina's Business and Economic Review* 10, no. 1 (October 1963):1–6.

Siegel, Irwing H., and Edgar Weinberg. *Labor-Management Cooperation: An American Experience*. Kalamazoo, Mich.: W. E. Upton Institute for Employment Research, 1982.

Simon, Bryant. *A Fabric of Defeat: The Politics of South Carolina Millhands, 1910–1948*. Chapel Hill: University of North Carolina Press, 1998.

———. "Rethinking Why There Are So Few Unions in the South." *Georgia Historical Quarterly* 81 (Summer 1997): 465–84.

Smith, T. Lynn. "The Redistribution of the Negro Population of the United States, 1910–1960." *Journal of Negro History* 51, no. 3 (July 1966): 155–73.

"South Carolina Mission Sparks Brisk Interest by Europeans." *International Commerce* 75 (November 24, 1969): 22.

"South Carolina's New Plant Boom." *Business Week*, March 26, 1960, 126–26.

"South Carolina's Upper Piedmont." *Industrial Development and Manufacturers Record* 132 (February 1963): 49–59.

"A Southern Curiosity." *Economist*, December 23, 1978, 26.

"Southern Hospitality." *Trends*, Winter 1975, 16–17.

Spero, Joan Edelman. *The Politics of International Economic Relations*. 3rd ed. New York: St. Martin's, 1985.

Stanley, Richard E. "Stimulating State Economic Growth through State-Organized, Government-Approved Trade Missions." *University of South Carolina Business and Economic Review* 14, no. 2 (November 1967): 3–6.

Street, James H. *The New Revolution in the Cotton Economy: Mechanization and Its Consequences*. Chapel Hill: University of North Carolina Press, 1957.

Stueck, William W., and James C. Cobb, eds. *Globalization and the American South*. Athens: University of Georgia Press, 2005.

Suggs, George G., Jr. *My World Is Gone: Memories of Life in a Southern Cotton Mill Town*. Detroit: Wayne State University Press, 2002.

Teter, Betsy Wakefield, ed. *Textile Town: Spartanburg, South Carolina*. Spartanburg, S.C.: Hub City Writers Project, 2002.

Thompson, Holland. *From the Cotton Field to the Cotton Mill: A Study of the Industrial Transition in North Carolina*. Freeport, N.Y.: Books for Libraries Press, 1906.

Tindall, George Brown. *The Disruption of the Solid South*. Baton Rouge: Louisiana State University Press, 1972.

———. *The Emergence of the New South, 1913–1945*. Baton Rouge: Louisiana State University Press, 1967.

Tomb, John O. "Should Industry Move South?" *Harvard Business Review* 31, no. 5 (September–October 1953): 83–90.

"Trying to Lure Foreign Investors to These Shores." *Business Week*, May 2, 1964, 94.

Tunley, Roul. "In Spartanburg, the Accent Is on Business." *Readers' Digest*, January 1974, 165–68.

U.S. Department of Commerce. *City Directories of the United States, White Plains, New York, 1928–1932. U.S. Census, 1930*. Series T626, roll 1666. National Archives and Records Administration, Southeast Region Facility, Morrow, Ga.

U.S. Department of Commerce. *County Business Patterns, 1951.* Washington, D.C.: U.S. Government Printing Office, 1952.

U.S. Department of Commerce. *County Business Patterns, 1956.* Part 6. Washington, D.C.: U.S. Government Printing Office, 1958.

U.S. Department of Commerce. *County Business Patterns, 1966.* Washington, D.C.: U.S. Government Printing Office, 1967.

U.S. Department of Commerce. *County Business Patterns, 1972.* Washington, D.C.: U.S. Government Printing Office, 1973.

U.S. Department of Commerce. *County Business Patterns, 1990.* Washington, D.C.: U.S. Government Printing Office, 1992.

U.S. Department of Commerce. *Fifteenth Census of the United States: Manufacturers, 1929.* Vol. 3. Washington, D.C.: U.S. Government Printing Office, 1933.

U.S. Department of Commerce. *Fifteenth Census of the United States: 1930.* Vol. 3, part 2. Washington, D.C.: U.S. Government Printing Office, 1932.

U.S. Department of Commerce. *Foreign Direct Investment in the United States: 1987 Benchmark Survey.* Washington, D.C.: U.S. Government Printing Office, 1990.

U.S. Department of Commerce. *Foreign Direct Investment in the United States: Operations of United States Affiliates.* Washington, D.C.: U.S. Government Printing Office, 1985.

U.S. Department of Commerce. *Foreign Direct Investment in the United States: Report of the Secretary of Commerce to the Congress in Compliance with the Foreign Investment Study Act of 1974 (Public Law 93-479).* Washington, D.C.: U.S. Government Printing Office, 1976.

U.S. Department of Commerce. *Local Area Personal Income, 1969–1992.* Washington, D.C.: Government Printing Office, 1994.

U.S. Department of Commerce. *Sixteenth Census of the United States: Manufacturers, 1939.* Vol. 3. Washington, D.C.: U.S. Government Printing Office, 1942.

U.S. Department of Commerce. *Sixteenth Census of the United States: 1940.* Vol. 3, part 6. Washington, D.C.: U.S. Government Printing Office, 1943.

U.S. Department of Commerce. *U.S. Census of Agriculture, 1954.* Vol. 1, *Counties and State Economic Areas, Part 16: North and South Carolina.* Washington, D.C.: U.S. Government Printing Office, 1956.

U.S. Department of Commerce. *U.S. Census of Agriculture, 1959.* Vol. 1, part 27, *Counties, South Carolina.* Washington, D.C.: U.S. Government Printing Office, 1961.

U.S. Department of Commerce. *U.S. Census of Manufacturers, 1947.* Vol. 3, *Area Statistics.* Washington, D.C.: U.S. Government Printing Office, 1950.

U.S. Department of Commerce. *U.S. Census of Manufacturers, 1954.* Vol. 3, *Area Statistics.* Washington, D.C.: U.S. Government Printing Office, 1956.

U.S. Department of Commerce. *U.S. Census of Manufacturers, 1958.* Washington, D.C.: U.S. Government Printing Office, 1961.

U.S. Department of Commerce. *U.S. Census of Population, 1920*. Series T625, roll 1178. National Archives and Records Administration, Southeast Region Facility, Morrow, Ga.

U.S. Department of Commerce. *U.S. Census of Population, 1930*. Series T626, roll 1666. National Archives and Records Administration, Southeast Region Facility, Morrow, Ga.

U.S. Department of Commerce. *U.S. Census of Population, 1940: South Carolina*. Washington, D.C.: U.S. Government Printing Office, 1943.

U.S. Department of Commerce. *U.S. Census of Population, 1950: South Carolina*. Washington, D.C.: U.S. Government Printing Office, 1952.

U.S. Department of Commerce. *U.S. Census of Population, 1960: South Carolina*. Washington, D.C.: U.S. Government Printing Office, 1963.

U.S. Department of Commerce. *U.S. Census of Population, 1970*. Vol. I, part 42, *South Carolina*. Washington, D.C.: U.S. Government Printing Office, 1973.

U.S. Department of Commerce, Bureau of Economic Analysis. Gross-Domestic-Product-by-Industry Accounts, 1947–2007, database. http://www.bea.gov/industry/gpotables/gpo_list.cfm?anon=76097&registered=0 (accessed August 27, 2008).

U.S. Department of Commerce, Bureau of Economic Analysis. *Long Term Economic Growth, 1860–1970*. Washington, D.C.: U.S. Government Printing Office, 1973.

U.S. Department of Commerce, Bureau of Economic Analysis. "1947–97 NAICS [North American Industry Classification System]-based GDP-by-Industry Data," n.d., www.bea.gov/industry/xls/GDPbyInd_VA_NAICS_47to97R.xls (accessed August 15, 2008).

U.S. Department of Labor. *Employment and Earnings, 1979*. Washington, D.C.: U.S. Government Printing Office, 1990.

U.S. Department of Labor. *Employment and Earnings, 1989*. Washington, D.C.: U.S. Government Printing Office, 1990.

"The U.S. Market: A Good Catch for the Investors." *Vision: The European Business Magazine* 102 (1979): 43–53.

Voght, Geoffrey M., and Ray Schaub. *Foreign Languages and International Business*. Washington, D.C.: ERIC Clearinghouse on Languages and Linguistics, 1992.

Vogl, Frank. "The Spartanburg Example: How an Old Southern Town Became 'Euroville.'" *Europe*, May–June 1979, 26–29.

"Wary about Importing Foreign Work Rules." *Business Week*, September 29, 1973, 66.

Watson, Douglas J. *The New Civil War: Government Competition for Economic Development*. Westport, Conn.: Praeger, 1995.

Weinstein, Bernard L., and Robert E. Firestine. *Regional Growth and Decline in the United States: The Rise of the Sunbelt and the Decline of the Northeast*. New York: Praeger, 1978.

Weinstein, Bernard L., Harold T. Gross, and John Rees. *Regional Growth and Decline in the United States*. 2nd ed. New York: Praeger, 1985.

"Welcome, Y'All." *Forbes*, November 15, 1974, 113–14.

Whayne, Jeannie M. *A New Plantation South: Land, Labor, and Federal Favor in the Twentieth Century Arkansas*. Charlottesville: University Press of Virginia, 1996.

Whitehurst, Clinton H. "Industrialization in South Carolina's Rural Piedmont Counties: The Plant Location Decision." *University of South Carolina Bureau of Business and Economic Research: Essays in Economics*, no. 13 (August 1965): 68–73.

"Why Foreign Companies Are Betting on the U.S." *Business Week*, April 12, 1976, 50–59.

Wilkins, Mira. *History of Foreign Investment in the United States to 1914*. Cambridge, Mass.: Harvard University Press, 1989.

———. *The Maturing of Multinational Enterprise: American Business Abroad from 1914 to 1970*. Cambridge, Mass.: Harvard University Press, 1974.

Wingerd, Mary Lethert. "Rethinking Paternalism: Power and Parochialism in a Southern Mill Village." *Journal of American History* 83 (December 1996): 872–902.

Woodward, C. Vann. *Origins of the New South, 1877–1913*. Baton Rouge: Louisiana State University Press, 1971.

Wright, Gavin. *Old South, New South: Revolutions in the Southern Economy since the Civil War*. New York: Basic Books, 1986.

Writers Program of the Work Projects Administration. *A History of Spartanburg County*. Columbia: South Carolina Department of Education, 1940.

Interviews by Author

Dr. Paul E. Foerster, January 30, 1998; September 24, 2002, Spartanburg, S.C.

Dr. G. B. Hodge, September 24, 2002, Spartanburg, S.C.

Mr. Douglas E. Jones, March 16, 2002, Spartanburg, S.C.

Rep. Liz Patterson, March 16, 2002, Spartanburg, S.C.

Dr. Douglas Romine, March 15, 2002, Spartanburg, S.C.

Rev. B. Snoddy, March 14, 2002, Spartanburg, S.C.

Philip A. "Pat" Tukey, January 30, 1998, Spartanburg, S.C.

INDEX

Politics and Culture in the Twentieth-Century South

A Common Thread: Labor, Politics, and Capital Mobility in the Textile Industry
by Beth English

*"Everybody Was Black Down There": Race and Industrial Change
in the Alabama Coalfields*
by Robert H. Woodrum

Race, Reason, and Massive Resistance: The Diary of David J. Mays, 1954–1959
edited by James R. Sweeney

*The Unemployment People's Movement: Leftists, Liberals, and Labor in Georgia,
1929–1941*
by James J. Lorence

Liberalism, Black Power, and the Making of American Politics, 1965–1980
by Devin Fergus

Guten Tag, Y'all: Globazation and the South Carolina Piedmont, 1950–2000
by Marko Maunula

Printed in the United States
147840LV00002B/1/P

9 780820 329017